THE CAMPAIGN
FOR PRESIDENT

THE CAMPAIGN FOR PRESIDENT
1980 In Retrospect

Edited by
JONATHAN MOORE

A Project of the Institute of Politics
John F. Kennedy School of Government
Harvard University

BALLINGER PUBLISHING COMPANY
Cambridge, Massachusetts
A Subsidiary of Harper & Row, Publishers, Inc.

International Standard Book Number: 0-88410-836-8

Library of Congress Catalog Card Number: 81-10801

Printed in the United States of America

Library of Congress Cataloging in Publication Data

Main entry under title:

The Campaign for President.

Proceedings of a conference held in Cambridge, Mass., Dec. 5-7, 1980.
   "A project of the Institute of Politics, John F. Kennedy School of Government, Harvard University."
   Includes index.
   1. Presidents—United States—Election—1980—Congresses. 2. United States—Politics and government—1977-1981—Congresses. I. Moore, Jonathan. II. John Fitzgerald Kennedy School of Government. Institute of Politics.

E875.C35	324.973'0926	81-10801
ISBN 0-88410-836-8		AACR2

CONTENTS

THE AUTHORS

The authors were participants in the Conference on 1980 Presidential Campaign Decisionmaking held in Cambridge, Massachusetts, from December 5 through 7, 1980, sponsored by the Institute of Politics, John F. Kennedy School of Government, Harvard University.

CONGRESSMAN JOHN B. ANDERSON, candidate for Republican nomination and National Unity Campaign candidate

MRS. KEKE ANDERSON, National Unity Campaign

DOUGLAS BAILEY, president, Bailey, Deardourff & Associates

KENNETH A. BODE, network correspondent, NBC News

BILL BROCK, chairman, Republican National Committee

DAVID S. BRODER, associate editor and national political correspondent, *Washington Post*

RONALD H. BROWN, deputy campaign manager, Kennedy for President

PATRICK H. CADDELL, president, Cambridge Survey Research

WILLIAM J. CASEY, campaign manager, Reagan–Bush Committee

ADAM CLYMER, correspondent, *New York Times*

JO–ANNE COE, Office of Senator Robert Dole

PETER DAILEY, deputy director (media), Reagan–Bush Committee

LES FRANCIS, executive director, Democratic National Committee

BETTY HEITMAN, cochair, Republican National Committee

ALBERT R. HUNT, correspondent, *Wall Street Journal*

ROBERT J. KEEFE, political consultant, Carter–Mondale Re-election Committee

DAVID A. KEENE, national political director, Bush for President

PAUL G. KIRK, JR., national political director, Kennedy for President

TIM KRAFT, campaign manager, Carter–Mondale Re-election Committee

CATHERINE MACKIN, network correspondent, ABC News

MICHAEL F. MACLEOD, campaign manager–treasurer, National Unity Campaign

EDDIE MAHE, JR., campaign director, John Connally for President

LYN NOFZIGER, press secretary, Reagan–Bush Committee

MARTIN F. NOLAN, Washington bureau chief, *Boston Globe*

TOM QUINN, campaign manager, Brown for President

JOHN RENDON, convention manager, Carter–Mondale Re-election Committee

JOANNE SYMONS, cofounder, Draft Kennedy Movement

RICHARD G. STEARNS, chief of delegate selection, Kennedy for President

ROBERT M. TEETER, president, Market Opinion Research

CARL WAGNER, director of field operations, Kennedy for President

JACK WALSH, national political director, Carter–Mondale Re-election Committee

RICHARD B. WIRTHLIN, deputy director of strategy and planning, Reagan–Bush Committee

INTRODUCTION

Jonathan Moore

On the first weekend in December following the 1980 election, twenty-six people who had played major decisionmaking roles in the various presidential campaigns gathered at Harvard University to explore how the whole campaign worked—to reconstruct and evaluate important decisions, the reasons behind them, and their consequences. This was the third such conference sponsored by the Institute of Politics at Harvard's John F. Kennedy School of Government, in an effort to achieve better understanding of the national electoral process.

From Friday evening, December 5th, through Sunday morning, December 7th, the participants gathered around a common table for the seven sessions which now comprise the chapters of this book. The discussions were led by journalists who had themselves played major reportorial roles from the early preprimary skirmishing through the general election itself. These thirty-two people are the authors of this book, and their transcript has been edited with an effort to reflect their own relationships and culture as well as to provide analytical insight into the nature of presidential campaigns and how they are run.

The conference was organized and the book coordinated by Elizabeth Pleasants, my principal assistant. The quality and volume of her work enabled this joint project to come off. Nicholas Mitropoulos, assistant director of the Institute and a shrewd political operative and observer, worked closely with the participants during the conference and with me in the production of the book. We are also grateful to the entire Institute of Politics staff for their contribution, especially Alan Mitter, Amy Gazin Schwartz, Larry Goldberg, Lori Forman, and Geraldine Denterlein, and to the student advisory committee, especially Dana Stein and Stephen Bates.

There are essentially two caveats which readers of this book should keep in mind. First, although there was excellent attendance by the major actors at our conference, not everybody came. No major campaign effort was unrepresented, and a conscientious effort was made by those present to fill in all perspectives; but it should be pointed out, for instance, that Hamilton Jordan, chief strategist of the Carter campaign, and John Sears, the early campaign manager of the Reagan campaign, were not present.

Second, as one moderator wryly noted, "No one took an oath," meaning that in some instances the participants may have indulged in selective recollection or guilefully remained mute. Examples where the reader should be wary of self-serving renditions or just plain gaps in the story include a failure to explore the impact of the Roger Mudd interview, the persistent anonymity of Kennedy's liberal Senate colleagues who urged him to get into the race, and a nagging sense that the real reason remained unrevealed for Senator Kennedy's not getting out of the race when the president had the nomination and the Democrats needed unity. Also, the role of federal largesse doled out by the incumbent, especially during the primaries, was barely touched on, and the Carter camp was not entirely candid about the way it used the hostage issue in the campaign.

On the Republican side, the attitude of unconcern over Governor Reagan's "gaffes" in late August and early September—having to do with Taiwan, the Vietnam war, evolution, depression, the Klan—lacked credibility, as did the failure to cite the worry that he might blunder in the debate with Carter as one of the reasons why that decision had been argued as strenuously as it apparently was. One is also left with the feeling that the story of the Reagan–Ford vice-presidential fandango at the Republican convention was never fully told. Finally, as Doug Bailey has observed, since the journalist session leaders naturally focused on news, some of the less newsworthy factors such as organization, advertising, and the use of money may have over the course of the conference gotten less attention than they intrinsically deserved. But on the whole, the individual analysts and raconteurs, aided by their newly friendly protagonists and the probing moderators, set a high standard of self-scrutiny.

Nothing in this long, complicated, bitter struggle for the presidency was as fascinating as its ending, when the major elements in the electoral drama combined in the last days to produce such a powerful outcome. The first factor in the terminal equation was the squandering by President Carter of his own most precious and potent political asset—the public image of his strong personal qualities of fairness, decency, and honesty, which were diminished by his perceived "meanness" and petty behavior in the campaign, particularly toward his opponent. In the last sorting out of political forces, the final making up of the voters' minds, this loss to Carter was almost incalculable; it removed the specific gravity without which he could not withstand serious external blows.

Second was the impact of a single, one-on-one television debate in the very last week of the campaign. With an indecisive, dissatisfied electorate—described as "volatile" the whole year—already inclined to cast its votes on the basis of personal qualities, the special characteristics of the television medium and the winner-take-all confrontation intensified this tendency. Watching Reagan's relatively informal, relaxed manner and hearing his simple, reassuring language, viewers didn't find credible the characterization of him as impetuous and dangerous.

Next, the traumatic re-entry of the hostages—which the campaign had been plagued by and flirting with from its beginning—not in the form of either triumph or tragedy, but an anniversary which perversely ritualized a feeling of frustration and impotency, to the president's great disadvantage. Then it became natural for the Carter record to become the focus. Having accepted Reagan and finding the president curiously diminished in stature and too sour about the nation's prospects and problems, the voters were encouraged to vent their frustration on the Carter administration's inadequate leadership and to accept, ruthlessly, Reagan's invitation to decide whether they were better or worse off than four years before. Thus the country's foreign and domestic inadequacies were more exposed and the blame more clearly targeted.

Finally, the problems of the economy emerged with full force at the end of the campaign, unleashed by the array of other factors and the psychology that they created. Perhaps it was inevitable that the devastating political impact of inflation would finally shape the out-come of the election, as many prognosticators had claimed it would. But the issue—always present and threatening—curiously did not really work to the challenger's benefit until it was part of the confluence of developments in the very last weeks which turned a potentially tight race into a debacle. In what proportions the landslide was a personal repudiation of the old and a conservative mandate for the new president must await more argument and more evidence.

F oreign policy was involved more prominently throughout the campaign than inflation, and it played a more explicit role in the behavior of candidates and the media. The seizure of the American Embassy and the imprisonment of the hostages provided the television networks with a bonanza which, though basically unrelated to the political campaign, affected it mightily. The publicity, the human drama, and the international stakes provided the occupant of the Oval Office with an opportunity to appeal to the innate patriotic and supportive instincts of his citizenry, to "act presidential" in dealing with the crisis, and to hang out in the Rose Garden, giving his opponent a chance to make the mistakes on the campaign trail. The issue galvanized the Iowa caucuses into a huge turnout for Carter, and much later, his support in the polls actually rose following the aborted rescue mission. But the hostage crisis proved a wasting asset for the president, helping him in the primaries but over the long run, without a genuine "October surprise," sapping his energies, exposing his efforts to manipulate the situation at home and ultimately his impotency to deal with it abroad; and it cost him on election day. International crises tend to boost an incumbent president's popularity and support over the short term, but time ran out on this one.

Except for the idiosyncracies of the hostage situation, however, the great issues of war and peace did not play a significantly influential role in the 1980 election. In its earliest stages, the campaign tended to influence foreign policy developments rather more than the other way around. Skittish over-reaction and fumbling of the Soviet combat troops in Cuba affair followed by the Soviet invasion of Afghanistan caused indefinite shelving of the SALT II treaty. Such events in a cooler, more rational noncampaign atmosphere might have underscored the value of such a treaty instead of junking it.

Foreign policy differences among primary contenders, although titillating, were not decisive. Howard Baker didn't get the anti-SALT benefits he'd anticipated, and John Connally flunked with his innovative efforts to deal with the Middle East. Kennedy's more liberal international stance probably hurt more than helped, and he did get burned by his critical comments about the Shah.

In the general election campaign, the grain embargo issue helped Reagan somewhat. The Vance–Brzezinski feuding created an impression of ineptness in the Carter administration's handling of foreign policy. The Stealth Bomber episode was manipulated to a draw. Any slight edge the Republicans gained in their Southern Africa posturing they lost by their confused jockeying between the two Chinas, if anybody cared.

The majority of the public, on the whole, liked Reagan's tougher stance toward the Russians but were skeptical for most of the campaign about his bellicosity; they supported a larger defense budget which Carter had already undertaken to increase; and they challenged the SALT II treaty while retaining a strong interest in pursuing nuclear arms stability through peaceful negotiations. Carter's warnings of the danger of an arms race went unheeded, and Reagan's assertions of the need for nuclear superiority went unchallenged. The major issue raised by the administration's announced new policy for a limited nuclear war fighting capacity attracted little serious interest or political effect. No one knew what to do about Poland or the Persian Gulf. And Carter was confounded by America's lack of influence and respect abroad, while Reagan hammered the theme.

Generally, candidates resorted to rhetoric on foreign policy, exploitative rather than constructive. They were genuinely baffled at the complexity of our problems abroad and convinced that because the public was, too, it would either be bored by or bite at excessive specificity by candidates about how to deal with such issues. Too often the normal impulse in both campaigns was to exploit assumed prejudices and emotions rather than generate serious, open, imaginative debate deserving of the common sense of the American people and required by their democratic function to understand and engender a viable foreign policy. Neither major candidate dared to point out that there are severe limits to American power in dealing with Soviet threats in the Middle East or that increased defense budgets contribute to inflation. Nor was our domestic political temperament during the national campaign perceived to welcome the assertion that economic and third-world forces are as important as military and super-power considerations.

On the other hand, the dark predictions that President Carter "would do anything to get re-elected" did not prove true—the Rapid Deployment Force was never deployed nor were Iranian ports blockaded or mined in an effort to create a timely crisis which could benefit the incumbent. Nor did the challenger intensify hawkish pressure which could have provoked adventurist and opportunistic actions by the administration. Both candidates had their own selfish reasons to be constrained, to be sure. But the point is that the conduct of American foreign policy during the campaign did not become dangerously overheated or de-stabilized by virtue of the domestic political competition. The most profound influence of American politics in 1980 on the character of American foreign policy was the voters' election of Reagan over Carter, itself, and the precise impact and consequences of this choice are not now calculable.

T he rampant power of television was demonstrated throughout the campaign, striking early with the Roger Mudd interview, which launched Kennedy as an unprepared challenger without clear reasons why he was seeking to oust the president of his own party, and set the networks' early negative tone of Kennedy coverage. It bestowed its favors capriciously—Carter took advantage of incessant coverage by the networks of the Iranian crisis, but on the very last evening of the campaign, their choice to review the year-long hostage ordeal in depth sealed his doom. Television's costs are enormous, increasing the threatening role of money in electoral politics. Approximately half of the almost $30 million in federal funds allowed each of the two major presidential candidates was spent on television. And television co-opts the functions and erodes the strength of political parties.

The networks spent millions to promote their ratings at the national conventions and sent thousands of television employees to them, overwhelming the delegates. Sometimes television seemed to manufacture its own reality, with interviewers and commentators assuming the identity of major players, shaping events, manipulating and manhandling genuine politicians. David Nyhan of the *Boston Globe* wrote that at times in Detroit network reporters "behaved in a way that suggested Howard Cosell climbing into the ring during a heavyweight fight, second-guessing the referee, asking the fighters to comment on each other's progress and getting in the way of every other feint or haymaker."

All this became melodramatically clear during the consideration of former President Ford as the Republican vice-presidential nominee, where the intense and ubiquitous reporting, gossip, speculation, logorrhea, and general furor on the screen snatched events away from Governor Reagan and his aides and threatened a loss of control of the only major decision the brand-new nominee had to make. In the Ford–Cronkite interview, having been aided by Republican operatives and negotiators who appeared to have taken leave of their senses, both men fell prey to euphoric extravagance, acting as if they were about to take the decision into their own hands, and galvanized Governor Reagan into tardy action. The real story here was the substantive viability and consequences of the job description being fashioned for Ford, and the quality of judgment involved in proposing it, and this was essentially missed by television, although print journalism did much better with it.

Bill Moyers commented that "Politicians deal in a world of complexity, and television deals in a world of simplicity," but the competitive nature of political journalism in general puts a higher premium on new developments and on being right first, on scoreboard and horse-race reporting, than on explaining the underlying meaning of events, examining issues, and analyzing the character of candidates. The press as a whole made bad predictions and reached premature conclusions during 1980. Bush was all but nominated after his Iowa victory. The drum-fire about Reagan's age liability didn't make a dent on the voters. Kennedy was characterized as the victor almost before he started, later pronounced politically defunct, then hastily resuscitated after his victories in the New York and Connecticut primaries. Both the print and electronic media pretended that the terms "closed" and "open" meant what they said rather than the opposite in describing the Democratic national convention, abused their use of polls, and along with the candidates shamelessly played the "lowered expectations" numbers game to the hilt.

Yet the media performed an incredible task in exposing the public to everything they could lay their hands on about the campaign, and generated torrents of information for the use of the electorate. Bill Casey states in the pages that follow, " . . . the power of the media is the most critical single parameter in the vote decision." Ultimately, the voters must be capable of intelligent discrimination and willing to sort their way carefully through a lot of diverse material in making their decision, but the information is available.

Despite the fact that political parties have, for a number of reasons, been getting progressively weaker and less influential in both their electoral and governance role in recent years, the rebuilding of the Republican party for 1980 is a factor which has to be cited in any effort to understand that election. As a number of this book's authors pointed out both during the conference and outside of it, the G.O.P. designed and executed a superb effort in basics: organization, computerized data and management techniques, recruiting, training, advertising, turnout, and, above all, fundraising. Following Vietnam, Watergate, and the Carter victory over Ford in 1976, the prognosis was bleak for the Republicans, who appeared divided, unattractive, and listless, even to some of their own. The new Democratic leadership was rooted in the South and was enlarging its centrist strength by moving to the right. Yet the precampaign program laid down under the leadership of their National Committee led by Chairman Brock put the Republicans in a strong position to challenge the incumbent Democrat, resist chewing each other up, and capitalize on opportunities as they developed in the course of the campaign.

By January 1980 numerous articles appeared remarking on the G.O.P.'s strength, its financial health, grassroots and base-broadening efforts, and victories in the off-year elections, but particularly noting the undivided, cohesive personality of the minority party. At the same time, the Democrats were characterized as debt-ridden, divergent, and purposeless, with an eroding electoral base and a leader with slipping support increasingly burdened by what were for him, at least, intransigent problems and unattractive choices in running the country. The "build up the challenger" game is normally played by the media at about this point in the political calendar — after all, presidential campaigns are even bigger business in a tighter race — but the contrasts depicted between the two parties were also true. Toward the end of the primaries, Republicans looked suspiciously like they might be putting it all together. Ford had stayed out of the race; Reagan seemed to be getting younger all the time; and his defeated opponents were, on the whole, gracious and supportive. On the other side, there were suggestions that Carter might have to resign to deal effectively with the nation's problems without the distractions of a political campaign; uncommitted delegates were emerging in numbers greater than predicted; Kennedy wasn't getting out of the race; and Mondale was being cast as a possible "consensus" candidate. Hamilton Jordan later expressed his frustration, to say the least, that "Kennedy would wait until the absolute last moment to hand over his sword—and then only after he had taken the last few whacks out of our old and tired political hides."

The Republican National Committee's budget for 1980 was $26 million, and national party organizations contributed over $17 million to aid their presidential, Senate, House, and gubernatorial candidates. The comparable Democratic figures were roughly half of these. Republican "institutional" television advertising developed simple, compelling themes aimed at middle-income nonvoters and emphasizing rampant inflation, weakness abroad, a failed liberal Democrat ideology, and a sense of resurgent, patriotic confidence. At the Republican convention, the nominee's acceptance speech resonated with optimism about America's greatness. At the Democratic convention, the only rousingly inspirational words were spoken by the defeated challenger. Reagan and Bush, and even Ford, joined together raising clasped hands in Detroit in impressive, if expedient, cohesion, whereas a month later Carter and Kennedy were circling around the podium in Detroit apparently unable and unwilling, respectively, to touch—let alone embrace—each other. Much of this contrast had to do with the advantages of the outparty, the skill of Reagan and his campaign organization, and chance; but part of the cause can be attributed to the institutional strength of the Republican party.

T here were several impressive disappearing acts during the 1980 electoral struggle. Jerry Brown, John Connally, and George Bush were special cases. Brown didn't have much of a chance with Kennedy in the race, in the minds of most political operatives and analysts; Connally was out after only four primaries, despite expenditures of $12 million for which he won a single delegate; and Bush held on long enough during the primaries and subjugated himself well enough afterwards to make the November ballot. Gerald Ford twice threatened to play a leading role in the drama, but, ever the reluctant dragon, a combination of his own hesitations and solicitations dissuaded others. He waited too long to enter the primaries, and when he hinted for an invitation from "a broad-based group in my party," it wasn't issued. At the convention, he resisted inquiries concerning the number-two job, then entered into negotiations to upgrade it, and eventually precipitated a mutual withdrawal. Billy Carter was another act, although of a different sort, which failed to materialize, much to the relief of his brother. The Plains, Georgia, entrepreneur's sticky relations with the Libyans in the midst of oil and hostage imbroglios were dubbed "Billygate," and on August 3rd a headline in the *New York Times* described the Billy Carter problem as the "Political Sensation of the Election Year." But the president's skillful handling at a press conference the next day effectively silenced the threat.

The strongest nonperformance of the year, however, was that of John Anderson and the National Unity Campaign. His showing in the primaries was tantalizingly marginal in the sense that it didn't provide quite enough evidence of success or momentum to make a run as an independent candidate a compelling decision. The clue to the future might have been found in the results of the March 18th Illinois primary. Running in his own home state, with crossover voting privileges to benefit an "independent" candidate, and following a strong showing in Massachusetts, Anderson only got 36.7 percent of the vote to Reagan's 48.4 percent. But winning better than a quarter of the vote in five primaries, combined with a perception of widespread lack of enthusiasm for either of the likely November contenders and his own philosophical and personal commitment, the urge became seductive. Anderson announced his independent candidacy on April 24th.

From then on, he suffered from several persistent problems: a system which gives the advantage to the two major parties and makes it difficult for other entrants; intensely related difficulties in raising funds, getting television exposure, and demonstrating enough popular support to be regarded as a genuine rather than a protest candidate; and an inability to put together a clear and cohesive ideological or programmatic alternative to the other two candidates. During the primaries, Anderson was credited with a fresh, direct, candid style and unconventionally sensible and nonexpedient policy positions. As he qualified for the ballot in state after state and moved up in the polls, speculation was rife that he could do well enough in states where Carter had a narrow lead over Reagan to swing the electoral votes under our winner-take-all system to the Republican challenger. There was even intense hypothesizing about Anderson winning enough states outright—Massachusetts plus just one or two of the states Ford took from Carter in 1976, one projection had it—to throw the election into the House for its decision and perhaps even reverting to the Senate in the event of deadlock in the lower body.

Admittedly, our scandalously obsolete and dangerous backup system to deal with the lack of a clear majority in the electoral college itself perversely stimulates scenarios which would activate it. But these aspirations or apprehensions about the Anderson candidacy — which only fleetingly, if ever, suggested that he could change the direction of American government or win the presidency outright — are now hard even to recall. The Anderson campaign won a decision by the Federal Election Commission to qualify for partial, retroactive public financing, but was frustrated in its struggle to get into the debates. Gracious, fair, with sights high, John Anderson never won the image of a viable candidate and got wiped out by the big boys, their resources and their own fight. On November 4th, he received 5,719,437 votes, 7 percent of the total national vote, and no electoral votes. The highest vote percentage he polled within a single state, Massachusetts, was 15 percent.

L ooking back at the campaign in its various parts, structural and behavioral, considering how well it worked overall, what the weaknesses and strengths were, it's not a particularly pretty sight. It produced confusion and exhaustion; cost scads of money; at times seemed curiously separated from the challenges of governing ahead — not to say detached from reality; appeared to place unnatural demands, hypermetabolic pressures, and peevish tests on the candidates; and finally only about half of the eligible voters cast their ballot.

At the end of a typical eight-event day, during another seven-day week, in the fifteenth month of campaigning, while brightly spouting boiler-plate rhetoric in fear of losing momentum or making a mistake, candidates gave the impression that their brains had turned to pudding. The Democrats squabbled about making their convention a more deliberative body, but at the cost of changing the rules in the middle of the game. Political Action Committees and independent expenditures replaced individual high financiers. Media organizations functioned both as major actors and shapers of politics and as the enterprising businessmen which they, in fact, are. Fed up with cynicism, abandonment of traditional values, and corruption in political life, a band of evangelical religious leaders joined the fray, but too often contributed more of the bigotry, television promotion, money hustling, and negativism already rampant in electoral politics, instead of wisdom and healing Christian charity. The phenomenon of three born-again Christians on the ticket, incidentally, should be attributed more to accident than to a new electoral religiosity in the land or the single-minded discipline of the zealot—indeed, each of the three proved their sophistication, pragmatism, breadth of knowledge, and sensitivity in various ways.

The public at its worst combined an attitude of irritation and anxiety about confusing and threatening events around it and one of exuberance at the prospects of returning to a simpler, more promising age; it seemed poised between demanding that government be smaller and less intrusive and that it do the impossible. Or as George Will has observed, "You cannot tell people over and over that government is a klutz that cannot help Cleveland, and then suddenly say: Oh, by the way, give the government $1.3 trillion for military assets and support its attempt to do something about Cuba." Given the electoral uncertainty and impatience of the American people, we may be in a period when our presidents are more likely than not to be summarily tossed out of office in their first shot at re-election.

That's the bad news. On the other hand, the process showed flexibility and pluralism, tested the stamina and resourcefulness of individual candidates and their organizations, provided them plenty of opportunity to expose their qualities and relate to events, and disseminated a plethora of information and criticism. The system "worked." The people spoke. The transition of power occurred smoothly. The new government is hard at work, trying out new ideas within an institutional framework which still endures. Nothing we learned about 1980 suggests concrete change in the electoral process which would be clearly beneficial and feasible to implement. Even so, from the pages of this book we can reasonably conclude that some improvement in the way we nominate and elect presidents would be a good idea, and we should not simply heave a sign of relief that the ordeal is over and put it out of our minds until it's again too late to act.

While keeping in mind some of the trouble that "reform" has already gotten us into, efforts to improve the process might follow three basic guidelines. First, assess the drawbacks as well as the benefits of change, and don't bite off more than can be chewed and digested. Neither the excesses of the present system nor its capacity to improve itself should be overestimated, and meddling too ambitiously can result in no change at all. Second, seek changes consistent with the strengthening of the role of political parties, which despite their weaknesses can be an antidote for the fragmentation of American political life. Stronger parties can help to reconcile disparate interests and build coalitions; to resist the separatism of campaigns run independently by "professionals"; to perform critical linkage tasks relating campaigns to governance and connecting candidates, issues, and ideology; and to bring individual citizens at the grassroots closer to their own institutions of government. Third, synchronize different kinds of recommended changes so as to avoid the discombobulation of their running headlong into each other. Over the past several years, for instance, reforms in delegate selection procedures have produced a proliferation of more costly state primaries while campaign finance reforms have restricted the money available to nominating campaigns.

Proposals abound in various categories for renovating the structure of our nominating and electing system. The overall campaign is too protracted and should be shortened, and although this is very difficult to accomplish, it should probably take priority over efforts to "order" the primaries by regional or time-zone groupings. The ratios between "bound" versus "unbound" and primary-elected versus party-selected delegates should be shifted in favor of the latter categories, while maintaining some balance. Greater participation by elected officials would help in providing continuity between electoral and governing processes and in making the conventions more deliberative, but they can't be unduly pampered into delegate roles. A national primary will be promoted and should be prohibited. All of these courses involve difficult judgments about how much uniformity to impose from above on a pluralistic system which must have muscle, vitality, and individuality at the state level, and it appears better to proceed by party rather than Congressional action.

The awful problems of financing political campaigns will continue to plague us. Money should neither be allowed to run amuck nor be banished from the system—the latter attitude ignores human nature, freedom of expression, and the need for a democracy to pay for the reciprocal dynamic of exposure and education between the citizens and the officials who must both represent and lead them. In addition to proposals which encourage increased access to television by political candidates and public service broadcasts about election campaigns, the Institute of Politics Campaign Finance Study Group has made recommendations which would raise the limits on individual contributions in order to offset the amount of money coming from political action committees, increase the overall spending limit, and abolish state-by-state limits. It was only subsequent to the conference that produced this book that a Federal Elections Commission audit disclosed that the Reagan campaign, in some measure of post–Iowa panic, had overspent its New Hampshire limit by about 150 percent. The amount of overspending was paid back, but as Ken Bode has pointed out since, "Those dollars were vastly more valuable to them in January and February of 1980 than a year later." The story hardly validates the efficacy of this particular feature of the current finance rules.

Finally, the system for counting the votes of the general election needs attention, if not in the form of a direct popular vote, then by abolition of the electoral college itself and some more rational form of fallback than throwing the decision into the House of Representatives if an electoral majority is not achieved.

The legitimacy of our democratic process of choosing presidents must be proven both by the way it tests those qualities actually needed for the job and by the extent to which it avoids providing so many disincentives that our most able and qualified leaders are dissuaded from running in the first place unless they are out of a job, excessively well-heeled, or in possession of bizarre ego drives. The authors of this book were not asked to address these two standards explicitly, but there may be derivative counsel to be gained from their discussion, and in any event efforts to improve the system will benefit by keeping them prominently in mind. Ultimately, even more than the structure of the system, the values and behavior of the participants—campaign operatives, party people, big and small funders, media commentators and managers, government legislators and regulators, and the candidates and the voters themselves—will determine whether these two criteria are honored truly or in the breach. That, of course, will rest upon the maturity and selflessness of the whole society, which could improve as we spend still more time working at our democracy, spurred by the more explicit shortcomings of its institutions and intensity of the problems it faces.

It *is* inadequate and self-serving for some of our campaign decisionmakers to conclude, as they do at the end of this book, that in the final analysis it's all quite properly left in the hands of the candidates and the people. Unless they are willing to point out at the same time that a good deal of their own activity can be interpreted as designed to frustrate rather than facilitate that purity, it's a cop-out. In other words, it should be made clear that neither the candidates nor the people are now fulfilling their responsibilities adequately in the electoral process and that they require more help from other components of the system in the way of less parochial and more idealistic performance. We are actually in danger of over-emphasizing the performance of the presidential candidates in the course of campaigns even as we over-rate the power of our presidents during the course of their terms. In both cases, we have a system which can only work pluralistically, with all of the components reinforcing one another, with leadership provided not just from those at the top but throughout the society, as required in a nation made up of its own governors, as ours still pretends to be.

It may be that most voters for Reagan reached their decision in 1980, as our authors suggest, in repudiation of President Carter's record. That's a perfectly sound basis, as long as it's accompanied by a sense of reality about the complex challenges and limited power of the presidency. It may be that the people who voted for Reagan in 1980 did so largely because of their instincts about the personal qualities of the candidates, and that's not a bad basis either, particularly given the bloated rhetoric, superficial treatment of confusing issues, and conniving and manipulating done during campaigns, as this transcript shows. It's no accident that the most non-manic candidate just got elected president. The point is that the people—all of us—have got to work harder at it and with a larger vision. *We* are being tested by the electoral process, not just the candidates and our various procedural and structural devices, and all the most skilled tinkering with the system will not matter a whit without basic changes in the attitudes, values, and behavior of all the supporting players.

Cambridge, Massachusetts
May 1, 1981

1 BEFORE THE PRIMARIES

The Bush Challenge. The Connally Camp. Dole's Bid. The Anderson Plan. Baker's Problems. The Reagan Strategy. Bush and Iowa. The G.O.P. Favorite. The Democratic Nomination. Brown as Challenger. Carter's Approach. Pressure on Kennedy. Carter as the Incumbent. The Kennedy Draft. Carter's View. The Hostage Crisis. Des Moines Debate. Reagan in 1979. The Other Republicans. 1979 for the Democrats.

ADAM CLYMER (correspondent, *New York Times*): Nineteen seventy-nine, which is basically the period this session is going to cover, was probably a more active year before the election than ever before. Whoever does this job four years from now may have to deal with 1982 and 1983, the way campaigns get longer and longer. We are arbitrarily going to limit our discussion to 1979. There isn't anyone here from Phil Crane's campaign to complain that that leaves out his announcement of candidacy on August 2, 1978.

I want to start this session with a reminder of two things that I want to return to at the end, and I hope you will think about them as we go through. First of all, this preprimary, precaucus year did seem to be more important than it's been in the past, and I'd like you to think about whether that, in fact, was so. If it was, was it because of things that politicians, state parties, or candidates did, or because of things that we and the newspaper and television business did? Another thing I'd like to go around the table on at the end, after we've kicked around 1979, is: What had your candidate accomplished relative to what he might have accomplished in the course of that year, and what singular problems or opportunities did you see as the election year began?

I think I'd like to start by going around and asking people, at least one person from each campaign, to talk briefly about what the opportunities were at the beginning of 1979. There wasn't anybody who ran for president in 1980 who didn't have people around him and around this table thinking he might run in 1979. Even if they hadn't all decided, there were people working for them or thinking about it or assessing the situation. The best way to start is with the Republicans, going around the table briefly. Bob Teeter, in 1979, was working for George Bush. What made any of you folks think that your fellow could beat Ronald Reagan, and what had to happen for that to occur?

— THE BUSH CHALLENGE —

ROBERT M. TEETER (president, Market Opinion Research): I think there was never any certainty whether Bush or anyone else could beat Ronald Reagan. I think the key was that you had to get yourself in a position so that if something happened and the opportunity that Ronald Reagan could be defeated presented itself, you were the alternative to Reagan.

LYN NOFZIGER (press secretary, Reagan–Bush Committee): They kept thinking he'd die!

TEETER: The real sense of it was to become, among all the other candidates, the alternative to Ronald Reagan. There were a number of people who were firmly committed to Reagan, and there were a number of people who objected to Reagan and didn't want to vote for Reagan or see him as the nominee. The first problem in the Bush campaign was to become the *one* other Republican who was running against Reagan; in some way to get Baker, Dole, Connally, and the other candidates out of the race so that you could sooner or later have Reagan one-on-one. There was an effort then to build on Bush's popularity within the party. He had been chairman of the National Committee; he was well known among the party people and reasonably popular among them. We simply followed the rules that everyone has come to know that primaries and early caucuses are far and away the most important—they're everything now. What it takes in those early ones is a number of dedicated people within those states, campaigning full time, and probably, in order to become that alternative, establishing some uniqueness. It seemed to me then, as it does now, that there are probably three ways that you can establish that uniqueness. First, you may have some candidates who simply, by the force of their personality, may be unique and different from all the others. Second, you may have a candidate who has a message that is more unique than all the other candidates in the primaries. It seems to me that that is what President Carter did in 1976, and I think it was difficult to figure out how to do that with Bush against Baker and Connally and Dole, who were not ideologically very different. Certainly none of them, with the exception of maybe Connally, had that unique force of personality that would break them apart from the pack. So the third way, the real way to do it, was to win some early caucuses and early primaries. And that alone would break you away. Almost the entire effort was to build some kind of an organization that would allow you to do that, during that period in early 1980.

KENNETH A. BODE (network correspondent, NBC News): Wasn't there also, in the case of Bush in particular, an effort to position yourself so that you didn't alienate Reagan's support?

TEETER: Yes.

BODE: So Reagan was the one who stumbled?

TEETER: Absolutely. There was a very definite effort to make sure that Bush didn't become an anti-Reagan candidate or a stop-Reagan candidate, a vehicle for the people who were against Reagan.

—THE CONNALLY CAMP—

CLYMER: Eddie Mahe, tell us how this looked from John Connally's perspective.

EDDIE MAHE, JR. (campaign director, John Connally for President): If you accept Bob's premise that there are three ways you position a candidate, with John Connally the force of personality is the obvious one that you are going to use. But perhaps we thought our situation was somewhat different, in that we felt we had to take on Ronald Reagan head-to-head at some point because his base and our base were too much the same. We were not competitive with Baker or Bush, the so-called moderate wing. Our strength was going to come out of Reagan's strength and so we felt that we had to take him on, which we tried to do at a national level. We could not attempt to take him on just in Iowa—setting aside the problem of getting Governor Connally to spend three months in Iowa campaigning in kitchens—we felt we had to take on Governor Reagan nationally. We could not alienate his people because that obviously would work to our disadvantage, but we had to be more than just an alternative. We had to be preferable to Governor Reagan at some point with the same base that he was going after.

CLYMER: How did you see that you would make him preferable to Reagan?

MAHE: Probably by sheer contrast of force and personality. If you accepted that a dominant issue in the campaign was the subjective issue of leadership, then John Connally personified leadership to many different people. One of our big strengths was that people were scared of Connally because he had a reputation of being very tough. The best example of this that was ever put to me was by former Governor John Love of Colorado when he came on our National Steering Committee. He said, "I've been against him too many times. This time I'm going to just get on the right side to begin with." That feeling was out there in the minds of a lot of people. Even those who did not like him would not question his capacity to be a strong leader, and we felt the head-to-head comparison on that dimension ultimately would work to our benefit.

—DOLE'S BID—

CLYMER: Jo-Anne Coe, how did Bob Dole think he might get the Republican nomination as he looked at that prospect early in 1979?

JO-ANNE COE (Office of Senator Robert Dole): We saw ourselves not only as an alternative to Ronald Reagan but as the choice beyond Reagan. Dole himself has even said, "I'm the younger Ronald Reagan. If you're looking for a younger Ronald Reagan, I am he!" Beyond that, we had felt that there was a group of voters out there who had not yet identified themselves with any candidate—more or less a coalition of voters that could very personally identify with Dole such as the farmers and veterans and handicapped that he had worked with on a one-to-one basis over the years. We felt we had an opportunity to reach out to them that some of the other candidates might not have. That was the base of our strength that we were hoping to develop further.

—THE ANDERSON PLAN—

CLYMER: Mike MacLeod, how did John Anderson think he was going to do this?

MICHAEL F. MACLEOD (campaign manager—treasurer, National Unity Campaign): I think it's safe to say that our particular strategy at the beginning of the year had less to do with mechanics than with ideology. In retrospect, this may have been a mistake, but we viewed, and I think properly so, the distinction between John Anderson and all of the rest of the candidates as principally ideological. Most professional observers felt at the time that there was just no way that a so-called moderate or progressive Republican could indeed do well in the primaries.

Back in 1979 when he declared, I remember standing by as he made his announcement statement, remembering what Oscar Wilde said about second marriages—that they are the triumph of hope over experience. And yet I felt as we looked through the nominating process and the state laws and some thirty-five states that were having Republican primaries, that there was a certain amount of opportunity there that perhaps had not been tapped before, and that rested

6 THE CAMPAIGN FOR PRESIDENT: 1980 IN RETROSPECT

principally in those eighteen states where some measure of crossover voting was allowed. In the first four primary states where we chose to focus our early efforts—New Hampshire, Massachusetts, Illinois, and Wisconsin—three out of the four offered a certain amount of promise for us to dilute the traditional conservative Republican primary vote (and these are my own words and I should make that clear). In retrospect, it didn't work as well as it should have but I must say, in January, as we sat there poised to strike in New Hampshire in the February primary, I was reasonably optimistic. Looking backward to a November Harris poll that showed that only 1 percent of the American people knew who John Anderson was—and with all due respect to my friend and candidate, I'm sure that most of those 1 percent were confusing him with Jack Anderson—and having just come out of the Des Moines debate where he had done extremely well and seeing a tremendous wellspring of financial support.

CLYMER: We're trying to focus more on 1979, particularly at the beginning of it—was there anything singular that made it look doable in the year before the primaries?

MACLEOD: I'll defer to anyone else who has a different opinion, but I don't think that there was really any distinction, in my own mind, for us until 1980. We really started way back on the wrong side of the curve, for a variety of reasons. I think the principal reason was the lack of money, and it really wasn't until 1980 that I saw a real shift in our own potential.

—BAKER'S PROBLEMS—

CLYMER: Doug Bailey, how did Howard Baker think he might be the one to beat Ronald Reagan?

DOUGLAS BAILEY (president, Bailey, Deardourff & Associates): Let me try to answer your very first question first, which I believe was what did your candidate accomplish in 1979 compared to what he could have accomplished.

CLYMER: Try to save those for the end.

BAILEY: But I think it governs everything that I'm likely to say about 1979 as far as Baker was concerned, because the answer is practically nothing. We spent most of 1979 discussing when he ought to get in the race. And I don't mean in terms of formal announcement, I mean in terms of organizational questions about getting off the ground. I think Baker is perhaps the principal political exponent of the notion that everything will turn out right in the end and, frankly, looking back over the last two years and seeing where he is now, maybe he's right. (*Laughter*)

We did have a thesis. It was clear that no one was going to take the nomination away from Governor Reagan unless that person became *the* alternative. In Baker's strategy, he had to do one more thing than just that. He also had to directly contest George Bush and beat him. That was not evident in early 1979 because Bush's strength frankly was not evident in early 1979. Maybe there was a Baker assumption made incorrectly by a lot of people to dismiss the Bush candidacy as serious and as a major factor, and that caused a delay in making decisions to get into the race. The theory essentially was—and I'm interested in hearing some of the comments by the people around the table on this, but I remember many discussions between people in different non-Reagan Republican campaigns—that somehow there was a magical 35–40 percent that was an automatic Reagan vote in virtually every Republican primary, but for him to get above that would be very difficult. So he would do well in early primaries and not well in late primaries, and the key was to survive long enough; and I think it was an underlying thesis of the Baker campaign to be the survivor so that when it came down to two people, it would be Reagan and Baker. But we had the additional problem as 1979 wore on that we had to beat George Bush or it was obvious to us that Bush would become the survivor.

ALBERT R. HUNT (correspondent, *Wall Street Journal*): Doug, we can get some of the particulars later, but was there in early 1979, given the experiences of '72 and '76 when candidates who had started so early and been out there in the Iowa and New Hampshires and had done so well, was there a feeling with either Baker or with some of the people around him that somehow the pendulum might swing back in '80 and in fact you could be an indoor candidate—a Senate candidate, if you will?

BAILEY: Well, I don't think quite that way, but there was another thing working in Baker's case which caused a delay. Teeter talked about uniqueness and how any candidate, to survive in the early going, had to generate some uniqueness. Baker, I think, believed, and in one sense correctly so, that he was in a position of responsibility unlike most of the others that were running. So it was very tempting to think that continued Senate responsibilities in the leadership role would help him establish that uniqueness which constantly was an argument against getting going early organizationally. I think it's also fair to say, and he would, I think, now agree with this, that his concept of political organization is vastly different than anybody else's who has been through the process of Republican primary politics, and that was a battle waged in his mind in 1979 as well.

BODE: How did you all regard Baker's position on the Panama Canal as you began plotting where you stood ideologically with the Republican-based primary voters?

BAILEY: Seriously, in the long run, because doing battle one-on-one with Governor Reagan, if it ever got to that point, would be a major, major issue. In the early going, it would have been a major issue in the South and not necessarily a major issue in the North. That was part of the decision, frankly, to bypass the Southern primaries. The other part of that decision which is dominant was that we had to beat Bush and we had to take him on where he was strong in the early going, or otherwise we wouldn't get anywhere.

TEETER: I think you should comment for just a moment on what role you thought a potential SALT debate would have. That was obviously a major factor in Baker's life at that point.

BAILEY: I'm not going to kid you and say there was no discussion of the pluses and minuses of SALT from a political standpoint. But I would say clearly at the outset that Baker's opposition to SALT was a very strong personal opinion and the question then was whether he should stay in the Senate to fight the SALT treaty or get out and campaign. As a practical matter the decision essentially was to stay and fight the SALT treaty. There are a whole lot of other things imposing on that, but again one way of establishing uniqueness was to take on the president over a major issue in the Senate and beat him. The fact is—whether it was Baker's fault or to Baker's credit that the SALT treaty was so soundly defeated—that it never came to the debate which could have allowed him to establish that unique quality on one issue.

—THE REAGAN STRATEGY—

CLYMER: Dick Wirthlin, which of these guys looked, early in 1979 and maybe again in September, like the biggest threat to Reagan's nomination?

RICHARD B. WIRTHLIN (deputy director of strategy and planning, Reagan–Bush Committee): That changed as the campaign progressed. As you'll recall, Connally came out of the box very strong, very early. In that initial phase of the first four months of 1979, even when Connally was getting good kudos in the press, we felt that Baker potentially was our strongest contender outside of Ford. The decision that we were somewhat concerned about all through 1979 was that Gerald Ford might grasp the gauntlet again and mount a primary challenge. If that had happened, it would have changed the whole chess board for us. But early it was clear to us that aside from Ford, Baker had the base, the name identification, and the reservoir of goodwill to make a fairly strong challenge should he have decided perhaps to have mounted his campaign somewhat earlier than he did. By the end of the year, by December 1979, however, Baker's star faded politically. While Bush wasn't garnering a good deal of public support then, we felt that potentially Bush would be our strongest opponent, even prior to the Iowa debate, for three reasons. We saw Bush doing things organizationally that gave us pause for concern. We monitored very carefully the amount of financial resources that he was gathering. And he was showing some momentum, which of course didn't come to full-blown political impact until after the Iowa vote.

CLYMER: Did you do anything different in the Reagan campaign as the targets of your concern changed?

WIRTHLIN: Through most of 1979 we felt we had one major and paramount opportunity, and that was to use the primary to build the coalitional base and begin establishing the issue agenda for the general election. That pretty well overrode a lot of the decisions we were making in terms of the announcement, for example. We felt there would be an advantage in not officially declaring early, but late, so that we would have maximum impact. Secondly, the things we discussed and the topics the Governor addressed when he did announce were specifically designed to appeal to a group of voters who were outside the direct purview of the Republican primaries.

CLYMER: We haven't heard of the North American Accord since then, have we?*

WIRTHLIN: Who knows? We may again.

BILL BROCK (chairman, Republican National Committee): Was anybody thinking in any of the campaigns about "sweating" Reagan by trying to wait him out and let him announce before they did? Did that enter into anybody's conversation at all?

MAHE: Clearly, we never had that option. We had too many negatives to deal with, and there was no way we could outwait Reagan. Our strategy was just the opposite: to get out front and get out hard, making him, in effect, come against us. By having reached that point when he came in, it would not be seen as the race being over because Governor Reagan had announced.

BROCK: It seemed to me that he had an enormous advantage by being able to hold back, and obviously I think it worked.

TEETER: I don't think there was anybody else strong enough to do that. If he'd had a formidable opponent who was anywhere equal to him, they might have been able to do it. Ford could have done it had he run at some later point. But Bush, for example, couldn't get the organizational support or the money he needed unless he announced. He was actually in a situation where he had to inch his way up the ladder.

---

*The North American Accord refers to a proposal advanced by Governor Reagan early in his campaign to establish cooperative economic relationships between the governments of Canada, the United States, and Mexico.

BAILEY: It probably won't surprise you to learn that there was active consideration given within the Baker campaign to waiting longer and, in fact, conceivably waiting until after the first round of primaries, which is one thesis that I think was also considered by Ford.

TIM KRAFT (campaign manager, Carter–Mondale Re-election Committee): As one of several people who watched Senator Baker in 1979 with great interest, I'd like to ask Doug Bailey a couple of questions. One, was there a definite commitment at the outset of 1979 on the part of the senator to run for President? And two, was some hard thought given with reference to the 1976 campaigns as to how valuable that Senate minority leader position was in terms of nomination politics vis-à-vis the organizational and fundraising decisions—that is, to get out there and build a war chest and establish credibility and winnability in, say, Iowa and New Hampshire and Florida and the other early states?

BAILEY: To answer that question, Tim, I've got to go back to the very first meeting that I ever had with Senator Baker, the first time I ever met him. It was just after the 1978 elections. I was automatically taken by the man and his potential. But I was also struck, I've got to tell you, by the fact that the only decision in relation to the presidency that had been made was the decision in Baker's mind that he wanted it. And as a practical matter, the decisionmaking process in the first six months of '79 was just horrendous, largely because Baker was not surrounded by people. He had not put a team together either in terms of professionals or fundraisers or whatever. He did not have the people necessary to make the decision. Was there hard thought about the Senate? Yes, about the pluses and minuses of staying or getting out. In retrospect I'm not sure that a particularly intelligent decision was made there, but there was an awful lot of consideration. It was very difficult, and if you know Baker, as you do, one of the things which I find so appealing about him is that he is a man who is not irrationally committed to any course. You say over and over again, and people at this table have written over and over again, that maybe it's not a very good system if the only candidate who can make it is one that is irrationally committed to the presidency. That was not the nature of his commitment, and frankly that attracted me to him as a candidate and as a potential president but not as a political success story.

DAVID S. BRODER (associate editor and national political correspondent, *Washington Post*): Could I ask Bill Brock whether, from his viewpoint as Republican chairman in '79, it looked as if the Republican party was structured to produce a Reagan nomination or if there were strategies that could have had a different outcome?

BROCK: I thought Reagan was probably a six-to-five shot for the nomination but no better. In other words, he had a slight edge over the field, but I did not believe that it was foregone, by any means. I thought probably Bush and Baker were the only ones who had any real chance to pose an alternative unless Ford got in, which would of course have been a very real contest. But I watched campaigns doing what I thought maybe they shouldn't have done, and I thought by the end of '79, the only possible alternative might be George Bush and I frankly didn't know whether he could do it. I thought it depended entirely upon his ability to win the Iowa caucuses.

—BUSH AND IOWA—

CLYMER: Let's focus on that for a second. It seemed to some of us that indeed the Bush campaign was focusing entirely on the Iowa caucuses, and to some extent it also looked as if the Bush campaign, to a very considerable degree, was the 1976 Carter campaign without the substance. That there was a look at the timetable, a look at what kind of support Carter got at an Iowa straw poll at a dinner that made him look good, and by God, George Bush would go to every meeting where six or more Republicans gathered in Iowa and hope that he'd win a straw poll. The Bush campaign looked very good organizationally in 1979, but was the candidate explaining to himself or to the voters why he ought to be president?

TEETER: I don't think he was nor do I think his success depended on doing that. I think you're correct in saying that to some significant degree the Bush campaign was the Carter campaign of 1976. That's why I pointed out a few minutes ago that those early primaries and caucuses are important, and the unique breaking away from the pack would come from the fact that you won the Iowa caucuses. Then you would have the opportunity to create the message when you had the awareness and attention of the press after that. I really don't think that was a requirement prior to Iowa.

MAHE: Was there any preparation as to what the message was going to be?

TEETER: Yes and no. There was a great deal of issue preparation. There was a great deal of substantive preparation. I don't think it was ever agreed upon well at any point what kind of central theme or message there was going to be. I think there were a lot of details but no real central theme.

HUNT: Can I just touch on something Tim Kraft said earlier? I would be curious as to how the Democrats handicapped the Republicans in 1979—who you thought were the strong candidates and who you feared the most.

MARTIN F. NOLAN (Washington bureau chief, *Boston Globe*): And is it true that there was the opposite of Lyn Nofziger's description—when they all light candles and pray for Governor Reagan's health?

CLYMER: What do you think of that, Tom?

—THE G.O.P. FAVORITE—

TOM QUINN (campaign manager, Brown for President): Having grown up in California and having been there when Ronald Reagan was governor and having worked as a reporter for a TV station in Sacramento back in 1966 when he was running in the primaries, it was obvious to me that Ronald Reagan was one of the most effective campaigners in the country. I was always amazed that people thought he could be beaten in the Republican primaries. Maybe I have even elevated his campaign abilities beyond reality, but my first political experience when Jerry Brown asked me to run his campaign in 1970 was to go back and read all the internal memos of the Pat Brown campaign in 1966. All the political wizards around Pat Brown wrote little memos as to how they had to help Ronald Reagan win the nomination and somehow damage George Christopher, his opponent, because Reagan would obviously be a pushover. After Reagan won they were delighted, and they had this whole advertising strategy based on having a real governor, not an acting governor. That one theme was made into a commercial. I think it ran only once, with Pat Brown leaning down to a little black girl and saying, "You know, it was an actor that shot Lincoln." Well, there was a psychology there of underestimating this guy that I saw in the Carter campaign this year. It always seemed to me that Ronald Reagan was the strongest potential Republican nominee.

CLYMER: Carl Wagner, in Kennedy's office even early in the year there was plainly a little thought about running for president. Who looked like the toughest Republican then?

CARL WAGNER (director of field operation, Kennedy for President): I think the sense was Reagan was clearly the strongest guy. The coalescence not only of the forces within the Republican party but countervailing forces which had developed since 1976 in American politics generally argued for his candidacy more than that of a moderate candidate. In addition to that, the issues that were developing late in 1979 lent themselves, at least in my judgment, to the Reagan campaign more than to a moderate campaign. Having said that, it was my own view in 1979, more so early than late, that the possibility of the emergence of a moderate candidate in the Republican party was a serious option. Bush or Baker—and in my view Bush—was the more serious candidate principally because of earlier and better organization. I thought Bush would win in Iowa by virtue of what he had done in 1979. I was surprised by how early he'd been there and how well he had done it, although I didn't know whether he could capitalize on that and move to New Hampshire, Massachusetts, and then to Illinois. I had no idea of what the thinking inside the Bush campaign was, but by no means did I think by virtue of the structure of the Republican party, the primaries, or institutional forces in the country, that this option was impossible. I thought Bush was impressive because he had considerable support among some very serious and I think weighty institutions in the Republican party.

CLYMER: Pat Caddell, what did it look like from your perspective?

PATRICK H. CADDELL (president, Cambridge Survey Research): From our perspective, I think that there was no question, given the general cohesiveness of the minority party—particularly as conservative as the Republican primary voters seemed to be—that Reagan was the odds-on favorite. What was very clear was that he had run against an incumbent President in 1976 in a party which, by definition of its minority status, tends to be more cohesive and more institutionally leveraged, and he had almost taken the nomination away from Gerald Ford. It didn't strike us that any of the other candidates, once you got to the primaries, was going to have the kind of strength that Ford had had. In thinking about a general election, which was at that point not our singular concern, we had some other preferences of people to run against, but people we never thought we would get a chance to. The foremost person was Governor Connally, just because of the problems that he had and so on, but we never really took that seriously. The person that we were most concerned about as a general election candidate was Howard Baker, for obvious reasons. He had a position, he's a moderate, he came from the border South. As 1979 wore on, we were constantly amazed at Baker's lack of startup in taking that on.

CLYMER: Weren't there at least some times when no matter how good he looked for the Republican nomination in 1979, Reagan looked like an easy candidate to beat in the general election?

CADDELL: Well, he certainly looked a lot easier to us than Baker did, and Bush was an unknown. Frankly, you looked at Reagan at that point and he carried a lot of negatives, as most of the candidates did. He was better known, but he seemed to us to be a candidate that in the general election might well be limited in his constituency, particularly compared to a centrist candidate in a general election. The thing we were most hoping for had nothing to do with the eventual winner of the Republican primaries—that we would not have a long Democratic contest and particularly that the Republicans would go through a blood bath or process where the campaign would become so competitive that it would last a long time. Then the candidates would be forced to deal with one another as we had seen in our party and in the Republican party in 1976. We wanted someone to emerge against Reagan so the campaign would go on to some extent.

BODE: Pat, as you were toting up Reagan's negatives, what were the dominant ones?

CADDELL: For one thing, we weren't doing any extensive surveys. We had done some work on Reagan in 1976 and we knew that he had some particular problems, but we didn't have extensive information. We could see that even at that time in early '79, he was running on favorable ratings in the 40th percentile as a general election candidate, and the incumbent was not enjoying particularly high ratings himself, which is the kind of person you would like to run against.

BODE: So your people were praying for Reagan from your own point of view?

CADDELL: Well, again, I wouldn't use the word "praying," but we were hoping that he would survive. The reasons were ideological ones to start with; we felt we could cut him out, and hold the South if we had to.

NOFZIGER: You just wanted him to die in the general election!

CADDELL: I'm not sure, given the way you phrase that. The person we were most afraid of was not a candidate in the race; it was Gerald Ford. I was convinced from the outset that if Ford were the nominee of the Republican party, we were going to lose and lose badly. When you looked at Reagan, particularly compared to someone like Ford, you saw someone who had weaknesses among Democrats, moderates, and independents. Reagan had weaknesses in the Northeast industrial belt at that point more than he had in the West. And we felt pretty secure that we could at least contest the South fairly well. We didn't think that he would draw as well as Ford in the North, particularly with constituencies that we had had difficulties with Ford in 1976.

—THE DEMOCRATIC NOMINATION—

CLYMER: Let's shift our attention—and the Republicans will get their chance to throw some rocks at the Democrats—to the race that got, to the frustration of the candidates and many of the people they represent, a great deal more attention in 1979 than the Republican contest: the race for the Democratic nomination. We began 1979, again an arbitrary date, having come out of the Democratic mini-convention in Memphis in December of 1978, a mini-convention in which the Carter folks won every vote they wanted. But if there was ever a Pyrrhic victory in public relations terms, that was their victory in Memphis because Senator Kennedy gave what is probably one of the great political speeches of the era. This was the "sometimes the party must sail against the winds" speech, and White House aides of my acquaintance were jumping up and down in the back of the room cheering, occasionally looking around the room to see who else had seen them.

KRAFT: Hey, don't look at me!

CLYMER: You weren't in the back, Tim. There was plainly a potential for a contest for the Democratic nomination. One of the things that I personally have been most curious about—and I'll take one prerogative from the chair—is was there ever, Tim, a strategy contemplated at the White House of killing Kennedy with kindness, of doing so many things for him that he would appear to be a total ingrate? Your proposing his National Health Insurance measure, putting Archibald Cox on the First Circuit Court of Appeals, and so forth. Did anyone argue that this was the way to deal with the possible challenge to the nomination?

KRAFT: Not very persuasively and not really. Perhaps this was weird. There was a feeling that this president had taken on tough issues and was applying himself intelligently and with industry and that we were making some progress and that he would be the best candidate for the Democratic party to renominate and the best hope for re-election. You start with this parochial, home-team, self-sustaining vision and then you question the credibility or the credentials of any challenger. I think that all goes without saying. But as to the sort of nomination strategy in light of a potential challenge by Senator Kennedy, part of our thinking was governed by a review of the Ford–Reagan relationship in 1975, in which we thought that Ford was perhaps too tentative in his declaration and his efforts to seek renomination. He was perhaps not definitive enough, and too solicitous of Reagan in an attempt to establish some sort of relationship, some friendship, or some accommodation. That in turn did not deter

Governor Reagan or his partisans; it may have even encouraged them to think that President Ford did have weaknesses, that he was vulnerable, that he was takeable, and that they would proceed in that direction. We did not want to adopt that course.

We also had the startup, as you all know, in February of 1979, of a campaign plan that had been conceived in the fall of 1978 before the midterm convention. We wanted to get started on all the elementary steps—fundraising which is so difficult at $1,000 a clip, and the initial organization in the primary and caucus states which takes more lead time and more startup effort than one might think at the outset. We wanted to be ready to take on any challenger as the season progressed in 1980.

CLYMER: Did Memphis and the mini-convention and any of your analyses of it change anything you did in early 1979?

KRAFT: Not really, primarily because there was no Shakespearean dilemma on the part of the president as to whether or not he would run.

CLYMER: We got that impression!

KRAFT: And the staff was ready to go with him, the initial organizational decisions had been made. It was just a matter of the mechanics of startup and, of course, the mechanics of the announcement itself in the summer. So Memphis was a distant early warning that Senator Kennedy would be more actively considering the race. But I think an honest canvas of White House and attendant political supporters of the president would show a very mixed consensus on whether or not we actually thought Senator Kennedy would run. I see some hindsight here about how well we knew he was going to run since Memphis; but from January to June, we did not know.

—BROWN AS CHALLENGER—

HUNT: How did you view the Jerry Brown thing?

KRAFT: Well, starting with '75-'76—you know, run everywhere, prepare thoroughly, anticipate the toughest possible opposition—

here was a Democratic governor from the largest state in the country that certainly had taken our measure, clocked us a couple of times in the spring of '76. You don't take him lightly, and you monitor his preparations very carefully: his fundraising efforts, his inroads into Democratic organizations, the people he put into New Hampshire and Florida. To be utterly candid, we became a little less concerned as we saw a rather slow startup in the fundraising efforts and a less than thorough and comprehensive effort in those early states which we felt a challenger would have to start in early to catch up and defeat the incumbent Democratic president.

CLYMER: Tom, when most of us talked to Brown in early 1979, he sounded for all the world like someone who was going to run for president, or were we just getting him on the odd days of the week? If that wasn't coincidence, why weren't you in more places worrying Kraft?

QUINN: I don't think Jerry had decided, really. He wanted to be president. He wanted to run. I think inside of him he expected to run, but he didn't want to make that final kind of commitment. There were a lot of us urging him right after the re-election in 1978 to get moving, but he wanted to wait. I remember, since we're talking about 1979, on New Year's Day up at Lake Tahoe reading a boxload of material Jerry had sent up to me on the balance-the-budget amendment and constitutional convention movement. We had quite an internal debate in the governor's office in the tail end of December, beginning of January. He wanted in his inaugural address in 1979 to come out and propose that. His logic was that Kennedy was a certain candidate, and he had to do something to distinguish himself from Kennedy. There were some of us who felt that if Kennedy were going to be in that race, Jerry could not win. There was really only room for one challenge to Carter.

CLYMER: The balanced budget device was a campaign tool for Governor Brown.

QUINN: Of course it was.

CLYMER: Lots of things are obvious, but now some people are saying that they weren't.

QUINN: No, no. I don't think anybody said that. I think that he believed in the balanced-budget amendment—believed it too much—to the point where he wanted to set up a nationwide committee to promote the balanced-budget amendment and the constitutional convention argument. That went through several months of discussion, during which period there should have been the establishment of a campaign committee. He probably didn't make up his mind for certain until something like May or even June—very late in the year. I would say probably within one month after he said all right, we had the exploratory committee set up. I think this was probably about the beginning of July. So there hadn't been a go-ahead from him, and that created the delay; even when the committee was set up he didn't want to announce, because it would be a commitment. He wanted to hold the option of pulling out, so nothing really began in our campaign until probably September. About the time it was really all over is the time we launched ourselves.

JOANNE SYMONS (cofounder, Draft Kennedy Movement): Tom, I never could understand that visit he made to the legislature on the balanced-budget thing, the way it was not prepared for and the resulting carnival. Was that just a "let's go to New Hampshire tonight" kind of decision?

QUINN: It's strange. From the outside when the world looks at politics, it's probably all organized, but ours was like a lot of the other campaigns I'm hearing about here today when you talk about what thoughts we had, what ideas, what strategy. We had the problem that Jerry was enamored with the constitutional convention concept, but nobody who worked for him was, and when that happens to a campaign you have difficulties. I mean, the candidate either has to bring the staff along or the staff has to convince the candidate, and we had this internal conflict dominating the internal discourse until probably very late in 1979. That's something Jerry did pretty much on his own. I learned about his decision to go probably not more than a week before he went, maybe less than that. Everybody—Gray Davis, me, Richard Maullin—we all argued against it. He insisted on doing it. In retrospect he was right in one key analysis, that Kennedy was going to be a candidate, with that as a given, I think it follows that he had to find some way to distinguish himself from Kennedy. Maybe in retrospect we all should have figured out a way to make this balanced-budget amendment work instead of trying to hope it would go away.

CLYMER: We've heard about one thing a candidate did that was indeed widely perceived at the time as a campaign device, although I believe I've got assorted on-the-record denials that it was ever thought of for that reason or in that context. But a much more significant political event, I think, both in terms of your campaign and others, Pat, was the time the president spent at Camp David in early July of 1979 and what my colleague Frances Clines of the *New York Times* calls the "cross of malaise" speech. How much was this performance, this approach to the country's problems, pointed at the 1980 election?

—CARTER'S APPROACH—

CADDELL: I don't think you can take anything that was done in 1979 by anyone in public office who was running for president, as the president really was, and not say that it didn't have some tinge or consideration of 1980 politics in it. In that particular instance, though, I do not think that was the major thrust of it. You had a president who, all spring, had been wrestling with the problem of becoming steadily unpopular in ways that he had not been in previous years of his administration when he had also not been particularly successful in his political ratings. There was a growing sense of frustration, too, of not having command of the country or even the attention of the country. This broader set of factors influenced his decision to go to Camp David; it had little to do with specific electoral politics, although, as I said, everything certainly was constructed in that environment.

CLYMER: In another context, Paul Kirk, what Carter did then—the speech he made and the Cabinet shuffle that followed—was this a significant factor in Senator Kennedy's deciding to run?

PAUL G. KIRK, JR. (national political director, Kennedy for President): Yes, I think it was. Probably the final significant event during that period starting with the Memphis speech that you mentioned, which was not meant as a campaign device. Here there was a Democratic incumbent of his own party, someone whom Senator Kennedy had supported in 1976 perhaps more than others in the Senate had, and whom Kennedy wanted to do well. The Memphis speech was basically the leveraging speech on events that occurred in 1979—with the economy, with energy, health, and some foreign policy matters that Carter articulated—as to whether or not we really had our own house under control and whether our global neighbors thought so. During that time there were people coming to Senator Kennedy and asking him to consider running, and there were personal questions in terms of the family and its concerns. I don't think his final decision was made until August, but I think basically he felt the "malaise" speech after Camp David violated the spirit of America, the things that he thought the American people wanted to do and feel about themselves. Coming from the number one office, from a member of his own party, the speech was basically an indictment of a lot of things Senator Kennedy believed in. I think fundamentally it was the turning point of his decision, even though that decision was not finalized until perhaps a month later.

CLYMER: Who asked him to run? Who said, "The Democratic party needs you as a candidate, we need you. If Carter runs, Democrats won't turn out and we'll all go down the tubes."

—PRESSURE ON KENNEDY—

KIRK: Although I wasn't in his office at the time, I know he was hearing from various quarters of the Democratic party—from those in the Senate body as well as many in the House who were concerned about the direction the country was taking—as to whether or not we'd be better off in 1981 as a country if President Carter were re-elected, and, further, what the fate would be of a lot of Democrats in terms of the 1980 elections.

CLYMER: Carl, you were in his office?

WAGNER: The most difficult thing in politics is to structure a campaign that is consistent with and responsive to events—the tenor of politics. I don't think there have been many years when as dramatic a change has occurred in both the nature of the debate and the spirit of it as there was in 1979. It's important to consider this at least in terms of Senator Kennedy's thinking about 1979 in terms of pre-July and -August and thereafter. First of all, Senator Kennedy's consideration of the presidency was influenced by the need he felt to manage the national political debate on behalf of the constituencies around which he had organized his political life, principally in the Senate. It should be remembered that going into 1979, Senator Kennedy was probably one of the most consistent supporters of the president in the Congress on a number of issues. That is not to say that late in 1978 and parts of 1979 he did not become very troubled about the drift of the political debate in general, and specifically about the course the administration had taken on three or four issues of rather prominent concern for him. I spent an enormous amount of 1979 negotiating on his behalf with various agencies of the administration or its representatives, not on the logistics or tactics of campaign politics, but on substantive politics, trying to seek out and secure agreement on energy policy, or health policy, or economic policy.

NOFZIGER: Was it then that you asked him to run?

WAGNER: My point is that those were his concerns over the course of at least half the year.

CLYMER: I don't think, Carl, that anyone at this table is disputing his concerns. . . .

WAGNER: No, but my point is, as that debate drifted rather considerably from where he thought the Democratic party ought to be, prominent institutions in the Democratic party—

CLYMER: Who?

WAGNER: Trade unions, activist Democrats, basically liberal Democrats, elected officials—

HUNT: Were there members of the Senate and House?

WAGNER: Yes.

HUNT: Who in the Senate asked him to run?

WAGNER: Most of the people who came to Senator Kennedy in 1979, especially in mid-to-late 1979, and expressed either interest in him running or encouraged him to run did it in the context of whether or not Carter and/or the Democrats could win against the Republican challenge.

HUNT: Was one of those people Robert Byrd?

WAGNER: Not in 1979.

HUNT: Not in 1979 at all?

CLYMER: Scoop Jackson?

WAGNER: I don't like this! Why don't you direct these questions to Joanne Symons?

CLYMER: I don't think we're going to get an answer, although on the last point at least we didn't get a denial.

QUINN: I don't think there was one single Senator who asked Jerry Brown to run. (*Laughter*)

CLYMER: I'm not sure the next question is any easier to answer.

WAGNER: Oh, terrific!

CLYMER: As Paul says, at some point in August the Senator decided to run. Why didn't he get a campaign, why didn't he start putting an organization together, why did he permit this zoo that the Florida Democratic party had created to drag him along and damage him? Why did he let his campaign consist basically of newspaper interviews, not get a pollster, not get a television man? Did he, did you, think it was going to be easy? He always said it would be difficult, but you ran the campaign at the beginning as if it would be easy.

WAGNER: No, Adam, the Senator didn't really decide to become a candidate until August and, as a matter of fact, late August; then he announced a campaign almost within thirty days. In October we established a campaign, and sixty days later he was an announced candidate. It may have been that the conclusion should have been reached earlier, that the structure should have been built earlier, but there was not much lag time between the decision and the setting in place of a campaign.

CLYMER: What was done in September of 1979 to produce a winning campaign?

WAGNER: A number of things were done in that thirty day period. A lot of things had to be thought through very quickly. First of all, the context in which the challenge to the president was stated, how that was articulated, took a lot of time. Secondly, the goals of the organization defined in terms of thirty-seven primaries. Which ones? Where? How? What? The team of people to be brought in to work to organize the campaign in those primaries and the leadership of the campaign to handle it was really resolved very quickly. I don't know how much time these other presidential campaigns took to think through the campaign structure and at least the entry focus; nevertheless, that is what occupied most of September. In addition to that, we knew we were operating under terrific pressure. The Carter campaign had been in the early states for six months—since spring in the cases of Iowa and New England. We knew we had to get in on a very broad basis and very quickly. Most of September and October was spent identifying political goals, primaries, and trying to structure staff and fundraising mechanisms.

—CARTER AS THE INCUMBENT—

BODE: At that point, how much thought was given and what were your conclusions about it with respect to Jimmy Carter as an incumbent president? He had a reputation at that point of not really being in step with his own party, not being a product of the party, and so forth. Did you think that he was the kind of president who would be able to make really effective use of his incumbency to ward off a challenge from somebody like Kennedy who was arguably more popular in his own party? Or was that not the question?

WAGNER: The greatest trepidation that I personally shared about the challenge was the president's ability to manage the debate and to structure the basis around which this election was going to be conducted. When we got into this race, to take a case in point, a number of the news organizations around here had done extensive polling on the leadership issue, and the results were about sixty–thirty in favor of Kennedy as "better able to lead the country." So on that issue Senator Kennedy beat the president almost two to one. That margin was, in my view, largely a function of Carter's handling of the issues that came before his administration, and conversely, Senator Kennedy's performance in politics generally and in the Senate specifically. Going into the race, I had no doubt that the administration would use what advantages it had, from the switchboard to patronage, effectively. But if you had told me in January of 1979 that when Senator Kennedy announced his candidacy, it would be the ninth story on all three networks following eight stories on Iran, I would never have believed it. And that was November of 1979. My point is that in a ten-day period the debate shifted radically, and it shifted in a way that became almost impossible for our campaign to influence that early on.

CLYMER: We'll get to Iran in a second.

WIRTHLIN: Carl, I was wondering why you didn't poll on Kennedy's weaknesses which could have been such a critical part of determining his political liability through 1979 and 1980.

WAGNER: Late in 1979 we did, Dick.

CLYMER: Before he announced?

WAGNER: No. But I'm not at all certian it was not anticipated. By no means did we expect the race to be anywhere near as easy as it seemed in the polls that appeared mid-to-late 1979. We thought it would tighten very quickly and be very tough.

QUINN: Did you ever consider delaying the announcement so as to miss Iowa and take on Carter in New Hampshire?

WAGNER: The dilemma of delay depended in large part on one of the substantial changes in the delegate selection system of the Democratic party after the 1976 election, which Tim could probably speak to, and that is the extension of the filing period to ninety days. The Pennsylvania primary was on April 27th, and the filing deadline was in January.

—THE KENNEDY DRAFT—

CLYMER: Were you also handicapped, Paul or Carl, in the possibility of any delay by the existence of the draft movements with which legally you could have no contact?

KIRK: Having made the decision to run and then getting off to what might be correctly called a less than fully prepared start, there was a discussion about the time needed to prepare properly in terms of a smooth entry and getting your ducks in a row. The senator felt very strongly that the president's organizational forces had already started to work in the real caucus states, forgetting the straw polls of Florida for a moment, and that there was a need for him to go out there as a candidate. We as an organization would have, in a sense, had to catch up with him as a candidate, because he, carrying the standard of the campaign, would have to catch up with the Carter campaign. If he could be out in Iowa, for instance, perhaps attracting people to his campaign there would help to pull us together as an organization so we could get a running start while the national campaign staff started to put other things together. That was a calculation and, like so many other things in hindsight, maybe you look back and say you should've done it another way. Waiting until after Iowa was never a serious consideration. I think the Senator understood fully what a president is able to do as an incumbent candidate and also understood the importance of the early events in the real primary process. So I think he felt he didn't have the luxury to delay it. While the campaign certainly wasn't a cinch, it was do-able, and he was prepared to go forward with it; the rest of us would try and make the best of it in terms of organization.

HUNT· Let's back up just a little bit 'cause I think we're kind of missing the draft movement here and what effect that had. I'd like to ask Joanne if she could tell us what you thought you all were achieving then. Did any of these Democrats that Mr. Wagner and Mr. Kirk won't name contact you and encourage you in your efforts?

SYMONS: No. It's sad. Certainly not from anybody here. But there were other Democratic state chairmen. There was a Democratic state chairmen's meeting in Memphis in 1978 prior to the convention. There was very little sympathy at that point—the antagonism toward the president astounded me—from the state chairmen of the president's own party. I'd like to go back for one second to 1978 because our great speech moment came in September 1978 at the New Hampshire Democratic state convention. Senator Kennedy was the keynote speaker and galvanized those Democrats to an extent that no one had done for a number of years in that party. Our idea was that by February or March Ted Kennedy could not announce against an incumbent Democratic president, but the need was rapidly growing. We didn't want to push it too fast because we hoped that the whole thing wouldn't be necessary. But we wanted to provide him with a way of being able to say that the party had called him rather than his being represented as trying to usurp an incumbent Democrat's place. Our original idea was he would be able to stay out until after New Hampshire, that the early contests somehow could be avoided so that we could start in a favorable spot, but that we could buy a little lowered expectation from the press with a write-in campaign. If that were successful, we felt there would be a delay in the attacks on the Senator's negatives. He was not an active candidate. If he could be successful in coming close to knocking off an incumbent Democratic president by the act of write-ins without being an active candidate, then that incumbent president would no longer be able to run for that party. We had a lot of problems obviously, but I will also tell you, you ought to try the experience of not having a candidate sometime. It's rather refreshing, but . . . .

CLYMER: I'm sure everyone here has wished that at one time or another.

ROBERT J. KEEFE (political consultant, Carter–Mondale Re-election Committee): I bet Tom Quinn knows what you mean. Which is worse, the candidate or the national staff?

SYMONS: I will never answer that question! Obviously we recognized very early that the people involved in the New Hampshire draft were pros. They were people who had made a lifetime out of New Hampshire Democratic primaries. In an uncoordinated effort, there is no control over what's happening in every place. In retrospect that kind of uncontrollable situation cannot work. But it was a remarkable experience because it genuinely was a party, grass roots movement in our state.

CLYMER: Paul, did this matter to the senator in deciding to run?

KIRK: I think perhaps it gave him some additional encouragement. I don't think that the draft movement, looking back in hindsight, received a lot of thanks from the Kennedy folks, but frankly I don't think it was decisive with respect to his decision. It added an element of encouragement, and when he did make the decision to run, then it was really a political question in terms of how to best integrate the finances. But it was not fundamental to his decision.

KEEFE: I'm anxious to hear what Bill Brock has to say.

BROCK: I'm fascinated with the candidate, but I'm wondering what the reaction was from Carter people at this time. At precisely this juncture, September–October, you had to know Kennedy was going to run. Now, how did you view it? Did you look on it as a contest that you could shift into an ideological battle where you could posture him at an extreme end of the party, or did you view it primarily in organizational terms where you simply use the brute force of the administration and the funding of the party and all that?

—CARTER'S VIEW—

KRAFT: You lead off, Pat. I've been biting my tongue for ten minutes.

CADDELL: Let me try to give our sense of it. There had been, as Tim said, no consensus in the Carter camp at the beginning part of the year as to whether or not Senator Kennedy would run. There were some fairly senior people who adamantly were convinced from the moment of that "the sail against the wind" speech that he was going to run, and there were others who just absolutely believed he would not. There were various tensions.

CLYMER: What did the president think?

CADDELL: That's a good question. I don't think he believed that Senator Kennedy would run. He felt that he had a relatively good relationship with Kennedy, which is something that Jackie Walsh might speak to because he had friends on both sides. In a sense, it was sort of a tragedy. It seemed to me that both sides would always read the worst intentions into each other's actions during that period of late winter and spring. If somebody didn't get a return phone call, I would hear from friends on the Kennedy side that it was because the Carter people were putting it to Kennedy, and any time Senator Kennedy said anything on policy, the Carter people would erupt and say, he's trying to really destroy us, and so on. It was that nature, often not involving the principals but involving people who were simply partisans on both sides, that added a certain amount of kindling to whatever the smolder was at that point.

The other thing I'd like to speak on is that we knew we were in an incredibly weak situation. By June or July, when the president went to Camp David, his job rating had dropped below Nixon's job rating in the Harris Poll; the gas lines existed; there was a sense that things were really out of control. In part what was going on that summer was, to take one of Carl's points, the need to assert something, some kind of control; but when we looked at the decision of Senator Kennedy to run, leaving aside the organizational questions and looking simply at the strategic things, we knew we were weak partly because we did not have a strong base inside the party. We assumed we would have one in the South, in the small towns. If you look at the Democratic party—no matter what the polls were saying at this point about who was ahead—Senator Kennedy was holding disparate parts of the constituency that were unlikely to stay in harness for a short time much less the five-month period remaining before the primaries; and you still have existing in the Democratic party an underlying division of North and South, small town and urban, and so forth. I saw it in 1976, and we see it again in 1980 in a very real way.

The one thing that we were glad about, in fact, was that Senator Kennedy, if he were going to run, got in when he did. Our feeling was that he had an enormous number of negatives that existed but were out of the picture at that moment. People had focused on Senator Kennedy as the alternative at that moment to a president they were very unhappy with. Even if you looked at the constituency groups you knew that there would be concerns, both in terms of the candidates themselves as well as issues and ideology, that were going to come into play here. So one of the great advantages we had was the five months or so, the half-year really, that existed from the moment that Senator Kennedy transformed the pre-election year from a situation where people were not very interested, to one in which the high levels of attention were more typical of the time of the first primary. Our feeling was—in a sense, it was the block-of-ice theory—that the longer he was not exposed to a real presidential campaign with the kind of media attention and challenge that would go on, the more advantageous it would be for him.

Our fundamental hope was that we would be able to make this essentially not a primary contest but a general election. Not only did we have a weak base in terms of the party, the president had done some things, as Carl pointed out, that had antagonized major elements of the party, particularly over fiscal and budgetary policy. The most activist elements of the party—the unions, different interest groups—were, to say the least, unhappy and unenthused by what we had imposed on them. Our feeling was that if at that point the race took on the connotation of simply being a referendum on the president or a primary where people would exhibit most of their frustrations, we were doomed. In fact, this would be, as I've described it since, the "wolf at the door" which, for over a year, we were forced to try to keep away. And our intention from the beginning was that the media would help with this. Because Senator Kennedy was so well known and such a force in the country and in the party, we hoped that many people would begin to view this as not simply a choice in a primary process that would yield someone down the line but, in fact, a real choice for president. We had to get it to where we could bring to bear, first of all, a comparison of personalities. Secondly, we could emphasize, if necessary, the ideological differences because if we did not dominate the activist wing, we dominated the centrist part of the party in terms of number, in terms of voters.

BROCK: Did you think that dominating the center of the party was that important? This is part of the problem that we had to wrestle on our side too. I think Reagan's advantage on our side was that he was the only candidate with a philosophical base. That was Kennedy's advantage, too, or at least that's the way I was looking at it from our side, and I was wondering how you were going—

CADDELL: The numbers are different, Bill. One of the things that had taken place over the last few years was a change in the numbers. If you look simply at Democrats—and primary Democrats nationally, not in individual states—clearly the most activist elements of the party were liberal and were Senator Kennedy's. But if you looked at all Democrats, there had been fairly significant shifts on substantive positions, not necessarily in a defined ideological way by those voters, but at least in terms of how they had come to view issues. The rise of inflation is an issue for many Democratic voters, questions of government spending, and so on. The center of the party had, in fact, moved to the right to some extent on at least the most important issues since 1976, even though we were suffering from the problem that large numbers were unhappy with the way the president had handled things. Our basic situation was that we had to have a choice between candidates. We had to keep the focus on that basis. From the beginning that was our intention and, as I said, the thing we were most glad about was Senator Kennedy getting in early. We're all familiar with the rules, the pressures that Carl describes, the organizational and filing needs, the getting-started problems, and so on, which would push you toward an active candidacy. At the same time I think some of us felt that those were the very things to avoid if you could help it—if you were Senator Kennedy. In a perfect world, you would like to wait until the last minute, jump in quick, and then get into the primaries or whatever, but he had been sucked in by the process himself. At that point, we felt that it was going to be a really tough contest.

—THE HOSTAGE CRISIS—

CLYMER: We've got some timing problems of our own, and there were two questions in particular that I'd like to take around the table. Carl has pointed out, certainly, an event that changed the attention that the race got in November and December: the seizure of the American Embassy in Teheran and the hostages. This curtailed everybody's ability to get on the television news. In that sense it helped Governor Reagan. As long as the American public thought President Carter was handling the situation well, it plainly helped him. In conversations I've had with several of the candidates represented here and certainly people who work closely with all of them, it's my strong impression that every 1980 presidential candidate, except President Carter, thought that President Carter had made an enormous mistake, and that he would be held responsible for the Embassy's being seized. And yet, certainly at no point in 1979 did any candidate address that issue in those terms. Did any candidate seriously consider a detailed, point-by-point attack on the president for the hostage seizure?

MAHE: Yes.

CLYMER: Why didn't you do it? Why did you decide not to in 1979?

MAHE: Well, recall that when that thing took place we already had all the grief we needed with one foreign policy speech, so it didn't seem to make sense to take on another one at that point.*

CLYMER: Tom.

QUINN: I think the feeling was that it was unpatriotic to criticize the president at that point. No matter how accurate or cogent or per-suasive your arguments, the president was cloaked to the flag very effectively. We saw what happened when Kennedy made what really was a fairly innocuous comment, I think, by criticizing the Shah in San Francisco on that TV show. In fact, it was left in the cutting room floor, and a UPI reporter or someone later in the night finally picked up that comment. I'm not sure what it was: something about how the Shah had had a reign of terror in Iran and was really a des-pot. It was nothing really attacking Carter directly, and yet it was played up as though somehow Kennedy had attacked America.

CLYMER: Doug, did Howard Baker consider doing it?

BAILEY: No. As you know, Adam, he did give a speech on Iran in Iowa which was filmed and then turned into a commercial. But I think he certainly intended to go out of his way, and I think he did

---

*The speech referred to was given by Governor Connally on October 11, 1979, which outlined a nine-point Middle East peace plan, recommending Israeli withdrawal of territory occupied since the 1967 war in exchange for an understanding by the Arabs of Israel's right to exist and a return to oil price stability.

always, to say that he was not going to criticize the president, and the speech was not critical of him. It was not particularly supportive of the President, but I don't believe he ever considered breaking ranks, even though he was appalled.

CLYMER: Bob, did Bush think about it?

TEETER: No, definitely not in 1979. It seems to me that the crisis was still new enough that Carter did have substantial—I mean almost total—support of the country on it during November and December.

CLYMER: Isn't one of the reasons he maintained total support was that no one criticized him?

TEETER: I don't think so. I think any criticism of him at that point would have backfired. He had the support because it was an immediate crisis, it was new, it was still getting the top of the news coverage every day, and you had American lives involved in it. Also, as in all foreign policy crises, everybody is really afraid to talk about it because they don't really know as much as the president—at least they *feel* they don't. They have no idea what may happen the day after they say something about it. I don't think there was any consideration whatsoever in 1979. Obviously, Bush later in '80 at the time of the Connecticut primary, that week, did go into it. But not at all in 1979.

WIRTHLIN: Ronald Reagan didn't hesitate, of course, to take the president on quite critically on other matters. But on the Iranian situation he never seriously considered attacking him primarily for three reasons: first, in December the situation was still unfolding, and we didn't know which way it was going to develop. Secondly, there was the strong desire to support the president in a time of crisis, and there was a strong rallying-around-the-flag phenomenon he did enjoy at that time. Thirdly, we felt that there was time to see how that situation would develop with greater knowledge.

NOFZIGER: Well, Dick, I think there's a fourth reason, too, and that is we were always very careful—and I wasn't in the campaign at the time—we always were very careful to avoid making him look any more trigger-happy than he was already portrayed. Clearly, one thing you don't want to do is get into a situation where it looks like he supports some aggressive action.

CLYMER: Paul, did Kennedy, before his statement in San Francisco that caught all the flack Tom referred to, did Kennedy consider making a prepared, thought-out criticism?

KIRK: I don't know whether it went that far. I think it was a real dilemma for the Kennedy campaign. One of the questions obviously that brought him into the candidacy was the one that Carl had mentioned and I alluded to—about the capacity to lead and the fears of people about where they were as a country. It was our feeling that a lot of the American people had transferred those fears into empathy with their fellow Americans who were under seige over there. If there was anything that you did to undercut that opportunity to show leadership, or jeopardize the hostages, it would be not only counterproductive politically but might indeed have serious ramifications. No one knew when it would end or even if it would, but at that point it was much too ticklish to make any full-scale attack.

BROCK: If you are going to look at Carter as your fall opportunity, you have to keep your debate focused on those issues in which you have the high ground: inflation and unemployment. We knew that a year, two years, in advance. We didn't even want to talk about anything else.

SYMONS: I would just like to throw in a word on the Shah statement since it's been mentioned. In New Hampshire that was the single most devastating thing that happened to our campaign. The *Boston Globe* picture showing crowds in Iran hanging signs saying, "Hurrah for Kennedy" or something. We had people gathering petition signatures out on the street the weekend right after that statement was made. It was the first weekend out on the streets, and the first time I have experienced having people physically assaulted. We had people who got spit on. People turned; they felt that the remark had been traitorous, and it was devastating.

CLYMER: Tim, not quarreling for a moment with the view that the president's basic objective in 1979 and 1980 was to get the hostages released, you had a presidential campaign on. Did the hostage situation seem to you to be a problem or an opportunity in the campaign?

KRAFT: There was an academic forum sometime in December, and that same question came up. I think the question was, Do you have any input on the strategy affecting the hostages? or something to that effect, and I said, honestly, none whatsoever. Those of us in the campaign know about as much about the hostage situation as we see on the evening news. I can't tell you at what point Pat polled or got any feedback on the reaction of the American people on the situation.

HUNT: But was there any feeling, way back in the first couple of days after the seizure, was there a feeling in the beginning, even though you weren't involved in the policies, that this might be a real political liability rather than the plus it turned out to be?

CADDELL: It's interesting, because I think the day that the hostages were seized, which was a Sunday, we were at Camp David discussing campaign strategy and working on the campaign; that was the same day Chicago Mayor Jane Byrne decided to support Senator Kennedy, which occupied much more comment.

BROCK: How did you arrange that, by the way?

CADDELL: I don't know.

KRAFT: Carl Wagner did that! (*Laughter*)

CADDELL: Our first reaction, in fact, was not very much at all. Don't forget this had happened earlier in the year: a brief taking over of the Embassy, and then they gave up and everything went back to normal. During the first hours of that first day we felt that's probably what would happen again. We were concerned that what we were dealing with was another example of a perception of being hurt overseas. It was not for a week or so that things began to clarify and we realized the Americans were not going to come out. I remember talking with some of the press; it was still unclear at that point exactly what would happen. I don't think that the situation changed dramatically in the president's favor. I went through at that time and looked at the public polls because opinion was unfurling very quickly in the surveys being done. The president didn't really start to move with that crisis until he actually did something. It was his decision to freeze the assets, to expel the Iranian students, and so forth. It took several days to see the issue as having enormous political impact, at least in terms of seeing the president's numbers move, both his rating numbers and his numbers in relation to Senator Kennedy.

—DES MOINES DEBATE—

CLYMER: You did use the issue in at least one plainly political context at the end of the year, when President Carter announced that he had to withdraw from the debate in Des Moines because he had to work full time on the crisis in Washington.

CADDELL: You mean, the memo with the "I would like but I . . . .

CLYMER: Well, since you bring it up—

CADDELL: I was sure it wasn't going to pass, Tim, so I thought we should get it on the table first!

KRAFT: Senator Kennedy asked the president to debate on a Thursday, the first of November, and the hostages were taken the fourth of November, and on the sixth of November the president agreed to debate. The wisdom of not debating occurred only twenty days later in Iowa as the crisis unravelled. In the public press generally, the issue hadn't emerged. We polled Iran as an issue on Sunday, Monday, and Tuesday of that week, and it was a very small issue in terms of the public press. There had been one story, as I recall, but by Wednesday it really moved.

HUNT: Can we finish up with this debate decision? I really think the debate decision was obviously very important. Could Pat and Tim just give us some idea of how that evolved?

CADDELL: Frankly, I don't think the president had been particularly enthused earlier about debating, but there is no question— and this got lost in the reaction to the memo—that in fact Tim and almost all the political advisors to the president at that point wanted him to debate for a variety of reasons. There was, in fact, a feeling that not to do so would hurt in Iowa; it would hurt us with the *Des Moines Register*. The essential decision to stay in the Rose Garden campaign was at that point not a brilliant conceptual or nonbrilliant conceptual decision. It was in the president's mind, a day-by-day sort of situation, and one that he felt very strongly about, even though it was one that would lock us in later to very real difficulties in the primaries. The rise of the debate issue would haunt us one way or the other all through the rest of the campaign.

The last point about Iran from my perception is what it did to President Carter in the spring in terms of the quick rise that he had in public opinion approval. The people had earlier seen him being a strong leader, which was the thing that they later became most unhappy with him about; it overturned several years of fairly concrete attitudes. It seems to me that in some ways this situation forced the American people to come to some fundamental decision about why the president was so different during the crisis than he had been before. Faced with the alternative of deciding that he had always been like this and they simply had been wrong, or that the crisis had changed the president, I think as we would later find in our work that the public opted for the belief—and I think it's a cognitive, realistic one—that they, in fact, had been right all along. Yet the crisis *had* changed Jimmy Carter. It made him a different president. The event would go on and not be resolved, of course, and people fully expected to see the same or the new Jimmy Carter evidenced when other issues arose. This caused some real problems because when the economy went the way it did, and people began to see Jimmy Carter in the same ways they had prior to the Iranian situation, it added a sharper, hostile edge to their feeling than had existed previously.

CLYMER: I'd like to press Tim's question on the Reagan folks. What basically did you think you were establishing? It looked at times like the campaign of an incumbent. You started late, and you didn't get out very often then. There was something of President Muskie's "don't you feel better already" air to it, but nevertheless you were still ahead. I'd like for you to discuss that briefly, Dick, and conclude with one of the things I mentioned first; we'll go around the room for the other candidates. What had you accomplished by the end of 1979, and what singular opportunities or problems had 1979 built for you?

—REAGAN IN 1979—

WIRTHLIN: All through 1979, it was very clear that we did have the luxury of pointing toward the general election, and that conditioned every strategic decision we made concerning organization, the issue agenda, our relationship with the other opponents, and the kinds of things we were doing and saying about the incumbent president. In terms of what we accomplished in 1979, I think that perhaps the most general and significant thing was that even with a large number of very visible, strong, articulate opponents, in several critical ways we ended the year 1979 stronger politically than we started it. Specifically, about the middle of December, we took surveys for the first time in four critical key primary states and found that in Vermont our lead over the next most popular opponent was 26 points, in Florida it was 23, in Illinois it was 28, in Massachusetts it was 19, and in New Hampshire it was 43 points.

I think that the success of Ronald Reagan and his campaign was due to the following things established during 1979: to begin with, I strongly believe that John Sears developed with great skill an issue agenda that served us well during the primaries and provided an excellent base for the discussions in the frame of reference of the general campaign. Specifically, we very carefully viewed and tested and assessed analytically the crisis of confidence that was sounded by the Carter administration in the summer. We did some psychographic analysis to test countering themes that might be used in the general election, and we found that there was a sense of malaise among many people in America. Nevertheless, it was strongly indicated—again taking cues from some of the hypotheses that John Sears developed— that we could counter it strongly by speaking rather hopefully about an America that can deal with its problems if challenged and if led by leaders who were strong. Very early, then, we sounded the theme of leadership which was developed consistently in the early primaries, and of course that was the tagline on all of our advertising that Peter Dailey developed and used through the 1980 election. The North American Accord idea served us extremely well in the opening phases of the primary. We did pre-post analysis of those who heard the announcement speech or were aware of the idea, and it did broaden our base. It crosscut very well, as we hoped it would, with moderates and liberals, ticket splitters, Democrats and Republicans, and it established a tonality that helped us a great deal as the primary campaign progressed. Also in terms of issues, it was again early that we dealt with the basic idea of appealing to people's basic values, particularly the family, the neighborhood, the workplace. Ronald Reagan, going back to the 1966 election, has had a very unique appeal to blue-collar workers, to those of somewhat lower incomes. This is an appeal that most Republicans don't enjoy, and we determined that the emphasis on the family and the neighborhood and values generally and an appeal for hope were very, very strong thematic elements that had good impact not only in solidifying that early support but also in building a base for a strong run at the presidency in November.

Secondly, in 1979, it was evident to us, and I think Pat would concur, that the Republican primary was not as strongly conditioned ideologically as was the Democratic party. From the very beginning, Reagan was getting rather substantial support from liberal, moderate, and conservative Republicans. Similarly, when virtually every tree in the forest fell on us after Iowa, we found that we had not only lost support among liberal and moderate Republicans in New Hampshire but also among the conservative Republicans. But by the end of 1979, ideology, which had concerned us the first part of the year as being a very heavy burden for us to pack in the primaries and through the general election, was found to be really not that heavy.

Thirdly, I think there were several accomplishments organizationally. The Citizens for the Republic (CFTR), which helped many candidates, served as an excellent vehicle for us to keep our activists involved. There were literally hundreds and hundreds of individuals, who even at the end of 1976 believed that Ronald Reagan should not only run for the presidency in 1980 but would be elected president in 1980. The Citizens for the Republic acted as an organizational focus for those kinds of individuals. It also provided a visibility for Ronald Reagan during that critical year of 1979. I believe that without CFTR it probably would have been more incumbent on us to announce earlier than we did, and it provided us with a very critical margin of a calendar which permitted us to push off the announcement until rather late. Next, Charlie Black put together a good political grassroots organization. He ensconced in the campaign individuals with experience, with a regional savvy that served the campaign extremely well not only in the primaries but through the general election. Also organizationally, we were able in 1979 to do something that was very difficult if almost impossible for us to accomplish in 1976: we finally were able to get some of the party activists and some of the congressmen and senators to come to our banner. That also proved to be extremely helpful. Finally, we put together a team that had worked relatively well together in 1976 and—

NOFZIGER: And we got rid of some of them. (*Laughter*)

WIRTHLIN: Lyn, what were the singular problems that we did face in 1979? There were two of them.

NOFZIGER: Nofziger and Deaver!

WIRTHLIN: Nofziger and Deaver, yes. Under one rubric! We clearly heard the beginning of the ticking of one of those time bombs, namely the purge of Mike Deaver and Lyn Nofziger, that led to what I can only describe as the cataclysmic reorganization of the campaign that took place on the eve of the New Hampshire primary. The second time bomb that was ticking away in our closet we didn't hear quite as clearly, and that was the explosion that came upon us in January in Iowa. I think that happened because we, like many football players, didn't give quite enough attention and care to the first game. We were already looking toward the playoffs, and because of that the whole thrust of the campaign was dramatically changed because of some of the seeds that were sown in our campaign in the latter part of 1979.

—THE OTHER REPUBLICANS—

CLYMER: Eddie, what had Connally accomplished?

MAHE: Unfortunately, the big thing that he had accomplished was that by the end of 1979 we'd lost. We had defined clearly what we had to do: John Connally had to be a national candidate; the package of negatives that we were carrying were such that we couldn't move in Iowa all by itself; we had to move the numbers all across the board. We had, in fact, been successful to some extent in accomplishing that for the first eight or nine months of the year. We had set a goal of having to be at least in the mid-twenties in various polls by the time Reagan came into the race. We were getting awfully close to that at the beginning of September; we were in the high teens and low twenties. John Sears was saying all the time that it was the intention of the Reagan campaign to control the agenda, and we felt that we wanted to try, to some extent, to set the agenda. We scheduled four major speeches in the month of October. He made all four of them. None of you could recall more than one of them.* Parenthetically, that speech did not start out to be what it ended up to be.

In point of fact, from then on we spent half our time going back and trying to explain or justify or clarify that speech going into the Florida caucus. And on November 18th at the Florida straw vote convention, we failed to reach the level of expectation—and with John Connally you can never fail to reach the level of expectations that we mistakenly set for ourselves. The original goal we had set was nothing more than to keep Governor Reagan below 50 percent. We achieved that one remarkably, but it had been decided that rather than keeping Mr. Reagan below 50 percent we could win. We not only failed to do so but only did marginally better than George Bush did down there. So we then went into the holidays on a downer—no chance to recoup, no chance to recover before we got into Iowa. We had, I think, the second best organization in Iowa. We never got credit for that. But there was no capacity to move one state because John Connally couldn't move one state. He had to move across the board. So basically, as I say, what we had accomplished was that we'd lost.

In other respects, we'd raised a lot of money, more money than anybody, and did not feel that we had even begun to really tap the amount of money that was available to us. Most of that money had come out of three states, and we hadn't even gotten cranked up in a lot of them yet. So we felt there was still lots and lots of money left out there. We did have a basic organization in fifty states. We had an in-depth organization in every state through Pennsylvania because we were convinced that we would either have won or be out of it by Pennsylvania. We never did see a way that it was going on beyond Pennsylvania, and I don't think it realistically went beyond Pennsylvania even though George didn't realize that for a few weeks.

The only way we could recover after Florida was to beat Governor Reagan in the South. We had to take him on, and we had to beat him

---

*See footnote on page 33.

down there. A lot of money and a lot of time and a lot of the effort that we put into the New England states we wrote off and threw what we had left into the South. One will never know, but if Ronald Reagan had won Iowa, I think we would have had a shot in the South. But when he lost Iowa, it geared and kicked his people up too much, especially in South Carolina and some of the other states, and they became far more intent than they were before they lost in Iowa. Consequently, the effort they made down there was too great for us to overcome.

BODE: A couple of times you've mentioned a package of negatives that Connally carried. I assume you're talking about negatives as they affect Republican primary votes. What were those negatives?

MAHE: It was different in different parts of the country. In New Hampshire, 12 percent of the people in an open-ended response identified the party switch as the big negative, and in the South that wasn't a negative at all. You know, down there they accept that and they have no problems with it. In the South, the problem tended to be different—primarily relating to the whole wheeler-dealer type problem plus the LBJ similarities which was a much bigger problem to us than it was in the Northeast. Again, maybe because the party switch was so dominant.

CLYMER: Doug, how about Baker? What had he done?

BAILEY: He made a very, very slow start, but by June there was a concept as to how to do it. There was an excellent national campaign plan, excellent in the technical sense. The assumption was a September announcement of the national campaign with a very late start in organization. But by September here were the problems: one, we didn't have the finances, largely because we did not have the top fundraising personnel to wage a national campaign so that we were forced by resources to make some choices. Secondly, in terms of organization of personnel, yes, there was an organization chart and, yes, a lot of the slots were filled, but frankly they were not very strong people and organizationally we did not have strong leadership at the top or much to fill in at the bottom either. Third, the assumption was that there would be a SALT debate, and it was clear by August and early September that there was never going to be a

SALT debate because Byrd would never call the treaty since it obviously did not have the votes. And fourth, there was the growing perception that Baker was in serious trouble which feeds on itself, so we were at that point forced into making rash decisions. How do you force yourself back into the ballgame?

One decision that was made—while the continuing debate went on in the senator's mind as to when he could afford to get out of the Senate—was to set a precise date for the announcement and base it on some immediate evidence following the announcement that all of these reports of Baker's inefficiency and disorganization were totally unfounded. The idea was to announce on November 1st and go to Maine on the 2nd or 3rd and win the Maine straw vote. And if anybody can really explain to me what happened in Maine, I'd be happy to hear it because I never quite understood, although I know of at least twenty different reasons as to why it fell apart. At any rate, that one event probably doomed Baker's candidacy more than anything else because rather than changing perceptions, it confirmed perceptions and made, for the first time, I believe, Bush a credible candidate even to his own people. I think that up to that point, the Bush organization had been extremely good at recruiting people, but there weren't a whole lot of people in the organization who really believed that it was going to happen. The perception was that Baker would win and that Bush would not; and when Bush won, it suddenly made him a believable candidate to his own people and made Baker really weak.

At that point, we were really in a fix and had to gamble, but if you know Howard Baker well he's not going to be outspoken on a lot of issues. He's not going to go around attacking people. He's not going to force himself into the ballgame that way. We made a heavy effort in the fall to recruit stronger people into the organization and leadership into the campaign, and while we did make some changes of significance I think frankly the heavy hitters that we wanted and I think wanted Baker would not join because I think the perception was strong that he wasn't going to make it. The Iran business in Iowa is an example of about as far as the Baker campaign would ever go to stir the pond trying to force himself into the ballgame. By the end of the year, obviously, we were desperate, and we had to beat Bush somewhere early or we were going to be out of it because we didn't have that much money.

CLYMER: Mike, succinctly, where was Anderson? What were your problems and opportunities?

MACLEOD: Talking about 1979 rather than 1980, I would suggest that it was a modest year for us, and our goals were modest. Our problem was perhaps unique. We were kind of like that girl in *West Side Story* who was always trying to join the Jets and never could quite make it. They wouldn't let her on the ballcourt. We had much the same thing in that the perception we were always fighting was that there were major candidates like John Connally who could raise more in the snap of his fingers than we could raise in two months. I think the two principal things that happened to us in 1979 give you an idea of just how accurate that was. The main accomplishment was qualifying for federal matching funds which took us far longer than we initially projected and took far more effort than we ever envisioned. The second was the candidate's decision to overrule the advice of his then principal campaign advisors who had suggested that he not participate in the Iowa debate in January of 1980.

CLYMER: Jo-Anne Coe, where was the Dole campaign at the end of 1979?

COE: By the end of the year, one major accomplishment was that we were dealing with a very, very effective U.S. senator in a campaign that was near its end. We had had severe management problems from the beginning, as well as fundraising problems. We planned on going into a number of the early primaries and we had, by early fall, a fairly decent organization put together. We had also—as it turned out, erroneously—the first candidate who came out and said that the Democratic candidate was going to be Senator Kennedy and not President Carter. We based a lot of our strategy on that. But by the end of the year when the Iranian crisis had erupted, all of a sudden we were dealing with a different situation. We had counted on spending some time out of the Senate with SALT occupying a lot of time on the Senate floor. We thought we could get away from the Senate. There had not been time for it previously, yet we found ourselves locked in Washington with the Windfall Profits Tax Bill soon to come up, and we found more problems piling on top of us. So as the year was coming to an end, I believe that it was a signal to the end of the Dole campaign.

CLYMER: Bob Teeter, what were Bush's accomplishments and problems? What had happened in 1979?

TEETER: He had three accomplishments. I think the first thing was that in contrast to some of the other candidates he had established an effective fundraising apparatus which was delivering the money he needed on a weekly or monthly basis to keep going and essentially do what we wanted to do in the early states. Secondly, the basis of an organization, particularly in Iowa, and in a number of the other early states, was there. There really were a number of infantry troops being recruited and on the ground. Thirdly,—and this is largely a tribute to Jim Baker, David Keene, David Sparks, and some others— he had developed a small but very effective staff. Not only was there the ability to raise the money but there was some discipline in how to spend it, and it was not wasted. The main problem at the end of the year was that the campaign was not much further along than it had been in the summer when we had spent four or five days working at it, trying to develop some kind of a theme or a message. The second major problem was the one that Dick Wirthlin mentioned a moment ago: we were a mile behind in New Hampshire and knew it.

WIRTHLIN: For a short time.

—1979 FOR THE DEMOCRATS—

CLYMER: Why don't we go to the Democrats. Tim, what did it look like for President Carter at the end of the year?

KRAFT: I think we had a very successful 1979. In 1978, we had laid out four basic tenets: start early, run everywhere, spend carefully, and anticipate the toughest possible opposition. Those tenets guided our operations in 1979. We did set up in February of 1979. We did want to raise $3 to $5 million by the end of the year. We had in effect raised a little over $3 million. We did lay the groundwork very carefully in those early states. We had good organizations. We had good campaign people in Iowa, New Hampshire and Florida, Maine and Minnesota, by mid–summer of 1979. So when the first perceived challenge came along from a possible draft candidate in the Florida caucuses, we were ready and took care of that so decisively that the subsequent straw challenge in Iowa just dissipated. So organizationally and financially, I think we prepared carefully and were able to execute in 1979.

Let me remind people here that we had a political problem in the summer of 1979 which we also addressed ourselves to—relatively successfully, I think—in the fall of 1979. You had to be in Washington in the summer of 1979 and be a Carter partisan to be absolutely shell-shocked within the Beltway consensus that the nomination was Kennedy's for the asking. For those of us who had looked upon the sequential line of primary and caucus contests and thought that we were in relatively good shape, it was amazing that day after day there were columns and talk saying that Kennedy's got it if he wants it. Of course this was supplemented somewhat by national polls showing a supposed preference by almost two to one in different states around the country, or in some cases nationally, for his candidacy. Our field organizations weren't quite picking up that sort of ground swell or unanimity, but we had to demonstrate to the political community that the president did have support in institutional politics and within the Democratic leadership, and we set out to do that.

Six major trade unions endorsed the president in the summer of 1979. Bob Keefe and Bob Strauss helped orchestrate a five-hundred-person dinner in October of 1979 that brought in Democratic leadership from all over the country, elected officials, trade unions, party leaders, and so on, as a sort of testimonial to the president. We went after mayors' conferences and NACO conferences and Democratic governors, speaking out periodically in an attempt to show the political world that the support was there and that any challenge would be met thoroughly and decisively. So at the end of 1979, we did feel like we were in pretty good shape. Although the Kennedy effort in Iowa geared up a little faster than we thought it would, fortunately a lot of the White House staff people were taking their winter vacations at that time and many of them did want to visit friends and family in places like Council Bluffs, Waterloo, and everywhere else, and they were able to meet that challenge. By and large, at the end of 1979, it felt like we were ready for the early going and we were able to execute.

CLYMER: Tom Quinn, what was Governor Brown ready for at the end of 1979?

QUINN: I remember the week between Christmas and New Year's, we were filming some TV spots, and we looked back on 1979 and both agreed that things went along very well. Only in retrospect, when we now look at 1980, can we appreciate 1979. I think we had two accomplishments then. One, we learned how to run a campaign without spending money. And two, we managed to get invited to the Iowa debates. Now our major setbacks were the debates being cancelled, not being able to raise any money at all, Iran and Afghanistan, and, I think most seriously for Jerry, the entry of Senator Kennedy. We felt at that time, and I think now even more in retrospect, that there was just no room for three candidates in the race. I still believed that if Kennedy had decided not to come in that Brown would have had the potential to give Carter a real run despite his coming in very late.

CLYMER: Paul, Senator Kennedy did come in. Where was he at the end of 1979?

KIRK: To the degree that a campaign going on before the race actually starts wants to lower its expectations, we were amazingly successful. We had, by the end of 1979, reversed the polls, and we were clearly the underdog. On the positive side we did put together in a short period of time a very good organization in Iowa. We obviously had made the qualifications in a relatively short time and started to raise substantial amounts of money. The thing that we did not do, clearly, was to live up to expectation, real or imagined. I don't think that anyone thought it was going to be a cinch. But in addition to running against an incumbent, in terms of press and public perceptions, we were running against the "will he or won't he" Senator Kennedy from 1968 on. The expectations left by his brothers that perhaps memory and history had enlarged a little bit were real factors to contend with, and we fell far short of that. In terms of the first impression that's so important in presidential campaigns, people's expectations were not lived up to. I think those were serious flaws that perhaps we never really recovered from.

HUNT: Paul, did you think the Roger Mudd interview was as devastating at the time as most other people did?

KIRK: At the time I wasn't sure. It was clear, Al, that it really was harmful in terms of a first impression. There were some mitigating factors around it in the sense that it was taped considerably earlier and aired only on the threshold of the announcement. It was well circulated in the written press, and it gave somewhat of a license, I think, to the electronic media to focus on a perceived inarticulateness. There were only some muffed lines by Kennedy on the air once in a while, the misstatement of "fam farmily" instead of "farm family" and so forth, which were partly our fault for overscheduling him. He was a guy that was not going to be an armchair candidate, and he had long days, but those verbal flubs were the things that ended up on the news and I think they became self-perpetuating for a while. It took a long time to get over. And I think also an important factor about the Mudd interview is that the number of times the American public will focus on a candidate during a campaign is relatively limited. Whether people saw it or not, they heard about it. As a result, if they saw a network clip that showed some less than articulate statement, then I think there were perhaps a few that said, Well, we've read about this fellow and he hasn't lived up to expectations. So I think the ripple effect lingered.

I don't think we ever felt that we would adopt an early knock-out strategy when you had an incumbent president, but we did feel that it was important to get some wins early and get off and running, and at the end of 1979 we knew the frustrations of not being able to break into the dialogue. We spent some time talking about policy and how we would move on in 1980, but we didn't adopt that until after the first of the year—in fact, after Iowa.

CLYMER: Thank you, and good night.

2 THE DEMOCRATIC PRIMARIES

The Iowa Caucus. Campaign Primary vs. General Election. Carter's TV Ads. Kennedy After Iowa. Agonizing Reappraisal. The Illinois Primary. The New York Primary. The Character Issue. Carter As Seen by the Voters. The Wisconsin Primary. Kennedy Stays In. Carter Statement on the Hostages. Kennedy's Resources. Polarization. The Debate Issue. Failure of the Rescue Mission. Out of the Rose Garden.

ALBERT R. HUNT (correspondent, *Wall Street Journal*): When we left off last night, Paul Kirk and Carl Wagner had taken Teddy Kennedy from 60 percent in the polls down to 30 percent in sixty days; Jimmy Carter, once he had gotten to 60 percent, courageously withstood the advice of Pat Caddell and Tim Kraft to risk it all by debating; and Tom Quinn and Jerry Brown were still discussing the constitutional convention. Let's take Iowa as the starting point. As the more focused Democratic primary and caucus period began, I'd like to ask each of you whether you were able to keep your eye on the general election or whether it had gotten so personalized that it became almost impossible.

—THE IOWA CAUCUS—

TIM KRAFT (campaign manager, Carter–Mondale Re-election Committee): I don't think it was either personal or parochial in terms of our campaign thrust, strategy, or execution. There was a political risk, in terms of subsequent primaries and possibly even the general election, in a decision made by the president to put the grain embargo on in response to the invasion of Afghanistan. This was certainly a risky thing to do in Iowa at the time, and it could've had its effect in subsequent states. I think that our overall message, conveyed by Vice-President Mondale and the First Lady and other speakers and representatives, was one that would be echoed in subsequent primary and caucus states: the Carter administration had tackled the tough problems, made some hard decisions, talked the truth and reality to the American people, achieved some successes on these goals, and was working on other programs to meet the problems of the country. It was a general, positive message, hopefully presidential in tone. I also think the organizational effort, the effort of our surrogates, was positive and not combative or hand-to-hand at that point.

HUNT: Let me just ask you a question about how you conveyed that message. We were all struck, as it got closer to the Iowa caucus, that there were a number of people who were receiving phone calls from the president; it was kind of difficult to find someone in Iowa who hadn't heard from him by January 21st. Did you all sit down in late December or early January and map out a strategy for how much time he would spend and how many groups you would bring to Iowa? Also, was there any fear that this would somehow be criticized or would arouse cynicism on the part of the press or the public from a person who said he had to stay in the White House because of the international crisis?

KRAFT: Well, I don't think we had x number of hours per day or week, or a budget for the phone calls he would make. We realized with some of the speaker phone calls that there might be some criticism there—as a sort of a nether world of participating in a meeting while not actually being there. But, on the other hand, we felt, given the nature of the caucuses and the need to generate and maintain support and enthusiasm, that it was a legitimate activity on behalf of the president. It didn't involve moving the whole apparatus out to the state. It took a far more limited amount of time than might be apparent from a rather exaggerated number of calls reported upon. So that wasn't a great public relations concern.

—PRIMARY CAMPAIGN VS. GENERAL ELECTION—

DAVID S. BRODER (associate editor and national political correspondent, *Washington Post*): I want to jump in on this point, because I think this is a crucial point. Caddell said last night that the strategy for winning against Kennedy was to make it as much like a general election as possible. The characteristic that distinguishes a general election from a primary is that the winner and loser don't have to end up liking each other or even dealing with each other very much. I'd like to ask Bob Keefe how he thought that kind of a primary campaign could be conducted and still end up with a Democratic party that was viable for general election? Was that ever a consideration in the decisionmaking?

ROBERT J. KEEFE (political consultant, Carter–Mondale Re-election Committee): I don't know whether it was a consideration in the decisionmaking, but I think that it was. When the campaign finally got started in January of 1980, there was great hope in all sectors of the Carter campaign that it would be over two to three months down the road and that there would be a long time to heal the thing and put it back together, which conditioned the way the campaign got started. Then as the campaign went on and it became more difficult to win, I think both sides stepped up the use of different kinds of artillery and made it more difficult to heal eventually and less time in which to do it. Does that answer your question, David? No?

BRODER: Well, I'll try it on the reverse side with Paul Kirk. I recall a conversation with Senator Kennedy on the plane just before Christmas. I asked him, if he were nominated, what it would be like in the general election with Jimmy Carter sitting in the White House while Kennedy was the Democratic nominee? His answer was, as I recall it, that you always assume that the tough fight is to get nominated and that the Republicans had a history of self-destructing in the general election. Were you really that naive about what you would face in terms of a general election campaign if you had been able to nominate him?

PAUL G. KIRK, JR. (national political director, Kennedy for President): On the threshold of Iowa, we had not focused at all, at that point, on the general election. Early on, there was a feeling that it would not be a cinch in the primaries at all, that it might well be a long, protracted struggle. As we got into the campaign and the roof started to fall in, Iowa then became more and more important for purposes of showing early viability. But the seeds of division, the rhetoric of the campaign, really hadn't built up. By the point at which it was known there would not be a debate, the attitude in the Kennedy campaign had shifted somewhat on the hostage thing from cynicism to feeling that the tactic or policy from the other side was a sham, given the flights to the White House by Iowa political leaders and the phone calls out of Iowa by President Carter, yet no "political activity." The feeling was not just that our campaign was being hurt, but that the process was being distorted somewhat. That, I think, built up some rancor within, which seeded possibilities for further division down the line. But it was not, at that point, so much a thought process within the Kennedy campaign; we were not saying then, "How're we gonna put it together in November?"

CARL WAGNER (director of field operations, Kennedy for President): Early on, late in 1979, we had to make a number of decisions about the tone of the Kennedy campaign. This is before the debate was frozen by Iran. There were calculations made about the campaign that went by the boards and were not even useful sixty days later. We got into a campaign running against Jimmy Carter and his record, and within thirty days, we're running against the president of the United States, every day, in the White House. So, a lot of the thinking that had gone into the structure and tone of the campaign was just impertinent, almost immediately. As a case in point, I can recall we dropped about a million pieces of mail in December or January. A lot of thought went into what this letter should look like, what the tone of it would be. And there were a number of people in the campaign who argued that the Kennedy campaign in the primaries shouldn't be driven hard left in a challenge to Carter, so that in winning the nomination, you could still put together a viable general election strategy. That sort of right–left focus of the primary debate occupied, I think, probably as much time, in terms of the calculation about the general election, as the question of the toughness of the argument with Carter.

CATHERINE MACKIN (network correspondent, ABC News): Bob, when you said that you thought it'd be over in two or three months, at what point did you all think that? Was it before the hostages were taken?

KEEFE: We're talking about January of 1980. The president was doing awfully well. The senator was doing very poorly. And when the thing got started, Carter jumped out of the box and bang, bang, bang. . . .

—CARTER'S TV ADS

ADAM CLYMER (correspondent, *New York Times*): I'd like to question Jack Walsh, and then somebody from the Kennedy side, in pursuit of David's point. Was there any time, for example, when television ads were being looked at, when someone came up with a piece of research that could be used to criticize Kennedy's voting record? Did anyone say, "Yeah, this might help this week, but in the long run, this approach will make it harder for us to get him and his supporters with us, and thus, harder to win the general election"?

JACK WALSH (national political director, Carter–Mondale Re-election Committee): In the fall of 1979, there was tremendous trepidation and confusion about how to run against a draft committee that would then just show up your negatives, but therefore you wouldn't have an opponent who had negatives. The assumption built into the summer and fall of 1979 said, "This will be a long, protracted problem if there are draft committees and Anybody But Carter Committees out there." But if a candidate gets in and it becomes a real political situation, it will resolve itself very quickly. It will be an easier situation to deal with.

CLYMER: Did anybody ever look at the "I Help Amy with Her Homework" ad and say, "This is useful, but that tactic might get us into trouble in the long run"?

WALSH: Pat did.

PATRICK H. CADDELL (president, Cambridge Survey Research): We considered that problem. Let me say something else about January that's also happening with the balance question that David's talking about. And Bob was right—we were looking, hopefully, to being able to resolve the thing fairly quickly. Senator Kennedy had said when he first indicated he was going to run that if he couldn't win early, that he was going to have to get out, and it had to be done quickly. And once the polls moved the way they did, it was our assumption that would happen. Let's not forget, however, that there was a common perception about the Iowa caucus being the first test, that it was a much closer test because it was assumed to be basically an organizational struggle with very low turnout and so on. The point was that the first ads and the first things that were done were generally on the president. There's no question that, in the campaign, we planned to emphasize those strengths that the public perceived about the president, which were mainly personal. And I think that as the campaign wears on, the ads take on a more and more difficult hue to them. The point was that, early on, we were trying to walk the balance between making sure that we won, and getting the thing over quickly, but trying to do it in such a way that it didn't open up the party any more than it already was at that particular junction.

In response to your direct question, was there anybody sitting down to question the ads, saying, "Hey, that one won't work" or "We shouldn't do that"? In fact, that did not occur, because Jerry Rafshoon wouldn't show them to anybody.* (*Laughter*) Jerry's situation was that he had pretty much carte blanche in terms of the ads. They were looked at by some people and decisions were made, but there are a whole lot of other people who wished to have say in it, perhaps, who should've had say in it, but who didn't.

BRODER: Could we hang on that point for just a second, because I think we're learning something rather interesting about the internal decisionmaking structure. Who was involved and who was not involved in that kind of a decision? Did the candidate see them?

CADDELL: He didn't. He had never seen ads, basically. No, seriously, he didn't see the ads for the primaries in '76 until after the pri-

---

*Rafshoon was media advisor to the Carter–Mondale campaign.

maries, as it turned out. One day he indicated that he had not ever seen them, so he decided he ought to see them. Basically, Hamilton saw them, Tim saw them, Jody saw them, I saw them. There was some discussion about them; it was not totally a free hand.

KENNETH A. BODE (network correspondent, NBC News): When Jerry Rafshoon was going to put the ads together, did you sit down with him and your polls and say, now this is what we know the public perceptions of Kennedy are and so forth? What were the kinds of advice you offered him in projecting, putting together some of the ads, like the "Amy" ad, for example?

CADDELL: Well, let me say the Amy ad came out of the half-hour film that Bob Squier had produced on the president which was an effort, at that point—given Bob's and Jerry's feelings—to give some sense of depth to the president, both as a person and as a president.

MARTIN F. NOLAN (Washington bureau chief, *Boston Globe*): I have to interrupt you. The slogan did not come out of the half-hour, though. The slogan that everyone remembers—"Husband, father, president: he's done all three jobs with distinction"—was that in the half-hour Bob Squier film? That voice-over?

CADDELL: No the voice-over wasn't. But in fact, if you go back, Marty, and look at the half-hour, the sentiment at that point in the film was, indeed, expressed, even if it wasn't—

NOLAN: The slogan wasn't. Is that correct?

CADDELL: Well, I don't think that—

KRAFT: So what's your point?

NOLAN: I think the slogan's the only synopsis of the half-hour film that's a one-line definition of what we're talking about—the "husband–father–president" business. Because Senator Kennedy, I do believe, took offense. Correct me if I'm wrong. (*Laughter*)

CADDELL: Look, we knew what our greatest strengths were. We were, at that point, at least somewhat aware of what Senator Kennedy's weaknesses were. As later we would prove, you can take these things even further. I would think that the first round of advertising that was prepared was, in fact, basically just playing up what we knew to be the president's strengths. Later, in Iowa, we would play up the international situation. In a campaign, you walk the tightrope between—and this is always the problem with primaries—those things that will continue to plant the seeds of division and hostility and also being successful. At that stage, it was a perception that we were certainly going to play to our strengths, obviously not without some subtle overtones, but that the major thrust at that point was mainly positive.

BODE: Carl, what was the reaction of Senator Kennedy and the Kennedy campaign to that whole wave of advertising that came out around that time, both on the senator's record and the advertising that seemed to suggest personal liabilities?

WAGNER: I think there were two reactions to the negative campaign run by the president, early and late—it was tougher late than early. One was the reaction of the candidate and the staff. But I think a far more consequential reaction was the reaction of many of the constituencies supporting the Kennedy campaign. I think there were negative feelings very strongly held. That was the reaction I would get from a state campaign manager who was in contact with either trade union leaders or liberal activists. I remember the reaction in western Pennsylvania when very heavy negative media hit. While it was very effective for the Carter campaign, the response by the Kennedy base in that state was very resentful, I think far more negative than it probably even was among the staff. That is not to say it wasn't also objected to there.

WALSH: I've got to add one thing, Carl. The problem with the general election thing, that David brought up, in the knock-out theory was this. The knock-out theory didn't come from the Carter campaign. All of the questions to us from the press through the fall were, "Can you survive the knock-out? He's gonna get you in Illinois." Kennedy says privately, "You'll be out of it in Illinois." Will you survive it? It was unbelievable the way it came at us. So the solution to the general election problem was "Get out by Illinois." Y'know, that's the way it was pushed at us.

HUNT: I want to pick up on something that Pat said a few minutes ago. When you filmed these commercials, whether we describe them as negative or not in the beginning, it was just a small group that really looked at them. I think it's accurate to say a rather small group made all the major decisions. Was there any fear on the part of you who were not part of this small group that the feelings they had about Senator Kennedy were making them go too hard? Or was there any effort on the part of any of you or on the part of the vice-president to try to convey a somewhat different and more positive message in the beginning? Was there any effort to get that thought across?

LES FRANCIS (executive director, Democratic National Committee): Well, we're taking it back eleven months ago. While Bob Keefe is correct—we had hoped that we could have the thing over with within a two- or three-month period—the fact of the matter was that nobody was betting that we would. In fact, in January of 1980, and in February and March, we were fighting for our lives because it wasn't at all clear that the thing was going to go our way. And I don't recall ever having raised questions about the contents of commercials. The ones that I saw before Illinois . . . we had a couple minor suggestions to make, but nothing major.

KEEFE: I think there was a bit of a sense in the campaign that, gee, this guy picked a fight, he doesn't get to set the rules. That really was a rather widespread feeling and I don't think that there was tremendous internal dispute over what the advertising was and so forth, what the message content was. I didn't participate in it, if there was.

—KENNEDY AFTER IOWA—

HUNT: Jack, why did you leave in mid-January?

WALSH: Personal. I didn't have the kind of internal dispute or conflict that a lot of people ask me about. We had a very amicable split.

HUNT: Did you get any sense that because you were from Massachusetts and up here and knew some of the people you were running against that there was some suspicion of you?

WALSH: No, it wasn't that. I learned a lesson I learned before in my life, which was, when you're working an incumbent campaign, and when pressure is put on the political situation and on the candidacy, the government, there's one question: Is the government going to run the campaign, that is, people in the administration; or will the campaign maintain its status? I came to the realization that the campaign wasn't going to be as important as the West Wing. But that's not negative. That was just education on my part.

HUNT: Let's try to get through Iowa. Right before those caucuses, Rick, you were really at rock bottom. Was there a feeling then that you had to, if not win, at least do very well or the campaign itself was in real peril?

RICHARD G. STEARNS (chief of delegate selection, Kennedy for President): As it turned out, the campaign was in real peril after we did not do all that well. But I think the problem was really set by the senator himself. He had inadvertently and unfortunately, in the fall, right after the straw caucus in Florida, pointed to Iowa as the first test of the campaign.

CLYMER: That very night in Louisville.

STEARNS: Right. And that, in a sense, set an expectation for the outcome in Iowa which was difficult for us to escape or explain away when the campaign did not go well. Carl probably came closer to having an intimation of what was going to happen in Iowa than almost anyone else in the campaign did, even including people who had done an effective job in a short period of time in putting a campaign in Iowa in place. I don't think any of us, as we approached the caucus within the last four or five days—again, Carl may be the exception—really thought we were going to lose badly. I think there was a sense that we were going to lose, but we thought that we would be left in some sort of competitive position. The results of the Iowa caucuses led to what we used to call an "agonizing reappraisal" of the campaign. It was a very difficult time. You may remember that at that point, all employees of the campaign went off the payroll. The campaign was financially—

WAGNER: I remember that! (*Laughter*)

STEARNS: The campaign was financially insolvent. A common part of the press view was that it was politically and intellectually insolvent after the caucuses as well. The campaign had somehow not found its distance from the president's campaign. And it looked, on January 22nd, as if we might not survive much longer.

HUNT: Was anyone inside arguing for the senator to get out then?

STEARNS: From what I knew, no. I think there was an argument as to what course the campaign would take after Iowa. Whether we would continue stressing what I would basically call the leadership alternative to Jimmy Carter, which was the tone that the campaign tried to set up through Iowa, as opposed to the thought that the campaign had to depart radically in an issues sense from the president's campaign, and particularly from his record. Most of the debate that I recall was over the direction Kennedy *should* go in what eventually became the Georgetown speech on January 28th.

BRODER: Ron, at what point did you become aware that there was such a debate about basic strategy and tactics regarding the contents of the campaign?

RONALD H. BROWN (deputy campaign manager, Kennedy for President): I became aware of that the day after Christmas at a meeting we had in West Palm Beach where all of these issues were discussed and where there was some pressure from some to make that jump toward a Georgetown speech earlier on. It turned out that that view prevailed after Iowa.

BRODER: Give us a summary of what the arguments were and why you think the decision wasn't made until after Iowa.

HUNT: And who the participants were on both sides.

BROWN: I guess there were about ten or so people at West Palm Beach. The outsiders were Congressman Paul Simon and one or two economists. From the inside were Paul Kirk, Gary Orren, Larry Horowitz, Sarge Shriver, Carey Parker, Bob Shrum, and myself. I think the arguments were clearly separated into political arguments and substantive arguments. That is, was it wise, in view of the fact that there was some concern about how far left the campaign wanted to be perceived in the public view, to get into gas rationing, to wage and price controls, to those kinds of issues at that point in time in the campaign? Clearly, there was some concern about moving in that direction. Others thought that we couldn't sit around and wait for the Iranian crisis to end; it was paralyzing the campaign. We were a hostage to that crisis as well, and we had to find a way to break out of it. One way was to do some dramatic things as far as direction and thrust and policy articulation. Frankly, leaving that meeting, I wasn't sure what the decision was. As it turned out, the decision was not to make that move at the time, a decision that history shows was changed after the Iowa primary, based principally then on political rationale. Clearly, there was nothing else left to do then.

HUNT: Did you have any sense around what position in that contest the senator was most comfortable with?

BROWN: There were several options. One option was to go with one or the other—either talk about wage and price controls or talk about gas rationing. Do you do them both at the same time? It was that kind of discussion. How much can you do now? There was some wavering, even during the meeting. I think that as people weighed it on each side, there was some shifting around. At one point, early on, my personal impression was, he was ready to go with one or another of those; probably not both. But there was a change either toward the end of the meeting or that evening, after it was over, and it wasn't until we got back to Washington for further discussion that I was really clear on exactly what we were going to do. The West Palm Beach meeting was not a decision meeting; it was kind of an input meeting, a discussion meeting.

BRODER: Paul, was it clear to everybody then that, because of Iran, you couldn't win the argument any longer just on the basis of leadership? Carter was now looking more like a leader, and you couldn't just say, "I'm more of a leader than the fella who's dealing with this crisis."

KIRK: No question, David. When the senator talked early on about wage-price guidelines—if you were really there at the table pushing them, you could really make a difference—it didn't wash. And it didn't wash, in part, because of the great overhang of Iran and, by that time, Afghanistan. So, we were doubly confounded by the flag-waving over the political landscape. I think it was becoming crystal clear that you couldn't just talk in that framework; there really had to be a division at that point to separate yourself and let the people understand the rationale for the challenger. In the meantime, for the first twelve minutes of all the networks nightly news for weeks, it seemed that Iran was the issue — and it wasn't until sometime later when the prime went to 20 percent one night, that the economy topped the news. So we were in the middle of a real squeeze. We still felt that if we went hard on Iran, there would be a tremendous back-lash on it. It happened that by the time the Georgetown speech was given, the Soviet troops had invaded Afghanistan. The senator felt strongly after the Soviet combat troops in Cuba incident that it should be pointed to as a vacillating policy which invited further Soviet incursions. But the hostage incident, as Carl pointed out ear-lier, together with a number of other factors, totally skewed any advance strategic planning and really brought us back to the draw-ing board.

WAGNER: The other thing, I think, to keep in mind is that you did not know, from day to day, how long it was going to last. As you all know, there were a number of times in the primaries where it seemed to be on the edge of resolution.

WALSH: Wisconsin. (*Laughter*)

WAGNER: Well, the calculation over the short run was even diffi-cult to make, not knowing whether, again, the assumptions you were operating on would radically change.

— AGONIZING REAPPRAISAL —

HUNT: After you were decisively beaten in Iowa, you did make the decision to go with the Georgetown speech, and you tossed in wage price controls, gas rationing, and everything else. Was there a feeling then that you had a month — through Illinois, through any time — to see if this worked, and if not, then you had to once again go through that agonizing reappraisal, and perhaps quit?

WAGNER: No, I don't think the decision was made after Iowa to look at it for another thirty days and see what happened in Minnesota, Maine, and New Hampshire, and then let's go through Illinois, and look again. After Iowa, the campaign had to make some radical adjustments internally. The strategy used to raise money had to be changed drastically. It was essentially decentralized; the state campaigns became an integral part, and the most successful part of it, direct mail—a much more ideological tool to raise money—came on line in January after the Georgetown speech. But the whole structure of the campaign, the organization and the financing of it, and in addition, the tone of it, for the reasons Paul suggested, were adjusted to meet the very dramatic political advantage enjoyed by Carter. We moved into the March 11 Southern primaries and the home-based New England primaries, but it wasn't done in the sense of whether we could make it through New Hampshire and look again.

KEEFE: Didn't the senator keep saying out loud, somewhat to your advantage, "I think that if I don't win in New Hampshire, if I don't win in Maine . . ."—you know, that was really happening pretty strongly. He kept setting the tests, I mean.

WAGNER: But you also remember that he began in January and February to say, "I'm in this till the first ballot."

KEEFE: Not until after he didn't pass the test that he had set for himself.

KIRK: That's true. He had mentioned that—

KEEFE: Seems to me that's the wrong thing to do, to say that "if I don't win. . . ."

KIRK: At a speech somewhere in Washington he was asked about the coming events which were Maine and New Hampshire, and I think he said that he had to win them. I would add that at the time— this is post-Iowa now, that the decision was made with respect to the Georgetown speech—there was concern about how long you could go on under the situation, a conceivable loss in Massachusetts and the ramifications that might have on the 1982 Senate race. Talk about sailing against the wind—there was a tornado! We were getting everything coming at us, and there were some in those sessions who talked—to respond to your question, Al—about how this is the way it's going to be for maybe an indeterminable period of time and maybe the thing to do is get out.

That was based largely on, I think, the feeling of some that this was a raw meat campaign, that the senator was being almost, you know, destroyed personally in terms of how the nation looked at him. We had a difficult time trying to combat all of that, and I don't think in the early discussions it came anywhere near the bottom line, but the clear sense that I got from the candidate himself was that in *his* mind the process was still distorted—the real dialogue hadn't been engaged in, and he was prepared to shoulder a lot of it, to tough it out, if you will. After the Iowa caucus there was a meeting at which it was decided that both on domestic and foreign policy, it was time to cut the cord and go with all of it, and I think the Georgetown speech was on the 28th of January or something like that. It was a matter of survival, and to see whether this would give his campaign further life and viability.

HUNT: What options did you think you had as far as dealing with the personal problems, the personal assaults on him? What did you consider?

KIRK: At least two options were clear. One, you could try to, in a sense, ignore those and stick to what the substantive public policy issues were. To some degree we tried that. The other was to engage somewhat in the personal dialogue, not so much in what he said publicly but perhaps through ads by others, emphasizing the need for compassion in public life, the fact that there were family problems but also family tragedies, and in those he moved in and filled voids and so forth. It's not clear to me still, but I guess looking back, perhaps the former option may have stood by us better because with the other you got rather a mixed message. The Carter campaign, the personal ads, kept coming, and it was a wrong ground on which to engage in any kind of dialogue, especially when the breakthrough hadn't come in terms of the policy content of the Kennedy campaign, and when the live news was such that we still weren't part of it.

MACKIN: With the discussion of Kennedy dropping out—I gather the first time that came up was in the private meetings at McLean right after Iowa, when some people in the inner circle thought that Kennedy should drop out—can you say now what went on in those meetings?

KIRK: I think basically not much more detail than I've mentioned earlier. There were not strong advocates for getting out at that point. But there were those, myself included, who said, you shouldn't engage in this conversation without exploring all the options, and that if things don't turn around for us, or if there wasn't a further boost in the campaign, given the kind of hammering he was taking publicly, dropping out was a question worth considering.

MACKIN: Was that the first time it was ever discussed, or was it discussed prior to that?

KIRK: The first time it was ever entertained as an option, I think, was post–Iowa, and the second discussion about it was on the threshold of giving the Georgetown speech.

MACKIN: Ron, after the Christmas meeting, how was it decided not to make the Georgetown-type speech then, or was it just inertia, just not getting around to it?

BROWN: No, it was decided by the candidate not to go at that point. The basic discussion was, do you wait to see what's going to happen in Iowa or don't you? The judgment was made, I think clearly by the candidate, that we would wait, and at that point, as Rick indicated, most of us did not anticipate the dimensions of the Iowa loss. So then you were in a crisis kind of situation after that, after that loss.

CLYMER: Either in Iowa or for sometime thereafter, here was a candidate whom a lot of people had encouraged to run, who was in trouble. Were you folks acting on a disappointed expectation? Did you ever have reason to think that more of those people who had asked him to run would come out and help: for example, John Culver in Iowa?

BROWN: It's hard to single out individuals in describing that disappointment. I can describe, certainly, my personal disappointment as being very profound then, about so many people, both elected officials and others who I knew had come to him in the summer and had urged him to run and who were not to be heard from when they were most needed. That was clearly a matter of disappointment within the campaign, but I think it was accepted. Although there was disappointment, there was not a feeling that the direction of the campaign or strategy would turn on the participation of those individuals who had said, please do it, and then couldn't be found. It did have an impact on how we felt, but I don't think that it colored the decisions made at that time—except in terms of how you put your strategy together in state campaigns, and that one objective is to get endorsements and to talk to people who can make it appear that you've got some forward movement in the campaign. We went to talk to some of those people; they either wanted to remain silent or had decided to support the president, so those kinds of experiences probably changed what we did in states after Iowa.

KEEFE: During the period of '77 and '78, the Carter campaign very actively set themselves up to take a Kennedy challenge by changing the rules in the timing of the primaries. That was very significant, I think, because as they came out of the problems in the North, bingo, they have to go South and get tromped. That was Mr. Stearns', Mr. Wagner's doing, there with the Winograd Commission. (*Laughter*)

STEARNS: Always willing to help. . . .

HUNT: It was semi-successful, wasn't it? I mean, there were more elaborate plans, some of which didn't come through.

WAGNER: The first primary would have been the Southern regional primary—if it had all worked out right. (*Laughter*)

KEEFE: There was some significant progress made by the Carter people in 1977-78 to make it a hell of a lot tougher to be challenged in 1980.

—THE ILLINOIS PRIMARY—

HUNT: After the senator won Massachusetts—didn't lose in his home state—the president won in the Southern primaries; then there was Illinois. I know it was a huge disappointment to you, Tim, when you didn't get Jane Byrnes' endorsement in November. When did you realize how lucky you were not to have it? (*Laughter*)

KRAFT: St. Patrick's Day Parade! We thought Illinois might be the Pennsylvania of 1980, in terms of being the breakaway state. In '79 we prepared political and organizational contacts there from the top to the bottom. In other words, we thought we would enjoy a close win in Iowa, we would hold our own in New England, we would win Florida, we would obviously win the Southern primaries, and then — enjoying a slight delegate lead—we would move into Illinois and hope that would be a breakaway state. This would confirm our winnability and provide a good delegate cushion and hopefully encourage the opposition to withdraw reasonably. We made contacts in the city of Chicago, Tommy Hynes being a primary example of a solid, good, early contact there, a Cook County ward boss. Alliances we very carefully cultivated in the fall of '79, and the organizational and party people that we had put together down state, led us to believe that we would do well there. There wasn't a lot of coverage of Illinois before the primary got there in terms of this groundwork, and we thought it could be a kind of surprise victory. We felt good about it, and we tried to keep out of the Carter administration versus the Jane Byrne administration business, in anticipation of needing unity in the general election.

BODE: Neil Goldschmidt wasn't too helpful on that.

KRAFT: Neil Goldschmidt was a valuable asset throughout the year, and I wouldn't single out one untoward remark.*

HUNT: Were you working with Richard Daley?

*The reference is to comments made publicly by Secretary of Transportation Neil Goldschmidt about Chicago Mayor Jane Byrne following Mayor Byrne's endorsement of Senator Kennedy's candidacy, stating his willingness to consider using his office to deny transportation project funds to the city of Chicago.

KRAFT: Yes, in the sense that we kept in close touch with the Daley family. They had a race of their own. We respected that. As you know, there was not a Daley endorsement, but again, if you had visited the 11th Ward in the weekend before the primary, I think you would have sensed a tilt to the Carter–Mondale campaign among its partisans.

WAGNER: In the 11th Ward?

KRAFT: Yes.

WAGNER: As distinguished from? (*Laughter*)

BRODER: Paul, Illinois is certainly an example of another place in which you weren't running against Jimmy Carter but against the president of the United States. Two questions: how did it affect your thinking that you were up against somebody who could mobilize all of the leverage of the White House and administration to build the kind of political network that Tim was just talking about? Second, looking back at it now, how do you explain what apparently was the misperception on both sides that the mayor of Chicago, as the head of that organization, was a valuable political asset worth fighting over?

KIRK: On the first point, I think there was, more than any time I can recall, use of federal largesse and probably more use of the cabinet in this political campaign. Although those things were written about, they were really hitting us hard. Day after day it became tougher and tougher. While we were on the skids and the president was holding on to the flag, the elected officials and other people who were important in the nominating process were either frozen or moving to his standard, and it took a very large toll in terms of the progression.

As for the mayor of Chicago, I don't think anyone on either side perceived her to be the mayor as her predecessor was the mayor. On the other hand, the fact that so many had encouraged Senator Kennedy to run and so few had stood up made us very grateful for Jane Byrne to say that she was going to be with Senator Kennedy. In a time when there were very few blessings, we counted that as a blessing. In terms of the Illinois situation itself, we didn't have any money, virtually no media, and we had basiclaly scrubbed everything in a lot of the states. The senator went out and spent time living in Illinois rather than trying to move from one state to another. We knew it wasn't going well, and we had to rely on the hope that she could do things in Chicago and Cook County. We had virtually no organization down state, and we had to rely on his personal presence, personal appearances, there to try to break through.

HUNT: After you lost as badly as you did, did you have any more of those meetings out at McLean or elsewhere about "should we get out"?

— THE NEW YORK PRIMARY —

KIRK: On the eve of the New York primary, or within twenty-four hours before, there was a poll in the New York *Daily News* which had us twenty-seven points down, and we ended up winning by eighteen points. At that point, by default we had come into sort of an industrial state strategy. We had already lost Illinois and we had Massachusetts and we were looking at New York and the numbers were, as I say, some twenty-seven points down. At that point there was another discussion as to whether this made any sense for anyone.

CLYMER: Was a withdrawal speech written?

KIRK: There was never a withdrawal speech ordered to be written. The senator never asked for one. There was a withdrawal speech that was written up as a possible option.

HUNT: Paul, did you feel at the time, and did Steve Smith feel at the time, that if you had lost New York, that really was it, there was no way you could—?

KIRK: I think when you look at the process as whole, there was no way financially that we could survive. As Rick mentioned earlier, we were bankrupt long before, and it was through the sacrifice and loyalty of a lot of staff in the states who were living off the land, and a hard cadre of people around the country who still believed in what the senator stood for and wanted to do, that we were able to hang on. Basically, the feeling was if we lost New York as badly as we were projected to, that the bottom was really out.

MACKIN: Can I ask where that discussion took place and who participated?

KIRK: Let's see. . . . That was in New York City at a hotel, perhaps the day before the election, and two of the senator's sisters were there. Joe Kennedy was there, I was there, Eddie Martin, the senator . . . there may have been one or two others.

CLYMER: Steve Smith?

KIRK: Steve Smith was not there.

NOLAN: There is something else that occurred during the New York primary campaign that had a great impact later on; at least the Carter people thought so. This is the famous turnaround in the United Nations Security Council resolution which had enormous impact within the Jewish community which was very active. I don't think myself that Carter ever recovered from it. When Secretary of State Vance took the fall for Carter—and you go out to Kew Gardens, you go to Ben Rosenthal's district and talk to people about what they thought of that—it was the beginning of the end for Carter in the Jewish community. Was it as bad as I thought it was?

KRAFT: Worse.

KEEFE: It wasn't the beginning of the end; it was the end of the end. The beginning of the end was much earlier. (*Laughter*)

KEEFE: Very cleverly planned plot that Wagner cooked up.

NOLAN: He did a hell of a job with that ambassador. Then he and Vance took the fall and it took several weeks for the president to realize, I think, how much political damage had been done. Did you feel—

KRAFT: Then, of course, there was a cabal of senators on the foreign relations committee that physically hauled Secretary Vance up to testify on the Friday before.

NOLAN: It turned around that weekend.

FRANCIS: The testimony was the Friday before the primary. The testimony had as much to do with what happened that Tuesday as the vote itself, I think.

KRAFT: That's still no excuse for Lou Harris to make a thirty-six-point error in the course of seventy-two hours just to be mean and personal about it. (*Laughter*)

STEARNS: Maybe Pat saw it coming. . . .

KRAFT: Don't get Caddell started on Harris! (*Laughter*)

STEARNS: I assume we're trying to mark turning points in the primaries. There are two reasons why Illinois was an important primary. First, if you simply look at the race in terms of the delegate numbers required to win the nomination, Carter won the nomination in Illinois. The cushion of 150 or whatever delegates that he took out of the state gave him an insurmountable lead that Kennedy under no conceivable set of circumstances would overtake before the convention. Second, Illinois was interesting, at least from my vantage point in Connecticut, as the peak and the end, so to speak, of the character issue as the transcendent obstacle Kennedy faced in trying to place a message before voters. The character issue began to lose its force immediately after the Illinois primary, and began to recede as an issue and continue to recede throughout the rest of the campaign.

—THE CHARACTER ISSUE—

KEEFE: Why do you think that was? I have my ideas. . . . I am just curious.

STEARNS: I was allegedly managing our campaign in Connecticut, and every poll there that we had taken showed nothing different than what the polls Paul referred to in New York were showing. Despite a lot of advantages in Connecticut, we were two to one behind the president. I thought the turning point came at the St. Patrick's Day parade in Chicago. The level of vituperation and personal insult directed at Kennedy reached an intensity during that parade that seemed to change people's attitudes. It was almost as if this man had been punished too much by the hostility that people saw on the television news that night. The only evidence I have for this relates to the fact that our offices were right across from the Civic Arena in Hartford. Three days before the primary, we leafletted the crowd leaving a sporting event at the Center. I remember on this Saturday, before the Illinois primary, we encountered probably the most hostile crowd I have ever encountered in any political campaign. Even leafletting for McGovern in a George Wallace rally was nothing like this crowd—people grabbing literature, ripping it up, spitting at you. It had snowed the night before, people picked up snow, threw it at you, challenged you to fights. I had never really seen anything so hostile.

KEEFE: What was the event? A wrestling match? (Laughter)

STEARNS: The day after the primary we leafletted—I think it might have been a basketball game—and the attitude had changed 180 degrees. The only thing I saw that had happened in the interval that seemed to make an impression on people was the St. Patrick's Day parade.

WAGNER: I agree with you, Rick, but I think two other things contributed to it. Within two weeks after Illinois, attitudes changed, and we saw this in some of our polling on two fundamental issues. One was the president's use of Iran, prior to Wisconsin primary, which followed Illinois by two weeks. While it may have worked in Wisconsin, Pennsylvania, New Jersey, California, and some big primaries coming down the road, it produced, at least in the Democratic electorate, a real question about how straight he was being in terms of the president of the United States versus Iran versus his pursuit of the nomination. That had never been an issue previously. Secondly, the recession was on line. It was beginning to lead the news. A whole set of issues were coming on-stream that had been really frozen out of the debate in January, February, and March.

BODE: Why do you think, Bob, that the character issue receded at that point?

KEEFE: As Rick mentioned, the president actually won the nomination in Illinois by building the delegate lead that was insurmountable, and the people in the press certainly caught on to that. That changed the character of the Kennedy candidacy from one of a viable campaign for the nomination to a protect movement against the president. That meant the issues were important and the personality wasn't.

CLYMER: Those were the times of the plucky Teddy stories.

KEEFE: Yes, that's right!

BRODER: Was there any perception of this change among the Carter people?

HUNT: Particularly after you lost New York and Connecticut?

—CARTER AS SEEN BY THE VOTERS—

CADDELL: Let's go back to the primaries in terms of the voters, which might be interesting for a second, as opposed to all the other things going on. We realized the situation was going to be somewhat more difficult as early as New Hampshire. We had always seen a difference between the East and the Midwest. One of the reasons why Illinois never budged was that Carter was always much stronger in the Midwest than he had been in the Northeast. The fundamental weakness that he had from '76 on was still underlying all those numbers in the East. That was not necessarily the situation in the Midwest, and the real difference was Midwest Catholics versus Eastern Catholics both in their perceptions about the candidates and the way they viewed the race. In New Hampshire we had found some difficulty in reconciling our vote-margin lead with what our information about the candidates would indicate. This suggested a much closer race. For a couple of days right after Maine, the New Hampshire situation was no longer a long lead for us. It was partly in reaction to Maine; it was partly in reaction, interestingly enough, to the president's State of the Union speech. While generally received very well, it caused some backlash particularly with women and other groups on questions of war and peace, ironically. What we were already beginning to see at the end of February when we first looked at New York was how precarious the structure of the situation was. As I said, our intention all along had been to keep it a general election. Every time we kept the focus on candidate choice, the margins would hold in a fairly wide fashion. Anytime it began to move off of that, we had some difficulty. What we saw happening in New York was happening even before Illinois.

Some days after the U.N. vote, we had a meeting. I think Tim Kraft was there, and Les Francis was probably there the Wednesday morning after Illinois when everyone was still savouring the massive victory there. We discovered that, in fact, the day before we had been behind in New York. The real problem first was the flood loss, the flooding of Jews away from the president in fairly significant numbers. Also, the president had taken a twenty-point drop in his favorable ratings over the period of two or three weeks prior to that. Attitudes about Senator Kennedy had not moved an iota. What we saw happening that last week and what we were most concerned about was as the economy began to soak in as an issue and as it became clear that Iran was not going to be resolved anytime quickly, we could begin to see the focus change in New York from a choice, again, in a general election context, to much more of a primary choice. And by late in the week, we could see it even further. By the weekend, our decline had extended beyond Jews and had gone all over the state. By Sunday we were looking at massive bleeding that was continuing to hemorrhage. We'd fallen already ten points behind, and it still looked like it was continuing to go down.

In terms of the statistical test that we were looking at in this period, we saw those characteristics that had dominated the early primaries—factors of trust, how trustworthy the candidates were, which had generally been the leading determinate for most people—go from being the most important to almost insignificant. One of the questions we had been monitoring on the president, that had concerned us all along, was the general protest question. That question took a massive turnaround, and in fact the weight—the importance—of that question for voters also went up. What you saw there was a whole structural change in the race. We saw this sort of protest edge beginning to really move as the major factor driving a number of voters, rather than the other factors we had seen previously. It was always something that we had been concerned about.

HUNT: Bob, after Carter lost New York and Connecticut, for whatever reasons, you thought it was basically a protest vote, did you have any fear that this could set off an avalanche where he could lose six, eight primaries in a row?

KEEFE: The schedule didn't project that he couldn't do what he had done so successfully in '76, and that is to win every day there's a primary.

BRODER: For Carter or for Kennedy?

KEEFE: For Carter.

—THE WISCONSIN PRIMARY—

HUNT: The next state after New York and Connecticut was Wisconsin. Within that time frame, two or three days after the New York and Connecticut primaries, was there real concern about Wisconsin?

KEEFE: Sure.

HUNT: And what did you decide to do about that?

KEEFE: Timothy can talk to that.

KRAFT: I mentioned last night that one of the four basic tactics or tenets of our strategy was to run everywhere. What that really did was have a balancing effect both in terms of our political strength and winnability, from start to finish, across the board. We hoped to do surprisingly well in Maine, and we won it—in the senator's back yard. The same night that we got clocked in Massachusetts, we won in Vermont. On the weekend, if you take a four-day period, we lost Connecticut and New York badly. If you throw in Virginia, which took place the preceding Saturday, we actually came out with a net plus of six delegates for that three states' contest. We knew Pennsylvania was going to be close; we knew we were going to walk away with Missouri, which took place on the same day. So this strategy, we think, paid off both in terms of perceived strength and delegate accumulation.

Now, at the same time that we were worried about Wisconsin — and we beefed up our media campaign there, we had a good organizational effort there by Kurt Wiley — Caddell was looking ahead down the primary schedule, seeing some problems in Michigan, seeing an opportunity in Indiana which he suggested to us that we should beef up in order to win decisively. In places like Texas and Indiana, we had more of a national campaign than the Kennedy campaign did — and I understand that they had financial constraints that were even more severe than ours at this point. So, by virtue of this gradual ball control, delegate accumulation sort of thing, we were never led to believe that "we would blow it." I mean not even super Tuesday and losing five out of eight scared the hell out of us at that point becuase we knew we had the delegates.

Let me turn the question around and sort of throw a bomb in the center of this thing, and bring up a point as the representative of the Democratic incumbent president. It became mathematically clear to everyone in the English-speaking world that the president had the nomination, barring death or disaster, and this was not long after Illinois and even after New York and Connecticut. I've often wondered about the rationale for a continuing Kennedy candidacy that was hard-hitting and extremely critical and very, very costly not only to the president but to the Democratic party, in terms of lost opportunities to raise money and prepare for the general election, say, between April of 1980 and August. What was the purpose for the continuing warfare given the mathematical impossibility of accumulating enough delegates to win the nomination and the almost foreclosed possibility of changing the rules of the convention?

—KENNEDY STAYS IN—

KIRK: A couple of things at that point with respect to politics generally. Because of the recollection of the president's record in 1976 where he was defeated toward the end of the primaries, where he almost blew it in the general election, the fact that New York showed that the Carter record, which was the reason for the Kennedy entrance to the campaign, had finally become the issue, there was still a strong feeling in the Kennedy campaign that as the primary campaign went on and the convention approached, ultimately people would make a decision within the party that the name of the game was the general election. As long as the Carter record on the economy and the foreign policy gaffes continued, the important thing would be November, and that basically the party later on in the primaries would realize that this was more than a one-time protest, that in order to be able to be viable against the Republicans, you needed a stronger candidate. It was our hope that with some wins in the remaining industrial states we would prove that in the states to be won in November, we would be the stronger Democrat.

In addition, this was the first time since the beginning of the campaign that there was an opportunity to engage the dialogue in *policy* terms. In the meantime, there had been the long trail of negative campaign ads and innuendos, and the seeds that were planted early along the trail were now flowers in that regard. Having a debate within the party, the senator felt, apart from what the numbers were at that point, was needed if we were going to be any better off as a party in 1981, or if we were going to have an opportunity to get the White House in 1981. These things couldn't be dusted over. They had to be debated. Combining all those circumstances, he was committed at that point to carry through.

KRAFT: Did he give himself a one-in-three chance of changing the rules at the convention?

WAGNER: Later on a much better chance than that.

HUNT: We'll come to that question later.

STEARNS: Can I say on Tim's point that for accuracy we should remember that Kennedy did at one point, in effect, offer to withdraw. He offered unconditionally to release his delegates in May, if the president would agree to a debate. I opposed that; I had other reasons for thinking that Kennedy should stay in, but it still staggers me today that Carter never accepted the offer. I thought that Kennedy had given away far too much. My assumption was that Carter would immediately grasp the opportunity and debate with Kennedy. And I think Carter would have been better served in the long run had he done so. Had Kennedy unconditionally released his delegates, I don't think anyone would have understood that as anything other than his withdrawal from the race.

—CARTER STATEMENT ON THE HOSTAGES—

HUNT: Let me just focus in for a minute, because I think this became a very important event on the morning of the Wisconsin primary. Patrick, I remember being with you the Sunday night before the primary in Wisconsin. You were upset; you weren't sure how well things were going; and you told me that you were going to spend some time talking to the president the next day and you had some ideas. Did the question of addressing the hostage issue publicly come up in your discussions then with the president, or with Jody Powell or Hamilton Jordan? How did that decision evolve?

CADDELL: The Tuesday decision was made late Monday night, apparently; in fact, I wasn't even aware of what would happen Tuesday morning. I knew from Jody and Hamilton over the weekend— and, of course, this was already getting out in the media—that there were significant things going on with Bani–Sadr at that time, and so on, concerning the hostages. My basic concern at that time was if progress was being made, if they thought they were going to get something, that it would obviously be more helpful than not if it came over the weekend. We were concerned about Wisconsin for the same reason that we'd been concerned about New York.

HUNT: What can you remember about the kind of message you gave the president that Monday when you talked to him? Did you tell him that there was concern out there, and did the question come up about what effect the hostage issue was having?

CADDELL: Well, we didn't start having concerns Sunday; we'd had them all week since New York. But we also had a sense that the thing did not look like it would go the way New York did. We thought it could get much closer depending on how it sorted out structurally. But Al, it wasn't a question of saying, "Oh, well, we're really worried out here, what can you do about Iran?" as much as some people might think. The point was we knew things were going on, and it was a question of how far they would go or what would happen. As of Sunday and Monday what was happening in Milwaukee and around the country was that there seemed to be real movement; Bani–Sadr had made his speech, and so on. If anything had an impact, I suspect that did. My personal belief from experience is that the very little that you're going to do at the very last hours of the day is not going to have much impact. It takes time for things to sink in. But there's no question that we were hopeful, and I was encouraged in the sense that the good news surfaced as quickly as possible.

BRODER: My recollection is like Al's. In the days of New York and Wisconsin you were saying that things were so loose that any event was likely to have a heavy impact. To what extent do you think the public shared the press perception that this was clearly a manufactured event on the morning of the primary?

CADDELL: I want to come back to that point, but by Monday night we knew that we had had some more movement; I mean, there had been some absorption of the "good news" and that it, in fact, was moving the race. That was coming along by Monday night. I was not involved in what was going on in the foreign policy end—someone else would have to discuss that—but clearly on Tuesday morning or late Monday night there had been a decision that the president would make a statement about Iran in response to Bani–Sadr's statement. And I think Jody Powell and I both agree and the president agrees and everyone agrees that it was a terrible mistake to have done it Tuesday morning.

HUNT: In retrospect?

CADDELL: In retrospect. Well, even that morning I was a little baffled because frankly it seemed to me that the primary was all gone one way or the other; you're not going to influence anything major like that on the morning of an election. We didn't quite see it yet as a negative, but clearly in retrospect we realized that it was a disaster because of the impact and of the fact that it had not bought us much that day.

HUNT: But Patrick, at that time, Monday afternoon and Monday night, weren't there some people telling the president that things were volatile out in Wisconsin, and you do have some indications of progress in Iran, and it ain't gonna help you any if you wait till

Tuesday night or Wednesday to announce it, so for the first time in your presidency you ought to have a 7 a.m. news conference? Weren't there political people saying that? (*Laughter*)

KRAFT: I would think that this question, this whole thrust, presumes control over events in Iran that have been patently lacking since November of 1979. I mean, nobody from Washington in the administration could dictate to the Iranian Parliament. I don't know that much about it, and I probably shouldn't have butted in. But there were two or three events that took place over there during the daytime, when it's the middle of the night here. On a seven o'clock announcement, they didn't get the text from Bani–Sadr's address or remarks until about four in the morning, when they were hauled down in the situation room to try to analyze this, to see if it was a significant step forward.

HUNT: Pat said earlier that the decision was made the night before.

CADDELL: Hold it a second. Now look, you can approach this thing from deciding you already know the conclusion. I'll tell you what we know. I did not know that the president was going to do a seven-o'clock-in-the-morning press conference. I went to bed Monday night knowing that we had had some progress, knowing that they were expecting something that night, and if they had something, there would be a statement. That decision was made sometime in the night. In the morning, once they had whatever the information was, the president decided that he would go, and Jody decided that they would go with seven o'clock in the morning. There was no cabal in Washington saying, my God, let's manufacture something and put it out on Tuesday morning. There was a sense of concern over the primary. There had been for a week. And there was pressure in the sense that if there was good news to get it out.

—KENNEDY'S RESOURCES—

BRODER: On the Kennedy side that same week, your people in Wisconsin were saying, "if we could just get the national staff to give us the candidate, to give us some resources." As a sort of case study of tensions between state level and national level staff, one, did you have any resources available in terms of candidate time, money, and other assets that you could have thrown into Wisconsin? And, two, if you did, what were the considerations about whether to throw them in?

KIRK: As for financial resources, we had virtually none, in terms of being able to do anything else through paid media. We might have had another part of a day of the candidate's schedule. It might have been shifted to Wisconsin, changing from what we had initially planned. I don't know. I think our basic feeling was that the numbers we had seen from Wisconsin were still pretty tough. I think our attention at that point was—

WAGNER: Pennsylvania.

BRODER: Three weeks later?

KIRK: Three weeks later. In terms of where we were in those major states, things weren't that easy in Pennsylvania either. We didn't want to get backed into a situation where, all of a sudden, after the New York and Connecticut win, Wisconsin then became the next "only if Wisconsin" hurdle. We'd been through that enough. Therefore I think if we had another day to spend, we decided that we'd go with Pennsylvania, as planned. I can remember within the Kennedy camp, there was a lot of talk about the 7:15 news conference which took place on April Fool's Day, and we thought it was probably the final act that the public would tolerate about what we considered at that point to be toying with the hostage crisis. Our intelligence assessment was that the Carter campaign had decided the only way to keep the incumbent's record from being the issue as it had in New York and Connecticut was to get back onto the hostage plane again, and to avoid having the dialogue about what was going on at home in the economy. We didn't resolve some of those questions; the people never really would make a judgment on what it was to—

BRODER: Tom Quinn, your candidate produced the other television spectacular in the Wisconsin campaign.* What was that all about? (*Laughter*)

---

*Mr. Broder is referring to a Brown campaign rally staged on the steps of the Wisconsin capitol, broadcast live in Wisconsin, and recorded for future use as campaign advertising, all under the direction of Francis Ford Coppola.

TOM QUINN (campaign manager, Brown for President): Well, unfortunately I was not there. I saw it after the fact. I think Jerry felt that Madison, and the big student population there, offered the potential for some kind of breakthrough, and I'm not sure what kind of breakthrough he thought was possible at that point, but he decided that clearly whatever he had been doing prior to that point had not worked and therefore became convinced that something very extraordinary and different just might grab attention. And he was right. (*Laughter*) I don't know what it did. It was interesting. I recall Carl calling me at one point, I guess about a week before the general election, was it?

WAGNER: Right.

QUINN: He was in Milwaukee, asking me whether Jerry would come on out there for Carter. I guess they had some polling data from somewhere, and I'm not sure if it was Pat's poll or not, showing that Jerry actually had some residual popularity in Madison, particularly, that seemed to mean something. They really wanted Jerry out there to campaign. I don't know. It was an effort to do something quite different, to get attention.

WAGNER: David, you raised the question of Wisconsin—why the major effort wasn't made there. I'd like to return to something I had raised earlier. After Iowa, our campaign was faced with, almost on a day-to-day basis, a terrific financial problem. One of the most impressive things about the campaign, quite frankly, in the end, was our ability to stay in the race financially. To raise close to $6 million, after Iowa, against the president of the United States, and through some very tough primaries. But, in order to do that, twenty-seven states, one of which was Wisconsin, financed themselves. I mean, staff in the states raised the money to finance the campaigns there. In some cases, there were campaigns of considerable magnitude. Now coming out of New York, we had to deploy effectively the resources we had at that time, and they were field staff that could be moved to another state; the state we targeted was Pennsylvania. The dough really wasn't there to wage the kind of campaign it would have taken to win in Wisconsin, which came a week later. We had to win in Pennsylvania.

E: Nobody knew early whether Wisconsin was going to count,
...er.

WAGNER: Exactly.

—POLARIZATION—

FRANCIS: There's one question I wanted to ask, as kind of a followup to Tim's question. He asked about staying in after it was seemingly mathematically impossible for Kennedy to win. I have a slightly different variation of that. With the Georgetown speech, with the decided turn to the left, or in the decision to stay in, you knew there was going to be some polarization. I mean, there had to be, that was going to be your hope to get back on top. Were there serious discussions about its effect in November on either Kennedy or Carter, whoever was to come out on top?

WAGNER: No, I think the strategy as represented by the Georgetown speech, and probably by the tone of the campaign as represented by the candidate's schedule, was thought through—and maybe not prudently—principally in terms of its impact in the primaries, to nail down the Kennedy base in the party, both politically and organizationally, and build off that as a basis to challenge the president in the big Eastern states and thereafter in the West.

HUNT: But by Pennsylvania, the nastiness really picked up, and from your perspective—to go back to the question that Adam asked some time ago—was there a feeling that this was the only choice you had or was there any thought given at all to the effect it was having after the primaries?

CADDELL: After New York, we knew this campaign was going to go all the way. It was a great concern we had always had that we would get into a string of steady losses, potentially, and it was obviously one of the great concerns about Wisconsin, given the fact that after that, there was a three-week hiatus before the next primary, which was Pennsylvania. We had known, even prior to New York, that Pennsylvania looked worse than any of the states we had yet been in. It seemed to us that there was a whole coalescing of forces that jeopardized the situation, leaving aside the delegate numbers, so that we could bleed to death all the way through the primaries. Pennsylvania, in my opinion, was the actual turning point. The week before Pennsylvania, it looked like it was going to become another New York. We were already down twelve points, heading into the very end of that campaign, as we could see it. Our choice then was, do you try to close that, or do you let it it go? We made a decision to try to close it, and that is when the campaign really moved to its most divisive point because that's when the man-on-the-street spots went on the air.

HUNT: Again, Pat, was there anybody inside—Mondale, or anyone else—who cautioned against going that route?

CADDELL: It was always understood what the price of that was going to be, Al, but you weigh it against the fact that if you don't do that, you may well just lose straight through.

HUNT: Uh-huh.

CADDELL: And given that choice, you know, you fight each battle, you try to look down the road, but you make the decision that you would try to save yourself today, and then struggle with tomorrow, tomorrow.

HUNT: But was there anybody who disagreed with that decision?

CADDELL: There was, I guess; I really don't remember well enough.

MACKIN: Are you saying that would have been the only way for you people to win?

CADDELL: In Pennsylvania, at that point, our problem was if we did not get the race back off of a protest and focused back to the candidates, there was no way we were going to win it.

MACKIN: So you had to take it back down to that level in order to be able to—

CADDELL: Well, we had to take it to some level to get it back focused on the candidates. Perhaps someone could come up with something that would have worked better, but the point of the matter was, that was on the table; that's what Jerry had prepared, and we went with it.

CLYMER: Pat, there's a dichotomy here, where Tim and Les are saying that after Illinois it was mathematically impossible to lose the nomination, and you were saying a week later that you still could.

FRANCIS: What I was saying was that it was mathematically impossible for Senator Kennedy to *win* the nomination.

CLYMER: Well, he was the other one running. I just find it difficult to understand the argument that we could lose and lose and lose, as opposed to the argument that the mathematics made it impossible.

FRANCIS: You didn't hear what I said. I said it was mathematically impossible for Senator Kennedy to win after Illinois. That is not necessarily the same as saying it was mathematically impossible for us to lose after Illinois, if somebody else were to get in and if they were to succeed in pulling things apart. If we were to lose, if another candidate were to emerge, those are all possibilities.

CLYMER: Who, who? (*Laughter*)

FRANCIS: Well, who knows?

CADDELL: We would see it later in the summer in terms of opening this thing and finding someone. Let's say we had lost Pennsylvania by a huge margin, had bled through and lost a number of the May primaries, and we had made a critical decision at the end of April to sacrifice in part our resources on June 5th, and had lost Maryland and Oregon and some of the states that many people felt, and the Kennedy people felt, they had an excellent chance of winning. At that point, you would be in a situation where other forces came to play. You had a wounded president, you had Senator Kennedy who was not going to be nominated, but forces were coming to play that would turn the applecart over.

HUNT: Were you in general agreement, Bob, with the strategy at this time?

KEEFE: I don't know that I would have been drastically different. The problem is that you have both logic and emotion. And you have political physiology; bad blood runs both ways. The bad blood was flowing toward the Kennedy campaign from the Carter campaign with "Gee, why doesn't he quit, it's all over. He's just hurting us all for the fall." Bad blood going the other way: "Why the hell does he insist on maintaining these personal attacks?" Those sorts of things really operate.

— THE DEBATE ISSUE —

BRODER: Could we revive Rick Stearn's unanswered question? You blunted the Kennedy drive, particularly the industrial state drive in Pennsylvania and Michigan. Then you come to May, and Kennedy offers to get out in return for a debate. Was any consideration given to taking him up on that?

CADDELL: Yeah, well not so much taking him up on that particular offer. For a variety of reasons, it did not appeal to many people. There was, after the primaries were over, in fact, a serious discussion for about twenty-four, thirty-six hours which included the president, and the president's inclination then was to have a debate before the platform committee.

HUNT: This was after the primaries.

BRODER: What were the variety of considerations that led you to do other than what Rick thought you had been given a great opportunity to do?

CADDELL: The general consensus was a feeling that those terms were not exactly as generous as Rick felt they were. Most of the people in the campaign did not perceive them quite as generously as he did. Basically the instinct was not to do it.

MACKIN: I was going to point out that it was not just the debate, but whoever won the most delegates. So, in effect, Kennedy could have come out on Super Tuesday as not having to withdraw.

CADDELL: Yes. The idea was, who had the most votes on Super Tuesday. We were looking at a situation where we knew that, given our resources, California and New Jersey just were probably not going to be there, and there was that little condition. It seemed to us to be a desperate move which just wasn't seriously considered.

BRODER: Paul, for the sake of history, I was told by Bob Strauss at that point that you had communicated directly with him. You said, "Don't miss the message in this offer. It is a way to wind this thing up on honorable terms." Is that correct, and were you in fact looking for an honorable way out at that point?

KIRK: After there was a negative reply on the debate, I did talk to Bob, and I said, "The trouble is, Bob, you mistook an olive branch for poison ivy," or whatever, and we kind of laughed about it. But the fact was that the senator did feel all along, and said so, that whether or not he got out of the race, many problems still existed in terms of the Carter candidacy, and we had to direct the dialogue around what people might be focused on in the fall. He believed it then and believes it still. A debate, we felt, would have been a political opportunity to turn things around with the states and with the focus; the party could have come to grips with its real problems. That candidacy really had a rationale. It was not, therefore, just hang in with no sense of what was going to happen in the fall. To the contrary.

—FAILURE OF THE RESCUE MISSION—

HUNT: Just one thing on that, again for the sake of history. Right after Pennsylvania, Ron, there was the dramatic failure of the rescue mission in Iran. Senator Kennedy basically held his peace on that; he seemed not to want to touch that issue.

BROWN: We had learned our lesson.

HUNT: And there was no thought given to raising that issue, to criticize him on what had happened.

BROWN: About thirty seconds of thought.

HUNT: And that was it? Okay.

KIRK: The only thing that flowed right off that, was the fact that after the rescue mission failed, the president said quickly that the situation now was "manageable," and he was coming out of the White House. We tried to get at that a little bit, but were also struck with some dismay that there really weren't heavier questions asked of his campaign, or by the media, as to whether he had given up on the hostages. How could the situation possibly be called "manageable"?

BROWN: But, Paul, I think it was really the reverse of that, in that we didn't want to touch on foreign affairs. I mean, it had nothing to do with being slapped again. We were finally focusing on domestic issues, on economic issues, and we didn't want to do anything that would take it off that track. On David's earlier question, and part of Paul's response: you know, you can't have it both ways on the winnability question. Many of us did think that there was still an opportunity to turn it around in political terms, and I would agree with Pat, and disagree with Rick a little bit, in that our aims were not all altruistic in the May debate offer. You know, we thought if delegates were released, there was a good chance we could get delegates who had been formerly pledged to Carter.

STEARNS: No, that's not true. Kennedy did not say that. He said he would release his delegates, irrespective of what Carter did or didn't do.

HUNT: Somebody mentioned a minute ago that the president did come out of the White House, finally, in May. How long had that debate really been going on in full force, and how did you finally reach a decision to bring him out after six months?

CADDELL: The debate had been going on for most of the campaign. The campaign itself was not particularly happy over having the candidate locked in the White House. We were having to carry the campaign with surrogates and the media, and so on, particularly when the great rise in inflation hit, and the Iranian thing continued, and the president began to go down. The damage that the president was taking among Democrats was enormous at that point. The campaign wanted the candidate, and that debate had been going on for some months. The problem was that we had painted ourselves into the corner; the question was how to get out of it, and the decision had been made that we ought to try to get out of it the first opportunity we had. The decision was that after the rescue mission was the best time.

HUNT: The decision had been made when?

—OUT OF THE ROSE GARDEN—

CADDELL: The decision had roughly been made a couple of weeks before, on the basis that if and when the opportunity presented itself and we found a way, we probably ought to get out of the Rose Garden, because we knew it was hurting us with the electorate. We still held off using the president very much at that point for two reasons. One was a severe money problem, the cost of moving the president around. In May, we had so front-loaded our spending in the early primaries that we were facing severe expenditure problems toward the end, and frankly, it had always taken us more money per vote to have more impact than it had taken the Kennedy people; again, the problem of running everywhere tended to add to that. The second problem in May was it was yet unclear what we actually needed once we started looking at those May primaries. The reason Carter didn't come out till he did was that, personally, I had some concerns—and I think maybe some others did—that he had been in the White House so long that he was rusty. If we just dropped him on the campaign trail at a point when things looked like they were going to hold up all right for a while, we would face the problem that he might do something that would cause problems electorally, or in fact, re-focus attention even more starkly on himself. And the truth of the matter is that the one campaign trip he took worked against us. We had been moving in Ohio. We finally poured our last bit of media on in Ohio, and we'd been moving up again. The "turn of the

tide" speech cost us in all three of the big states, following that trip.*
By the weekend, it had cost us five or six or seven points.

HUNT: Paul, going into Super Tuesday, did you think there was any
chance for Kennedy to win the nomination?

KIRK: Yes, basically on the political grounds that I mentioned earlier. I think we were quite sincere in saying that people would look
back on the primary campaign, find out that the things existing when
we got into the campaign still existed in terms of national problems,
that a debate had been denied the people, and the process had been
distorted. If we did well on June 3rd in a number of those states, it
would re-focus on the last chance for the party to speak. They'd be
mainly the states that the Democrats would have to carry in November; the problems on the economy were foremost and paramount;
and by June 3rd and into August, people would agree with us.

HUNT: Uh-huh.

KEEFE: At that time delegates were reasonably well selected and
the Democratic National Committee was getting out little questionnaires to them. If you read the questionnaires coming back from the
delegates, clearly the Carter delegates agreed with Kennedy's pos-
tures on the issues a helluva lot more than they did with Carter's.
And you did have a volatile situation in terms of what the convention thought about the issues. Obviously, there were other political
considerations that tied them to the president.

*The reference is to a speech by President Carter in Columbus, Ohio, on May 29, 1980,
in which he stated that "the tide has turned" on the nation's economy and that it would
soon be improving.

3 THE REPUBLICAN PRIMARIES

Reagan and Bush in Iowa. Reagan Lead Drops. Connally, Anderson, and Baker. Media Spending, Organization, and Turnout. Reagan After Iowa. The Decision To Fire Sears. The Nashua Debate. A Mousetrap. The Manchester Debate. Ford Considers Getting In. Connally's Refusal of Federal Funds. Dole Drops Out. Anderson in Illinois. The Chicago Debate. The Connecticut Primary. The Pennsylvania Primary. Bush in Michigan and Texas.

KENNETH A. BODE (network correspondent, NBC News): It is January 1980. We have eleven announced Republican candidates. One Republican candidate, Senator Wiecker, has already withdrawn. George Bush has travelled something in the neighborhood of 350,000 miles during the previous year. He spent 328 days on the road, which dwarfs Jimmy Carter's previous record for a pre-election year total. As Bush was fond of saying, he's seen the entire planting cycle in the state of Iowa. In the meantime, Governor Reagan is sitting on a three-to-one lead in the public opinion polls, and has taken a three-week vacation at the end of December.

BILL BROCK (chairman, Republican National Committee): There's a man who has his priorities straight. (*Laughter*)

93

—REAGAN AND BUSH IN IOWA—

BODE: Dr. Wirthlin, as a person who was involved in the campaign both before and after John Sears' departure, was the idea to keep Governor Reagan under wraps during that period of time a decision that was agreed upon widely in the campaign, or was that a John Sears decision?

RICHARD B. WIRTHLIN (deputy director of strategy and planning, Reagan–Bush Committee): I think it was primarily a John Sears decision. It wasn't only the national numbers that gave us a good deal of assurance that 1979 had been a good year for us, but more specifically, looking at the unfolding of the campaign process in New Hampshire and South Carolina and Florida and Illinois, we were very pleased with the progress that was made then. Also, it was evident that we did have an opportunity to really start running for the general election early, and therefore we could pick and choose with a good deal more discretion than we could have had the race at that juncture been more tightly contested. For the Republicans, Iowa, of course, was a first-time event. New Hampshire in the past had traditionally been the official kickoff of the campaign. We were dealing with a different system—a caucus election. There was some assessment as to what that impact might be in terms of developing what Bush described with such a vengeance as "Big Mo." Without any question, again looking with twenty–twenty vision hindsight, we learned, through the outcome of the Iowa caucus, that there's absolutely no substitute, none whatsoever, for the presence of the candidate in the state and organization in depth. The lack of Ronald Reagan's presence in the state, not only his decision not to debate but also the fact that he had cameo appearances, short appearances as he went and visited other states, set the stage for the loss which we suffered January 20, 21.

BODE: Dave, how did Bush's campaign size up the opportunities in Iowa?

DAVID A. KEENE (national political director, Bush for President): Well, we had a difficult time dealing with the opportunity that appeared to be coming to us in Iowa, for reasons that Dick has just outlined. We felt that it might not be necessary for Governor Reagan to debate, but we thought that he would be in there. It was as if the Reagan campaign were playing into our hands at many points, by publicly downgrading, or appearing to downgrade, the importance of the Iowa Republicans' voice in the nominating procedure. At the same time, we didn't feel that the Reagan organizational effort in Iowa was up to what we'd expected. You enter some of these things, knowing that there are a number of things that you have to do to have a chance to win. You also assume that everyone else is going to do all of them, and if that happens, you know you're still in trouble if you started out way behind. Then the other fellow's going to win. But you do them anyway, and hope that somebody else will do something wrong. We knew that we had to perform very well, very quickly, out of the box, to get the kind of coverage and the kind of media play that George Bush would need to put together a viable campaign once momentum really took hold after New Hampshire. It's often forgotten that momentum's good for maybe ten days or so, but a month is a long time. If you start out with losses in Iowa and New Hampshire, the fellow who's ahead is going to have a diffi- cult time losing his lead, and therefore we had to do very well, very early. So we decided not only on a heavy commitment of the candi- date's time, very early in Iowa, but on a heavy organizational effort. And by doing a number of other things in Iowa, we felt that we could initially eliminate the other contenders on the Republican side and try to structure a Reagan versus Bush battle as early as possible, perhaps as early as New Hampshire. We never really, in the early days, expected to go beyond that. We didn't expect to win the Iowa caucuses, but things just broke right, and other people did things dif- ferently than they might have done them, and as a result we did do much better than was expected.

ADAM CLYMER (correspondent, *New York Times*): Would you have been better off if you had barely lost?

KEENE: That's hard to say, because it depends on the play that you would get. There's no doubt that coming out of Iowa, we weren't prepared for what happened, and we made at least one sig- nificant error after Iowa, from the campaign side, that probably made it impossible for us to recover. But if we had barely lost, the story might have been the same, and the focus might have gone to George Bush anyway. If we could have kept the focus off our candidacy and still managed to watch Connolly and Baker and the rest fall by the wayside, that might have been the ideal world, but that's not possible.

CLYMER: What was the mistake you made?

KEENE: Somebody described presidential campaigns once as a soap opera with continuing development of the characters interspersed with events, and the story of George Bush had always been the story of this plucky fellow who nobody knew, out there, either trying to repeat the Carter strategy or just trying, through hard work and effort, to make some kind of impact. That was reported about George Bush even before the Iowa caucuses. There was no reporting in any significant way of the issue components of his challenge or his candidacy, or the reasons on a substantive basis why he rather than someone else should be nominated. When Iowa took place, the story there again was the success of that kind of thing. And momentum. You can't always control the enthusiasm of your candidate, but you can change the media quickly. If we were doing it over, I think that we would have scrubbed every commercial that was on the air and had a couple of very heavy issue commercials that we would have run to try and inject that component.

We weren't watching the nightly news. It doesn't matter how much or how long or how often a candidate talks about issues to small groups in Iowa, or answers issues-oriented questions, or talks in terms and substance of why he ought to be nominated, if the coverage is on the momentum and the horse race. I'm not really criticizing the media for covering it in that way because that was the story of George Bush. But perhaps—if we had realized that for all the time we had spent and for all the effort we'd put forth, the coverage, and what people were seeing elsewhere, was really the story of this plucky fellow working hard—maybe we would have changed it at that point. But we didn't; we let it drag, and that was the most serious mistake, I think, that we made.

WIRTHLIN: David, from what we were reading, I think it was absolutely essential for you to win in Iowa. If you had come close, I think the thrust and nature of the stories that clearly provided the bases for "Big Mo" would have led to a much different result in terms of the dynamic of the vote decision that we faced in New Hampshire.

KEENE: Right.

WIRTHLIN: As early as December, we did recognize the threat of the Bush campaign. You were running second to us in three of the five critical states. But the key to what later developed was found in the fact that Bush was very much unknown in December. The point was that those who did know him were strongly attracted to him. And when you have a candidate who is running very well among those who know him, the key that unlocks the door to political opportunity is visibility. And the kind of visibility that George Bush received on the 22nd, 23rd—

KEENE: Couldn't buy it.

WIRTHLIN: You could not in *any way* buy it.

KEENE: And we could not have accomplished our goal of eliminating the other candidates without that, either—whether we had won, or come within a point, or whatever might have been necessary, that was what we had to do. That that was the kind of visibility we got, without being able to fill in the blanks that appeared, may also explain the crucial importance of that first New Hampshire debate. There, people who finally got to know something about this fellow George Bush, saw this super-candidate coming out of Iowa who had done the impossible and had beaten the front-runner. When they saw him, however, they discovered that he appeared to be no taller than the rest of them. He put his pants on the same way. That allowed them to go back to what we knew from the beginning, that Ronald Reagan was not merely a front-runner by virtue of name recognition, but that he was respected and almost revered by a very large segment of the Republican party. That, in part, dictated our strategy early, which was to try and build a base for Bush and then get at those people who were saying, Well, in our hearts we'd like to go with Reagan, but maybe it isn't gonna work this time.

In Iowa, the questions were never about Ronald Reagan's views, about whether people liked him or didn't like him—they were frankly about whether he was up to it. By staying under wraps, he played into that. Perhaps the impact of coming out was arguably greater than if he hadn't been under wraps in the first place, but it was precisely that which helped us, because people said, Well, he isn't debating, he isn't campaigning—why isn't he? And he didn't have to say anything. At that point we began to pick up some of those people, particularly in Iowa.

WIRTHLIN: The success of that particular strategy, I think, was best reflected in the study we did in New Hampshire right after the Iowa debate, which showed that perceptually Bush was viewed as a more competent candidate, again without any underpinning of issue positions, but in terms of the perception that he was a more competent candidate than Reagan in a state where we were running forty-three points ahead in the middle of December.

ALBERT R. HUNT (correspondent, *Wall Street Journal*): What did that survey show right after Iowa? Did you do a head-to-head?

—REAGAN LEAD DROPS—

WIRTHLIN: Yes. We dropped from our forty-three-point lead in December to about a nineteen-point lead ten days before the Iowa vote. Two days after the Iowa vote, we were looking at a six-point deficit. In other words, there was a twenty-five-point shift against Reagan from the period from about the middle of January until about the 28th of January. And at that point there was a very, very serious discussion about the course of the campaign and about some of the assumptions that had been made concerning what our assets and liabilities really were.

MARTIN F. NOLAN (Washington bureau chief, *Boston Globe*): Can we get into that? (*Laughter*)

ROBERT M. TEETER (president, Market Opinion Research): It seems to me if you look at Iowa, in no way would it have been better for Bush to finish second than first. I mean I don't know of any election where that's true, ever, period. It just seems to me it is always better to win than it is to lose, and— (*Laughter*)

CLYMER: What sort of nut are you? Let's have another view! (*Laughter*)

TEETER: Iowa presented, in an accelerated fashion, the kind of culmination of everything that '79 and early '80 had been designed to accomplish. The problem is the one that David referred to. It's simply that if you worked in '79 and early '80 for that success and you get it, does that successful phase one then demand immediately a phase two or do you say that we've done so well that we'll do more of the same? That to me is the whole story of the Bush campaign in the primaries. There are some other things that we can go through here and give you a kind of inning-by-inning summary, but that is it!

KEENE: Phase two wasn't ready.

TEETER: There was no phase two which was demanded by a successful phase one, and instead the reaction was, let's do more of the same because it's worked so well up to now.

CLYMER: Let me ask one thing about Iowa and right around it. Basically, sure, it is better to win than to lose, and if you had won and had a phase two, that would've been fine. If you had lost by three or four or five points but everybody else had been way back, maybe the Reagan people wouldn't have got their act together. If you beat them in New Hampshire, then you've got primaries coming—week after week instead of their having five weeks to get their act together.

TEETER: My point is, Adam, I don't think we would have gotten the kind of shift Dick just described, nor would we have gotten those cover stories in the news magazines, had it not been a win. The fact that he won made it from just a good day for George Bush into a spectacular day.

KEENE: And we would have still had the same problem.

TEETER: That's right.

KEENE: Because for us, whether you're a few points ahead or a few points behind, the problem was exactly the same.

TEETER: We should get to the point that the Bush campaign spent a tremendous amount of its resources aimed at some of the phony events that go on, such as the nonbinding caucuses and straw votes, and it would be worthwhile to find out what some of these other campaigns thought of them. One thing I think that the Bush campaign did well was to spend a tremendous amount of money, effort, and staff time aimed at things like the preference straw vote in Florida, the straw vote in Iowa that had occurred earlier, the Maine caucuses, and all those things that really didn't mean much in terms of whether you got any delegates or whether you actually won a primary or not, but that were very important to what was going on.

—CONNALLY, ANDERSON, AND BAKER—

BODE: Eddie Mahe, your candidate spent a fair amount of time and money on at least a couple of those also. What did you think of it?

EDDIE MAHE, JR. (campaign director, John Connally for President): Our biggest effort in terms of spending money was in Florida, and we felt we had no choice. We opposed it; we opposed it every way we could, but Bill Taylor, state chairman of Florida, was strongly in favor of it notwithstanding what everybody else thought. We discussed it at some length in late June and early July, and made the decision that neither Baker nor Bush would be successful in stopping Reagan in Florida, and if in fact Reagan was to come out of that straw vote with 65 or 70 percent of the vote, that it would undermine our whole Southern strategy—and we could not tolerate that. So we committed whatever resources we had to commit, all of which were not effectively used, to keeping him below 50 percent. The only goal we had when we kicked that thing off was to somehow keep Reagan below 50 percent, so that he could not claim an out-and-out victory over the field. I felt at that time it was critical to do that, and I would make that same decision today.

BROCK: Eddie, your goal shifted, because John Connally—established a different goal for you?

MAHE: I would quote Mr. Wagner, I believe it was, in the earlier session: you cannot always control the enthusiasm of your candidate. (*Laughter*)

BODE: Bill Brock, what do you think of these phony events—the Florida straw vote, the Florida caucuses, the dinner polls—that predate the actual beginning of the nominating process—grab a lot of media attention, artificial but very real in terms of the candidates' chances? Is there anything that can be done about these things, or should they be just left to proliferate?

BROCK: I have mixed views. Thinking of it in terms of the system, I'm not sure that they're particularly helpful, but in terms of the party they are of enormous value. We built stronger parties by having these events. We raised a lot of money, we got a hell of a lot of volunteers, an enormous amount of enthusiasm—Maine was a classic case, but so was Florida. And our early primary votes were up 100, 200, 300 percent over 1976. And I think they contributed to that. I come at it from a totally different perspective.

As far as I was concerned, my only job was to build the larger and broader base, so that our candidates could go into this thing in November, regardless of whoever they were, with a winning opportunity. So we did our advertising carefully, to try to structure the debate, to establish the parameters on the economic issue. We set up the "Group '80" program to keep these guys talking to each other.* All of our efforts were designed to strengthen the party and use the primary process—in whatever fashion, whether it was the sweepstakes down in Florida or the Maine caucus—for that purpose. I was not averse to what was going on. I liked it. I'm talking strictly in terms of the long-term value of having a better base for whoever the nominee turns out to be. And in that case, it did some good for us.

BODE: John Anderson, it was pretty taxing on a candidate's resources when you faced these things, wasn't it?

CONGRESSMAN JOHN B. ANDERSON (candidate for Republican nomination and National Unity Campaign candidate): Well, they were in our case, surely, because when you talk about this prepri-mary period, talk about events like Florida, and even the Maine

---

* "Group '80" was organized by the Republican National Committee and was comprised of the principal managers of every Republican candidate for president. Its purpose was to prepare a plan for the post-convention campaign and to keep the party focused on the goal of defeating the Democrats.

caucus in December of 1979, and spending literally thousands and thousands of dollars for the purchase of dinner tickets and other devices of that kind, that was simply beyond any capability we had. As a matter of fact—not that I think it really mattered all that much as far as the outcome of the Iowa caucuses were concerned because we decided early that they were not the universe—the party caucus was not the most congenial universe of voters to which we wanted to submit our candidacy. I do recall, early on, giving some thought—because Iowa was a neighboring state, bordering my own home state of Illinois—to the possibility of trying to make an effort there; and, Jim Leach, congressman from the Davenport area, said that we were just light years behind. This was way back in late summer, I think. I talked to one very excellent political organizer in the state who estimated that at that time it would take me at least several hundred thousand dollars of expenditures to even begin to catch up with what George Bush had already accomplished in his early investment of resources in that state. So to that extent, you know, it just reinforced my conviction that we had to simply look beyond Iowa to New Hampshire as being the first place that we could begin.

BODE: One of the most significant early events in Iowa was the January 5th debate where the "Anderson Difference" began to emerge. Mike MacLeod suggested last night you almost passed that up.

ANDERSON: That's true, and I think he's to be congratulated for exhibiting that kind of candor. I found out that the campaign staff had actually vetoed my acceptance of an invitation to that debate on the grounds that since I couldn't make any kind of a showing at all in Iowa, to advertise my candidacy by even appearing in the state at a significant event would only further dramatize the extent of my weakness when I was inevitably defeated. I obviously chose to overrule that decision and appear, and it was really the first leg up that we got in the effort to become something more than simply an asterisk, which we were at that time.* It was that event, more than anything else, that helped us begin to climb out of the pit of total anonymity as far as nationwide recognition was concerned. So that was a significant event, not in the standings, because, as I recall it,

---

*In polling tables it is common practice to lump together candidates who receive extremely low responses into one category, labeled "Other."

we got only about 4 percent of the vote. We didn't campaign, made only one or two appearances in the state, spent no money whatever.

BODE: So, some of the candidates, Connally in particular and Bush, sought to wholesale that state to a certain extent. Iowa is a caucus state which traditionally has been an organization state; much more media money was spent in Iowa this time than had been in the past. What was your rationale for that?

MAHE: Well, we would take credit for having internally been by far and away—at least assuming that everything I was being told at the bars of the Fort Des Moines Hotel was accurate—the closest to projecting the total turnout in those caucuses. We did anticipate a massive turnout. At this point I can't tell you all the reasons why, but we just felt that it was something more than a handful of people turning up in somebody's living room that was going to make that decision. John Connally merchandises well in the mass sense, in a wholesale sense, in front of crowds. Our problem was all the way through that it was never totally translatable to television. We had also the organizational structure in place, but we still felt that we were looking at a massive turnout in those caucuses, and thus we should approach it like a primary.

HUNT: The Baker campaign was the campaign that really sailed in Iowa. Was your feeling—since you had no organization out there, virtually—that you had to do it not because that was your original game plan, to do so well in Iowa, but you had to do it in order to stop Bush?

DOUGLAS BAILEY (president, Bailey, Deardourff & Associates): Absolutely. We *had* to stop George Bush. In our thinking any vote that Baker might get is a vote that Bush might get. So you can't bypass Iowa without increasing George Bush's chance of beating Reagan in Iowa, and automatically becoming the alternative to Reagan in everything after that. Maybe it wasn't in the cards to beat George Bush in Iowa under any circumstance, but it wasn't even remotely considered a possibility to win in Iowa. But what we thought we might be able to do, with a massive media blitz, was somehow to drive up turnout sufficiently to get Baker advocates to the caucuses and either edge Bush or come in significantly close to a second place George Bush. In terms of expectations, and this is a game of expectations, that frankly would have been a Baker victory of sorts. Come the first of December, the practical fact of life is that we realized we had no organization of any kind in Iowa to speak of. We had a few people on a piece of paper; that was it. We got a good deal of help from Governor Ray, though not as much help as we had hoped for.

ANDERSON: It all seems so strange that he waited a relatively short time and then went to the state of New Hampshire and publicly endorsed Baker and yet he was unwilling to do so before the Iowa caucuses. Was a real concentrated effort made to get him to do that, and if so, why did that effort fail?

BAILEY: Yes, an unbelievable effort.

DAVID S. BRODER (associate editor and national political correspondent, *Washington Post*): Let's be honest and forthright. (*Laughter*)

BAILEY: I'm still waiting for the first secret of this campaign to emerge from anybody's mouth, and I'm not going to contribute one now, but let me say that—

ANDERSON: I'll withdraw the question. (*Laughter*)

BAILEY:—that an unbelievably strong effort was made, and if you found it a little bit peculiar that the governor would wait until New Hampshire to endorse, we had some similar reactions. (*Laughter*)

—MEDIA SPENDING, ORGANIZATION, AND TURNOUT—

KEENE: We, like the Connally campaign and the Baker campaign but perhaps for differing reasons, spent heavily on media—not just in Iowa, but in New England, immediately following Labor Day in 1979. The New England money was spent primarily because it was our feeling that there were going to be a lot of polls taken up in that part of the country. And again, we have to remember going back to that period, that our ultimate goal was to run against Reagan. But first we had to beat these other fellows. And Senator Baker was better known; Governor Connally was getting tremendous media play and had a good deal of apparent support. We felt that we had to drive George Bush's name recognition and position in those polls up a little bit. You couldn't do that nationwide the way we thought the Connally campaign was trying to do it, but we thought that if we massed our forces in a couple of places, we might be able to. If we began to rise there, it would be reported elsewhere, which would help us not so much with the broad public, which we didn't think was paying a lot of attention at that point, but as an assist to our organizers.

Our first step in Iowa and elsewhere was to make certain that our organizational act was together, that we had people on the ground to take advantage of whatever friendly feeling might develop. Then we used that media to help them recruit on a small unit basis, so from the standpoint of reaching people, it was very expensive. But from the standpoint of giving them the psychological edge and the sales tools that they really needed to go out there and get those people— particularly in Iowa—we thought it was an expenditure worth making.

The Reagan vote was solid. Before things started, we thought that it was around 40 to 45 percent in almost all of the states. We thought that it was largely self-motivated and that if you had a small turnout you would get a higher percentage of Reagan voters or caucus attendees or what-have-you to the polls than you would under any other circumstances. So what we wanted to do was, on the one hand, motivate people, and then have our organization there to grab 'em off, identify 'em, to the extent that we could, and deliver 'em to the polls. That's why we used the media. We didn't use it simply in the primary sense of trying to influence an electorate that we thought was going to show up. We tried to use it to improve, if you will, the attitude of the people we were then trying to recruit with our organizational effort.

BODE: Did you agree with Eddie Mahe that inevitably the Iowa caucus turnout was going to resemble a primary turnout more than a caucus turnout, first of all, and secondly, what was your assessment of the Reagan organization in Iowa?

KEENE: To take the first part first: we did not predict, didn't think it was going to go that high, and we were a little dumbfounded by the actual turnout that took place. We thought it was going to be higher than a lot of people did, but not anywhere near that. You have to go back to our assessment, though, of the nature of the Reagan vote as fairly cohesive and self-motivated. It was true that we didn't think that they needed quite the organization, in certain ways, that some of the rest of us had, but we did not think that the Reagan organization on the ground in Iowa was as good as we'd expected it to be or as it could have been.

HUNT: Was there any reconsideration going on within the Reagan camp? Was there any dissent over the issue of whether to participate in the debate? Was there any feeling of nervousness that maybe you were going to get sideswiped in Iowa?

WIRTHLIN: Yes. There were discussions held and concerns raised early about both decisions, namely, the presence of the candidate and the kind of visits he would make, as well as whether or not he should debate. But there was also discussion concerning how closely we should monitor Iowa. We did not do any survey research. Of course, it's difficult to assess a caucus turnout simply because you're dealing with such a small subpopulation. But as early as December, there were those in the campaign who recommended that we take a much more careful, critical view of the dynamic of that electorate than we did. We wanted to assess the organization carefully, and it was agreed that the resources needed to make an independent assessment of our organization would be better used in simply identifying and turning out the vote. I raised those questions with John Sears in December.

MAHE: Is it not also true you sent somebody in there to look it over and did not get a very favorable report?

WIRTHLIN: That is also true. We did agree that someone not directly involved in the organization should go into that state and make an assessment of how well the organization was operating, and the report did come back that our organization was not as strong as many people had believed it was in that state.

WILLIAM J. CASEY (campaign manager, Reagan–Bush Committee): One thing I could never understand, Dick is why there wasn't a better perception of the magnitude of the turnout in Iowa. Seems to me if there was any kind of an organization or any kind of telephoning, they would have known it was going to be a much, much larger turnout than there had been four years earlier. The whole planning, as I understand it, looking at it from the outside, was based on the same kind of a turnout that had been experienced in '76.

WIRTHLIN: History provides an imperfect guide to the present, but it does provide a guide, and the problem was there was no history concerning this event. It was a unique event, and while some estimates might have been made on turnout—and I think that the campaign did not assume it was going to be necessarily a low turnout—the magnitude of it caught everyone by surprise, even those who were monitoring Iowa with much greater care, as I recall.

KEENE: Looking at it from our perspective, Dick, we were trying to figure out what are these characters doing in Iowa, and why are they not doing other things? We got the sense that it was as if an early knockout strategy had been put together, but that Iowa had been taken for granted; that the resources and the best talent and other things from within the Reagan operation had been brought to bear elsewhere on the assumption that Iowa was in the bag. Had that happened, of course, then everyone would have said it was brilliant, because much of what's later viewed as brilliant and what isn't is really an accident of what does happen. But we couldn't believe that Iowa was actually being taken for granted, and we were always nervous that perhaps our assessment of what was happening out there was wrong for that reason. You always have a better reading of what your people are doing than what the others are doing. Our other feeling was that just perhaps, planning for breakthroughs, you had a whole series of dominoes being set up, but that nobody was paying any attention to the first domino.

—REAGAN AFTER IOWA—

NOLAN: What I'm curious about is, what's happening within the Reagan campaign all this time after Iowa? In that three weeks between Iowa and New Hampshire we know there was scuffling behind the arras and blood seeping out to the floor. What I'd like to know from Lyn Nofziger and Ambassador Casey is when they first heard the call.

CASEY: I don't really know what was going on in very great detail. Most of it I get second-hand. I think that there wasn't any great alarm at the top of the Reagan campaign as I perceived it and understood it at the time. Dick, you can correct me if I haven't got this straight—I understand that originally there were, right up until about three weeks before the New Hampshire primary, only six campaigning days scheduled in New Hampshire. Reagan himself said, "Hell, that's not enough, I want to spend more time here," and he just seized the bit in his teeth and spent better than twenty days. I think that's what made the difference. The polls in New Hampshire were very bad. I was satisfied that John Sears thought, the week before New Hampshire, that New Hampshire was lost. Lost. Reagan was out there, pitching around the state in buses. I give credit to the local grassroots organization that was put together, the spirit that Gerry Carmen, the Reagan state chairman, displayed in bucking up the morale—morale which was badly sagging after the surprise in Iowa. It really wasn't until the first New Hampshire debate that there seemed to be a movement that might pull Reagan out ahead.

WIRTHLIN: May I go back just a moment? There were serious concerns on the part of Ronald Reagan about the direction of the campaign prior to Iowa. When Lyn Nofziger was asked to take a new assignment that he didn't feel was one that he wanted to perform, and then when Mike Deaver was faced with the decision of either his leaving or to have Charlie Black, Jim Lake, and John Sears drop from the campaign, the governor, at that point, contacted myself, Paul Laxalt, and Ed Meese, and raised some very basic questions about the course of the campaign—prior to Iowa.* At that junction, he had indicated to us that should there be any move to remove any of the three of us that he would look very, very seriously on that attempt. That conversation, as I say, took place prior to Iowa.

---

*Deaver served as deputy director of the Reagan campaign. Until the day of the New Hampshire primary when they resigned, Sears was director of the Reagan campaign, Black was national political director, and Lake was press secretary. Senator Laxalt (R.–Nev.) was campaign chairman, and Meese was chief of staff in the Reagan campaign organization.

With the loss in Iowa, there were three things that came into sharp focus for us in terms of the strategy of the campaign: first, that the power of the media is the most critical single parameter in the vote decision. Without any question in my mind, the media created—and bestowed upon George Bush—a halo that was almost too heavy for any candidate to wear comfortably. Secondly, we re-learned a lesson that we had learned in 1976, but it was brought back with a force and a vengeance that really served us well through the entire campaign—namely, that our most effective, our most powerful, our most critical campaign asset was the presence, appeal, and campaigning ability of Ronald Reagan. We had put that asset pretty much under a blanket through Iowa. And, we resolved that that asset would be utilized heavily and that his time was the single most critical thing we had going for us in the campaign. The third lesson that came out of that period—December–January—for us was that we were dealing with an extremely volatile electorate. All of the past rules about how quickly and suddenly and massively the electorate moves had to be put on the shelf quickly. And we resolved not to take the vote decision for granted until it was counted and in the ballot boxes.

Lastly, we felt that the basic strategy of a quick knockout blow setting into force a series of steps that were already being planned could not be maintained. That is, it was agreed, after the New Hampshire primary, that we would not place ourselves in a position of putting all our chips on one state or one event, that we would run the primaries with backup options that would always provide us with a way out should events not unfold as we had hoped they might. So, for us, those were the major lessons, the major forces that we were looking at in what I consider to be the most critical period of the primaries.

BODE: Also, he was also just about to celebrate his sixty-ninth birthday, campaigning up in New Hampshire—

WIRTHLIN: That's correct.

BODE: And George Bush was on the cover of *Newsweek* jogging his three miles; John Anderson was doing his laps in the pool, all of which were setting the age issue in some relief with the voters. What were your polls showing you about how great a liability Reagan's age was at that point?

WIRTHLIN: Early on, mid '79, when we asked people the open-ended question, what they considered to be what they liked least about Ronald Reagan, the age issue ranked second in saliency, but even at that juncture there were only about 11 percent who were mentioning the age issue specifically. We made the assumption, and I think it proved to be correct in the course of the total campaign, that providing the American electorate with an indepth view of Ronald Reagan would not only help us overcome some of the other perceptual problems that we had, namely, that he doesn't care about people and so on, as well as put aside the concern that here was a man that physically wasn't quite up to becoming the next president of the United States. From that point, as the campaign progressed, as Reagan was viewed more and more intimately by the American voter, the concern over age fell off very dramatically. To the point where in September of 1980 we asked the question, "I'm going to read to you a list of phrases or words; tell me which of the three candidates—John Anderson, Ronald Reagan, or Jimmy Carter—is best described by these words," and one of the words we used was "vigorous." More American voters in September felt that that word applied to Ronald Reagan than it did, with all due respect, to President Carter.

—THE DECISION TO FIRE SEARS—

BRODER: The description that we've been given in print by John Sears of Ronald Reagan as a decisionmaker is capsuled in the phrase that he tends to be a ratifier of other people's recommendations. I'd like to ask the Reagan people here, in this crucial period when he was faced with these very tough choices about who was going to run his campaign and how it was going to be run, is that an accurate description of his own role in the process?

CASEY: My perception is that he made the decision himself.

BRODER: In a vacuum, or on the basis of—

CASEY: Well he certainly talked to people, to Ed Meese, to Dick, to Pete Hanaford, to Dick Allen, but I didn't perceive any of them playing the major role. And indeed, the key decision to make a complete shift on John Sears was Ronald Reagan's.

LYN NOFZIGER (press secretary. Reagan–Bush Committee): I might say initially that when he decided to go with John Sears, that was a decision he made, and the recommendations to him were certainly not unanimous. Who's laughing?

BODE: Everybody. (*Laughter*)

NOFZIGER: So I think Ronald Reagan is both. I think that he's a ratifier of recommendations which I think any good executive is, and I think when it comes down to where the going gets tough that he's perfectly capable of making his own decisions. He did with John; he did with Bill Casey, who kind of came out of the blue, you might say. I don't think there's any doubt about that.

WIRTHLIN: There's no question in my mind that this was a Ronald Reagan decision. He does gather information, and he gathers it from a wide variety of sources. He does consciously seek differing opinions. But, as I indicated as early as December, he had pretty well set a decision matrix on the board concerning John Sears. And I think we saw the same kind of ability to gather a number of opinions and then act very decisively once those opinions were in concerning the selection of the vice-president.

BROCK: Dick, was the decision then made literally like the day he got the results of Iowa?

WIRTHLIN: Concerning the change?

BROCK: Was it preset?

WIRTHLIN: It was preset. The matrix was, if John Sears attempted to squeeze out of the campaign, Paul Laxalt, myself, or Ed Meese, that he would look upon that move with great, great concern.

BROCK: Was Sears told that?

CASEY: But that was not the basis on which he made a change — that anybody was trying to squeeze anybody out. He made the change on the basis of dissatisfaction with the way the thing was going, the way it was being run.

WIRTHLIN: Surely, that was part of it as well.

CASEY: The other thing was that he stepped in and made a decision there to go with his local managers, on the advice of Gerry Carmen and the people on the scene instead of the advice he was getting from his national managers—to step up his schedule of campaigning in New Hampshire and to forego visits to Illinois and visits to the South, dealing with subsequent primaries.

HUNT: Mr. Casey, let's just zero in for a moment. Who called you and when did they call you about coming into the Reagan campaign?

NOFZIGER: What did you know and when did you know it?

CASEY: Ronald Reagan asked me.

HUNT: But when he asked you to come in, did he tell you he wanted you to run the campaign?

CASEY: He told me he wanted me to take a senior role and to help try to pull it together. And it wasn't until perhaps a week later that he decided to go all the way.

HUNT: In other words, when you were brought in, there was still the possibility that Sears would stay?

CASEY: He wanted to keep Sears. Definitely.

HUNT: He did want to keep Sears?

CASEY: He wanted to keep Sears. I was prepared to play the role of executive manager and let Sears stay and do the high strategy which he was supposed to be good at. Sears overplayed his hand and Reagan decided to clean house entirely.

HUNT: Well, that goes back to what Dick said. Didn't Sears make a move on Meese?

CASEY: Dick was talking about after Iowa. He said after Iowa Governor Reagan called in and said if anyone made a move on Laxalt,

Meese, or Wirthlin. The move you're referring to now on Meese — that might have occurred a week before the New Hampshire primary.

CATHERINE MACKIN (network correspondent, ABC News): Could we go back to what Mr. Wirthlin was saying the matrix was? Could you go forward from that? You said the matrix was if a move was made on you or Meese or Laxalt — and then you got sort of interrupted, and that conversation was mid–December.

WIRTHLIN: That conversation, Bill, was mid–December.

CASEY: The point I'm making is that the decision to make a change was well after that. And it was before there was any move made on Meese.

BRODER: Dick, was John Sears told that that was the matrix, to use your word?

WIRTHLIN: I really don't know, David. But the point is that there was concern prior to Iowa about both the direction and nature of the campaign and the personnel in the campaign. Iowa was the catalyst that raised the concern; the governor felt that he was not being given the opportunity to take as active a part in the campaign as he desired. He was concerned about the posture that the organization was beginning to assume under the direction of John Sears, namely, of eliminating those who had been close to the governor in prior campaigns. I cannot tell you if there would have been a change in the organization if we had won Iowa. That is a very open question. Nevertheless, it's my opinion that had a change not been made, the campaign would have encountered some very, very big rocks in the road down the line.

What we learned, Bill, as I remember when the change did occur, was that approximately 74 percent of the total allowable budget had been spent prior to the first vote being cast in New Hampshire. If the rate of spending had continued, the campaign would have been completely out of money by the first of April. Now, given that, plus the strong challenge that we faced from Bush, for example, in Pennsylvania, and Texas wasn't a rollover, we could have had difficulty in Illinois. A campaign completely without resources would have endangered, in my belief, the possibility of Ronald Reagan being nominated. The great and, I think, inestimable value that Bill Casey provided the campaign was to get immediate control of the budget, to focus on what was absolutely necessary and what was not necessary, and husband those critical resources so that we were able to meet the challenges of the next primaries effectively, but at very minimal cost.

—THE NASHUA DEBATE—

BODE: Let's go to New Hampshire if we can just for a second, because New Hampshire provided all of us with one of the finest pieces of political theater that any of us are likely ever to see, which was the debate in Nashua on a Saturday night where every media mogul you can imagine was in the audience crammed up in the gymnasium bleachers. And on the stage there were to be two candidates, Ronald Reagan and George Bush, and there turned out to be four cameos as well. I want to know first from the Bush people, how you got mousetrapped, what your contingency plans were, and why they didn't work.

KEENE: We were dumb.

CASEY: Now what do you mean by that word mousetrap?

BODE: Keene, I think, knows what it means. (*Laughter*)

CASEY: The question is whether you mousetrap yourself.

NOFZIGER: Did you find that building a better mousetrap was worthwhile?

KEENE: Well, we had mixed feeling about it going in. When the initial question of whether we wanted to participate in a two-man debate came up, we had a discussion about it. A number of people in the campaign were not, at the beginning, in favor of that. It was a mixed question: we weren't running that early against Reagan; we still had to eliminate these other guys. We didn't want to have our feet cut out from under us by votes that they were taking while we weren't impacting on Reagan's vote. By the same token, appearing on the platform with him alone helped to structure the two-man situation—even though on election day in New Hampshire, it wasn't going to be a two-man situation. So it was not something that was cut and dried as we went into it. Once we got into it, we then had pressures locally, and I have not been able to completely untangle all of what happened during that period, but once the two-man format was set, the newspapers and others were insisting that we go with that format.

BODE: For a moment, where did the original initiative for that debate come?

KEENE: It came to us from the newspaper. It was our understanding that it was initiated by the Reagan campaign, by calls to the newspaper.

BODE: Is that true, Lyn?

NOFZIGER: My understanding is that Gerry Carmen is the guy who recommended it, that's what Gerry says.

CLYMER: But isn't Hugh Gregg close enough to the newspaper—

BROCK: They were for Ford in '76; Gregg was for Reagan. . . .

KEENE: I said earlier that I hadn't untangled exactly what happened at the outset. As it went down the road, we were sitting around Governor Gregg's living room that day and not knowing quite what was going on. There were a number of phone calls back and forth, and we decided that a two-man debate would be preferable, but that we shouldn't be the ones who forced it. There was a decision that if there was a move to make it look like that's what was happening, our candidate should welcome the other candidates to the debate. It didn't quite happen that way.

BRODER: This is on the Saturday of the debate?

KEENE: Yes, this was on Saturday afternoon. There was a great deal of feeling at that point, and when we arrived at the high school, there was a request that Governor Reagan should meet with Ambassador Bush. Jim Baker went down for a pre-meeting. We indicated that we wanted to know what this was all about. At that point, we discovered that various other candidates were also present; we had not been informed about their presence when the meeting was asked for, and we then realized that there was a trap about to be sprung. . . .

NOFZIGER: Typical Sears trickery.

KEENE: We decided to go with our fallback option, which was to invite everybody up on the platform, and that fell apart on the platform itself —

BODE: Dave, wait. We've got the mousetrap baited now. You're going to the meeting, and you've got the other candidates, and who set the trap?

WIRTHLIN: I think that John Sears set it up. He discussed the options with me, and it was very evident that it was a win-win situation — either way we were going to look very good. The point I'd like to make is, I think there is strong evidence that it wasn't the Nashua debate —

KEENE: I agree with you.

WIRTHLIN: It was the Manchester debate that was the axial event.

BODE: I know what you are going to say, but can we stick with Nashua for now?

NOLAN: Congressman Anderson, you've known George Bush, you've served in the House with him, and Senator Dole, and Senator Baker. You knew him well, and the four of you are standing there, silent players, street mimes; and I was wondering, Bush is doodling like this the whole time and I'm saying, Why doesn't he just say, "Guys, why don't you come up, you know, come on and debate — you're all good Republicans." Why didn't he do that?

KEENE: Well there are some things you can explain and some things you can't. (*Laughter*)

ANDERSON: I was just going to offer this observation, in retrospect, and I don't want to contradict what I said in a very indignant press conference that I held right after that, but from a more distant mirror of history you get a sharper reflection. When I went out on that stage, I was really impressed with the fact that just minutes earlier, when we had that little meeting in the anteroom—the candidates, including myself and Ronald Reagan—that at one point, Governor Reagan had said that he was willing to go out on the stage and actually tell the crowd that he was not going to participate in view of the refusal of the Bush people to permit me and others to participate. The one who really became agitated at that point was Gordon Humphrey, who was there in the room also. "Oh, you can't do that; that would just be the most terrible thing in the world." You know, the governor has an acting background, and I don't say this disrespectfully, but he maybe fooled me because I thought he really was prepared to make that supreme sacrifice of giving up the debate altogether. . . .

WIRTHLIN: That was the case, John. That was not conditioned, not set up. One thing about Ronald Reagan is, he does have a strong sense of what's fair, and that feeling really was a sincere one; in my mind he would have been very much prepared to have walked out.

ANDERSON: Oh, I am comforted by the thought. (*Laughter*)

KEENE: Right afterwards when we were asked about what happened, we said we were bagged and we though it was a brilliant tactical move on their part.

MAHE: But you would not have been bagged if George had stood up and said, Sit down, folks, let's have a debate. I mean, you were not bagged.

KEENE: Well, sometimes you push the button and the missile doesn't go off. (*Laughter*)

—A MOUSETRAP—

HUNT: This is fascinating. When Sears called you to ask you about it, John, what did he say to you? Did he say, We've got George's mousetrap here?

ANDERSON: No, it was a very legitimate effort on their part to broaden participation, and he didn't know whether it would fly or not. He was always very careful to hedge his invitation to be there that evening. He said, We don't know whether this is going to come off or not but, gosh, we sure agree with you fellows 'cause we have been screaming and hollering and sending telegrams to Mr. Breen, editor of *The Nashua Telegraph*, protesting the outrage of the whole thing. He was very sympathetic with our efforts to broaden the scope of the debate. He was careful to be tentative about the whole thing, about not knowing if we got there what would happen.

BODE: What did you think was going to happen when you walked on that stage, the four of you?

ANDERSON: Oh I thought we were going to have a little charade, and we did have. We all stand there and smile and pirouette and turn to the crowd and beseech. . . .

KEENE: Organizing caucuses and budgeting money may not be John's strong suit, but in Nashua we were playing on his home ground because that is the kind of thing he does very well, and he outdid us on it. I think you are probably right. I know that it was not Governor Reagan who was doing these things because he is much more straightforward than that. We felt mousetrapped about it, but we didn't even really feel it was unfair—we admired it and wished we had been able to do it.

CASEY: I think there's been wide misperception here. I think the Bush people bagged themselves. This goes back to the afternoon of the debate. You recall that the paper was going to pay for the debate. The Federal Election Commission decided they couldn't, so— and I don't know whether this was Sears or Reagan—the Reagan camp said, Okay, we want to have a debate, we want to go head-to-head with Bush. Gerry Carmen, Reagan's New Hampshire coordinator, was a very strong factor here. So they asked the Bush camp to put up half the money, and they wouldn't do it. Next thing that happened, to my knowledge—I was sitting out in the audience—was I was told that Governor Reagan wanted to talk to me. I walked back to this anteroom and there was Governor Reagan and Mrs. Reagan, just the two of them, and the Governor said, I don't know how I can do this. They don't want to let these other fellows in the debate, yet I'm in the position of being responsible. I don't want to stand responsible for excluding these other candidates who have a strong feeling that they're entitled to be in the debate. And he said, If they don't back down, I'm not going to appear. I said, Governor, that's a very noble attitude but I hate like hell to see you give George Bush that kind of victory. If you don't appear, why, he's won the debate. Still, Reagan's state of mind was not to appear without the others. And then Bob Dole, Howard Baker, John Anderson, and Phil Crane all came in the room and the discussion was resumed. Governor Reagan was still saying that unless everybody was included—he wanted this open to everybody—unless it happens, he was not going to appear. Baker suggested that George Bush be asked to come in and discuss the matter in the interest of the unity of the Republican party. George wouldn't do that. He was sitting out there on the stage, and all the candidates got pretty mad at that. The publisher of the paper sent word that he would like to meet with all the candidates except Governor Reagan. That did not set well, and nobody went to see him. A messenger then came in and said, Governor Reagan, you got two minutes. Again, he came in and said, Governor, you got thirty seconds. Senator Gordon Humphrey said, Unless you get out there and participate in this debate, you've lost the New Hampshire primary, and it was still undecided what he was going to do. I didn't know when Reagan went out there and when he said he wanted to make a settlement; I didn't know what he was going to say.

ANDERSON: Well, we did know, those of us who went out on the stage with him did know that he was going to make a statement about his reservations about the manner in which it was handled.

CASEY: We knew he was going to make a statement, but we didn't know what the statement was going to say.

HUNT: You all knew that he was going to participate in the debate?

ANDERSON: Yes, and that we were just going to get a little exposure before we left—

BAILEY: Can I just add one word? It is very difficult to make Howard Baker mad. The Nashua debate may have been a win–win situation from Reagan's standpoint as you viewed it; it was a lose–lose situation from Baker's standpoint. I mean, he was an also-ran at that point and that just put the final nail in, no matter what happened that night. But he was genuinely furious, and he wasn't furious personally as much as he was furious on the question of party unity because he saw that as the first thing that had happened in the campaign which might break the party apart. I think it is a mistake here to be thinking, possibly with the exception of Sears, that all of this was some gigantic plot. I think everybody was completely caught up, frankly, in the emotions of the moment.

KEENE: On both sides, and Bill's absolutely right in that we played into it. In fact everything that we did made it worse, even though Bush wasn't approached to meet with the candidates until he was grabbed by the arm by Senator Humphrey on the inside of the auditorium on the way to the stage in a crowd of people ten minutes after the debate was supposed to have started. It was a bad day.

CASEY: I understood why George did that because from his standpoint it was the publisher's show.

KEENE: That's right. The publisher supposedly had a statement detailing exactly how it all happened that he was to read at the outset. By the time he got up there he was apoplectic and everything broke down, and I kept looking at my watch to find out when my plane was going to leave.

BODE: I had a conversation with the publisher afterwards who felt he had also been sandbagged. The result of all this was more than a two-to-one, better than two-to-one win of Reagan over Bush in New Hampshire. Dick Wirthlin, I know that in spite of the fact that the Nashua debate is the one to get all the attention, the Manchester debate was the one that made the difference, isn't that right?

—THE MANCHESTER DEBATE—

WIRTHLIN: I don't think there's any question about that. The Manchester debate was the key event that turned that election from George Bush to Ronald Reagan. As I've indicated, Bush led us by six points from the 28th through the 15th to the 18th of February. That lead of Bush's grew by nine points, so it was a period of great distress for the Reagan campaign. We had felt again by putting the candidates and especially Bush right next to Reagan, it would go down to Ronald Reagan's favor. The debate itself was not that beneficial, but two things were critical in terms of switching the momentum of that campaign from Bush to Reagan. First, the closing statement. One of the assets that Reagan carried early was an ability to articulate a vision for the country; and in his closing statement, which was finely honed, he did catch that vision and did enthuse a number of Republicans who had been sitting on the fence in terms of their vote decision. Secondly, as you may recall in the questions-and-answer period from the audience—prescreened questions—one individual stood up and said, "I was going to ask you a question about inflation, Mr. Reagan, but instead I think there's a more important issue to consider here, and that is your use of ethnic jokes."* Reagan responded to that, first with some anger. He controlled that, turned the question back, using humor to some extent in a self-deprecating fashion, and completely defused the question; the audience broke rules and applauded the way he responded.

I felt that we had probably got a slight edge in the debate, but I wasn't prepared for the results of assessing that debate, which we did the following day. First, we had a very wide audience; almost 40 percent of those who voted said that they saw the debate, and unlike some of the political commentators, almost nine out of ten said there was a clear winner. Thirty-three percent said that Ronald Reagan won the debate, 17 percent Bush, 14 percent John Anderson, and 12 percent Baker. In that same measure, we saw that we had closed the gap—we had gone from a nine-point deficit just before the debate to a two-point deficit right after the debate. In Nashua, we interviewed relatively early Sunday morning, and the turning point

---

*The questioner was probably referring to a widely publicized joke involving a Pole, an Italian, a duck, and a cock fight told by Governor Reagan, first to friends and aides and then to a group of reporters, on February 16, 1980, while campaigning in New Hampshire.

that occurred in the first debate led to a 45 percent Reagan to 24 percent Bush lead among Republicans, of whom only 12 percent had heard or seen any comments about the Nashua debate the night before.

BODE: Was it just too early to interview?

WIRTHLIN: No, it was too early for the secondary effects to begin to take place. As you remember, I don't think it was televized; I think it was carried on radio, and we started interviewing early, 9:00 Sunday morning.

CLYMER: The *Union Leader* was telling people about it by 9:00.

WIRTHLIN: That's right. We had conducted most of our interviews prior to noon, and at that point only 12 percent said they had heard or read about the Nashua debate, and among that population, we're looking at a forty-five–twenty-four lead. We felt that Bush did make two mistakes—perhaps the first two in what would seem to almost be a picture-perfect campaign up to that juncture, that gave us even additional points as we went into the Tuesday election. First, and David, this is a question I almost waited a full year to ask, we were very surprised that you used radio to try to explain away the events of the Nashua debate. We felt that simply added gasoline to the fire, focused on it, and rebounded to our favor rather than yours.

KEENE: I agree with that.

WIRTHLIN: Secondly, in 1976, perhaps the most painful moment for us had been the razor-edge loss that we suffered, and all of our data indicated that it occurred because we didn't have the candidate present in the state for the last two days. We were very sure this time around that Ronald Reagan would be in the state; he had campaigned vigorously and hard right through Tuesday morning, right through noon of Tuesday. The other thing that helped us expand that lead of forty-five–twenty-four was, in my opinion, the news covering George Bush, who had left the state forty-eight hours earlier, jogging in his LaCoste sportshirt in the sunshine of Texas with Ronald Reagan bundled against the cold, out meeting the New Hampshire voters. In other words, we saw George Bush commit what we felt would have been a fatal error for us both in '76 and in the Iowa caucus. Those were the two things that gave further boost to the momentum which, without question in my mind, was set in place with the first debate in Manchester.

BODE: As usual, when the press is involved in presidential politics, New Hampshire gets too much attention, and that's happening now. Right after New Hampshire come the other New England primaries: Massachusetts and Vermont, which have mixed results — Bush winning Vermont. The only person who regards these results as anywhere conclusive is Howard Baker, who drops out at this point.

BAILEY: Even more conclusive at this point, frankly, was the fact that Baker had no money and no likelihood of getting any money; he could not look down the road to a single thing in the near future which was a success, and it had been going from bad to worse. Bush had obviously won the Bush-Baker battle; there was some question as to whether Bush could win the Bush-Reagan battle, but Baker was dead. We even had the bad judgment in that period of trying to raise what we thought was a significant issue in the campaign on the same day that the campaign misplaced Dave Broder's luggage. (*Laughter*)

BRODER: Historically false. The luggage was not lost; the campaign may have been lost, but my luggage wasn't.

—FORD CONSIDERS GETTING IN—

BODE: Well, one person who seemed to be hearing different kinds of sounds out of all this was Gerald Ford. His interest was peaked a bit by the fact that Baker dropped out and there were inconclusive results. Bill Casey, Dick Wirthlin, and Lyn, were you worried much about Gerald Ford deciding at that point to get in?

NOFZIGER: I was an innocent bystander.

CASEY: I was scared to death.

BODE: Tell us about it.

CASEY: I would see Jerry Ford coming in with $18 million, all fresh, and us staggering to ration $2 million through the California primary. It was a scary prospect. For him it would be an uphill fight because of the numbers, but I was mighty glad when enough governors refused to go along, and he decided not to try it.

WIRTHLIN: Ford was the Damocles' sword, if you will, hanging over our head, both in '79 and through '80. I believe it was Adam Clymer's column which broke the story of Ford's interest in getting in.

CLYMER: On Sunday, March 1.

WIRTHLIN: We quickly added Gerald Ford's name to all the tracking that we were doing. We made an assessment within about a twenty-four-hour period that if Gerald Ford became an active candidate, he would strongly challenge us. In Wisconsin, for example, we showed that overnight we were again seven points behind with a Ford entry. Two things did give us some hope as that week progressed. The first blush was an enthusiastic one, from Republican voters, but as the week progressed we found that Ford support was becoming more and more thin. Within about a seven-day period we felt quite confident we could beat him in the event that he had made the decision to become an active candidate. We believed that he would pull support from the other candidates, and also that Bush would not bow out too gracefully.

KEENE: We made that clear, shortly after that column appeared, with public statements that President Ford could not expect us to roll over, that George Bush did not get into it as a stalking horse or to prepare the ground for anyone else. If the talk of a Ford entry caused anguish within the Reagan camp, it was like stabbing yet another knife into the body of our campaign because in '79 we had difficulty, as we were attempting to get support, with people who said that they were waiting for Ford or using Ford as a reason not to make a choice among the candidates. Then, following New Hampshire, the twin spectres of John Anderson on the one hand and the possibility of a re-entry by Gerald Ford on the other caused us some really significant problems. This was a period when we couldn't afford to have any problems. It was one of the factors that was seriously injuring our candidate's campaign.

CLYMER: I would like to ask something very briefly of Doug Bailey and Bob Teeter, who both got involved in the whirlwind consideration that Ford gave to running. As Dick Wirthlin pointed out earlier, 74 percent of the Reagan allotment had been spent by the day of the New Hampshire primary. That would have meant that if you could have raised it for Ford, you would have had four times as much money to spend as they would have. With hindsight, seeing what Bush did in subsequent primaries, what are the odds that if Ford had leaped in—would he have had a one-in-four chance of taking the nomination, one in ten? What do you think?

TEETER: You don't know. My guess is that he would have had a reasonable chance. I think it would have been a very difficult race all the way through. He would have had, I don't know, one-in-three or one-in-two, but he would have had some chance of getting nominated at that point.

NOFZIGER: I think there is an assumption here, though, that Gerald Ford could go out and raise 18 million bucks in three to four months, and nobody else was able to do it.

TEETER: If we wanted to talk about something that could split the party, that's it.

CASEY: I guess that is what stopped it. The point is that he didn't want to see the party get split. Not judging by polls, really, but just by the political support, I think that if Ford had been encouraged by Clements, by Rhodes, by Dalton, all of whom discouraged him, and by the New York leaders—if he had that kind of support, I think it would be even money that he could have made it.*

HUNT: Bob, did you think he was going to get in?

TEETER: Only very briefly. I thought during the discussions that I had with President Ford from '76 on that he would probably not run in 1980. They were periodic, leading us up to that week in March, the week of the 11–12th—it was about Wednesday of that week that

---

*William Clements of Texas, James Rhodes of Ohio, and John Dalton of Virginia are all Republican governors.

we had the long meeting in Washington. Between then and the final Saturday when he decided definitely not to run and made that announcement, there were some hours in there that I thought he might well get in. But overall during that period of time, say, from mid-'79 up to that Saturday in March, his general conclusion was that he would not run. There were some times between that Wednesday and Saturday that I thought he was wavering, and for a brief time, I think the decision was going one way and then the other.

CASEY: God knows he wanted to run. He was still wanting to run at the convention in Detroit. All he had to do, in my opinion, was to go out and say, "I'm going to do this." Then he would have had the support. He went to the New York county leaders who were still loose at that time, and he asked them to ask him to run; and these guys said, "Make up your mind, you ask us—but you take the plunge, and we'll decide."

TEETER: But he was not willing to run on that basis. I don't think he ever had been willing to go in front with it. He had made up his mind, for whatever reason, that only under certain conditions would he run. I don't believe there was much doubt in that meeting that it would be very difficult; there were some people who thought that it might be impossible. By and large, the idea was that he would have a very good chance of getting nominated, had he decided to run and go for it.

MAHE: What would have been the cost in party unity to do that?

BAILEY: That was the principal question, and by the time of the last meeting Saturday, that *was* the question. Even if he could succeed in getting the nomination, would he have something worth having, and if he couldn't succeed in getting the nomination, would Reagan have something worth having with the nomination? Despite any difference he may have ever had with Ronald Reagan, his attitude toward President Carter and the Carter administration governed that decision more than anything else. That was the absolute top priority as far as he was concerned, and I think he concluded that he was risking the re-election of Carter by running. That was more important than anything else in making the decision he made.

TEETER: That was the bottom line through the whole discussion. If you recall, it was on that Wednesday night, I think it must have been March 12th, that he made that speech in Washington to the House–Senate dinner, which was a pretty rough speech about Carter. The bottom line almost every hour through all those discussions was that getting Carter out of office was his foremost concern.

BROCK: From the point of view of a disinterested bystander, the roof was falling in, and what was panicking an awful lot of people, and it sure scared the devil out of me, was that we had the most remarkably coherent positive campaign I've seen in the Republican party in a long time. There was none of this bitter ideological split that can just tear us from end to end. With George and Howard and Reagan in the race, it was clean, it was upbeat, and we were hitting the right issues—everything was perfect. There was no way Jerry Ford could have gotten in that race without it being a stop-Reagan candidacy, and everybody knew it. It would have just blown the lid off that opportunity to keep us focused on the issues that we had to be focused on in November to win the election.

CLYMER: Moreover, I have interviewed President Ford on a number of occasions, and I've never previously had an interview in which he so clearly had in mind the points he wanted to make. When he said that Ronald Reagan was too conservative to win, it was not in response to a question of mine. He interrupted himself, answering another question, to make that point. Plainly he was saying that "Reagan's-got-to-be-stopped 'cause he can't win, and if you had only asked me, I'd be the one to do it."

BROCK: What was happening to Gerald Ford at that particular point was that George Bush had, in most people's mind, blown it in New Hampshire. Most people thought it was over with. I did frankly, and the old Ford gang began to get on the phone again; they were calling Jack Marsh and Bob Teeter and all the crowd and putting the heat on him, saying, You have to do it, 'cause Reagan can't be elected in November, and he was responding to that heat. And then, I think, on the second run of thought, he had to look at the consequences of his action. I think that's when almost everybody was worried about the unity side and began to make the impact that led him to the final decision, which was the right decision.

TEETER: I think that Wednesday, March 12th, was the only time he really focused on the mechanical problems of running—the filing dates and those things. The reason that week occurred when it did was the fact that there were two large state filing dates coming up, Ohio and California, and that was really the last time that you could file and have any arithmetic hope of getting enough delegates or preventing Ronald Reagan from getting enough delegates to win, and so the decision had to be made by the 20th or 21st. He either had to be in or out, and I think it was the first time he considered the mechanics of the situation. It brought to focus the stark realities of the decision, and the fallback decision was then not to run, and pray for rain.

—CONNALLY'S REFUSAL OF FEDERAL FUNDS—

BODE: While all this was going on, John Connally was heading for his Waterloo in the South, and one of the decisions he made along the way was to forego federal matching funds and raise the money from his own sources. You said you found some bottomless wells, yet you never really did see the bottom of the well on this one, Eddie. Could you tell us a little about Connally's decision to forego matching funds?

MAHE: That was a very easy decision. We were confronted with the same thing the Reagan campaign was confronted with, and we were shocked when they took matching funds. We were convinced all the way through coming into the end—and we were tracking their spending patterns, which were almost the same as ours—that there was no way, if you were confronted with the challenge all the way through, that we could beat Governor Reagan if we were under a limit and he wasn't. The only chance we would have is if they were foolish enough to take matching funds and we then survived in the South. In that case we could then just keep on going. You could see coming up in November and December of 1979 that they were going to soon be in very real difficulties with the overall spending limit. So at that moment, if we had decided to take matching funds, it would have ruled out any chance of winning because we were obviously in no position to do a knockout on anybody, and whatever chance we had was going to be overtime, and the only way we had time was to have the financial capacity to handle it.

BODE: Why did you place such a priority on South Carolina?

MAHE: Because it was first of the Southern primaries.

BODE: Were you positioned for Florida and Alabama and so forth, if you had won South Carolina?

MAHE: Yes, not as well positioned as we had planned on being, but yes, we had good organization. . . . I would amend that; we had dropped off Alabama in January, but we stayed active in Georgia and Florida all the way.

BODE: At one point in 1979, around September, when you were going to be on the cover of *Time*, I talked to you, and you said you now felt you knew how it felt to be like a man with a rocket strapped to your back. What happened?

MAHE: We had real force to the thing, pushing hard to keep it up, but when we hit that September–October time frame, we were in a glide path. We could not allow it to level out at that point, but it was difficult not to, and of course we felt that we were adversely impacted by the Iranian problem. When that hit, we had been generating, as David makes the point, a lot of good press, a lot of good publicity. John Connally was good copy; the television networks liked him, and we were generating a tremendous amount of coverage. But when Iran hit, we dropped out of sight as did everybody else. Also there was the network decision not to sell us any national advertising at that point, and we had no way to sustain a national campaign when we lost the television news coverage and we could not buy television spots.

—DOLE DROPS OUT—

BODE: So Reagan sweeps the South on the 8th and 11th; on the 15th of March, President Ford says he's not going to be a candidate, and Bob Dole drops out. When Bob Dole dropped out, he sent me a letter a couple of days afterward, and I'd like to just read it. It says, "Dear Ken: I would appreciate knowing how much coverage my campaign received by NBC from the date of my announcement to my final withdrawal. I've been told my total coverage by NBC amounted to fourteen seconds." I take it he sent that in good humor and not sour grapes, but did you feel in the Dole campaign that you just sort of—

JO-ANNE COE (office of Senator Robert Dole): Let me just interject a little bit more of his humor by saying we were obviously feeling all along that Reagan was the candidate to beat, and then of course Bush came along in Iowa. We had expected that we had a natural constituency in Iowa with the farmers, and then, of course, that fell apart. In referring to Ambassador Bush, Senator Dole said, "He's been quoted as Big Mo recently. Big Mo, Slow Mo, and No Mo, that's where we are." He also had a very serious concern that the campaign should have begun focusing more on the issues instead of the momentum of the individuals. Of course, he had been caught back in Washington working in the Senate, and for that reason I think he wanted to project more the issues, his experience, and so forth. He felt that the networks and print media and the like were not giving him coverage for what actually turned out to be Senate duties. I do think that he genuinely felt he had not received the coverage.

ANDERSON: The fourteen seconds was of his car breakdown wasn't it, stuck in New Hampshire? To recall the memorable phrase that NBC's Tom Pettit once employed when I ran across him in the snows of New Hampshire—he had a cameraman with him, and I was complaining bitterly about the lack of coverage of my efforts—he said, "Well, today you are within the zone of coverage." (*Laughter*)

—ANDERSON IN ILLINOIS—

BODE: Then we head for Illinois, which is not only John Anderson's home state but it's also a crossover primary state. Also coming right up after Illinois the next week, is Connecticut, which was one of your best states, and Wisconsin. At that point I remember talking to Mike MacLeod who was very optimistic. What happened?

ANDERSON: We were buoyed by the fact that in that March 4th primary in Massachusetts, even though George Bush won, we were only about 1,000 votes behind. On the same day we were about 800 votes or less behind Ronald Reagan in Vermont, a state which we really had no idea of winning. In Massachusetts, we had worked very hard and had some reason to think that we could even win. Vermont frankly was a real surprise. Now, from the beginning this was our strategy; this was the way we were going to get on board; this was how we were going to get in.

I think we ran out of time. Two weeks, literally, we had only two weeks between the March 4th primary in Massachusetts and the primary in Illinois, and it simply was not enough time. We did very well in that primary in the Chicago area, in Cook County, but we didn't have the time to go downstate, to go down to central Illinois, southern Illinois, where the Reagan forces were still deeply dug in from the 1976 campaign.

MICHAEL F. MACLEOD (campaign manager–treasurer, National Unity Campaign): The other precious commodity was money.

ANDERSON: You're quite right. We were outspent, I suppose, ten to one by the other candidates, the other principal candidates in the race at that point—namely, Bush and Reagan. I wasn't as conscious really about Reagan's spending as I was about George's, because—

KEENE: We didn't have anything against you in Illinois. We were beginning to get very concerned at that point that our progress toward a two-candidate race was disappearing, so we decided to do two things. One was to concentrate our candidate's effort in Connecticut, which really shaped our later campaigns in Michigan, Pennsylvania, and places like that. And because of the media coverage and the attention on your candidacy that occurred following the New England races, we concluded we were not going to be a factor in Illinois. We wanted to make sure we maintained some 10 percent of the vote, but we converted our Illinois campaign to an anti–Anderson campaign, and our spending there for those last ten days was really spending that was designed to keep you from accomplishing your objective in Illinois, rather than worrying about any of our own.

ANDERSON: I think, David, that that spending was more responsible for the fact that we then ended up with only 37 percent of the vote as against Reagan's 47 percent in Illinois, than the debate that took place—the League of Women Voters' debate which took place shortly before the election. I think some people have attached too much importance to that debate because it was not that widely viewed around the state of Illinois. As I recall it, it was carried on PBS in Illinois, it was carried on National Public Radio, maybe some of the Chicago stations. But in downstate Illinois where the strong Republican vote was, there weren't that many people who even saw that debate. So even though I did feel that I had been ganged up on that night by the other candidates, I still don't blame that event for the loss. I think it was more of the effective spending that you did on media.

BODE: That was the night that Phil Crane attacked you, and Ronald Reagan turned to you and said, "Come on, John Anderson, would you really prefer Teddy Kennedy to me?" Why didn't you say at that point, "Look, I didn't come here to debate pedigree, I came here to talk about issues"?

ANDERSON: Well, I did, in effect. I may not have had that instant retort you suggested which would have been suitable. But certainly duing the course of the evening, I made it quite clear that I felt that the issues were the important thing, and I remember saying that, you know, who are you to sit here and propose that I have to pass some kind of specially designed litmus test of loyalty in order to survive in this part? I did learn, incidentally, on the question of whether or not there was a cabal, and I think this was reported, that Reagan's Illinois coordinator, Don Totten, had gotten together with other people who participated in that debate and suggested that maybe a joint effort ought to be made to bring me down to size.

HUNT: John, at this point, when you lost Illinois, had you yet begun to consider the idea of an independent candidacy.

ANDERSON: The idea had been suggested, but it was really. . . . The nail was not totally in the coffin until Wisconsin. Again, we didn't have time, there were only two weeks from the Illinois primary until the Wisconsin primary. We still continued to cling to hope in Wisconsin, which was a crossover state, and we had to rely very heavily on that stragegy. I did campaign there. I know the media at the time wondered what I was doing wandering around places like Rhinelander, Wisconsin, and Stevens Point and up in the North, rather than concentrating where I should have, I know now, in Milwaukee County. I think we did make some bad mistakes technically in conducting that campaign, but it wasn't really until after that that we knew it was all over.

HUNT: Did you entertain any hope then, John, that if you could win Wisconsin you had any chance of getting the Republican nomination?

ANDERSON: Yes, I can honestly say that, foolish as it might seem to the experts around this table, we continued to cling to the idea that if Reagan were stopped in a fairly important primary—and I regarded Wisconsin as being one of those—that the reassessment of who could really win against Carter in 1980 would take hold in the Republican party and that things could yet change.

MACLEOD: May I add something to that before you go on? At the point, Al, that the Illinois primary was held, only about four out of the eighteen states where crossover voting was allowed had actually occurred of the thirty-five states holding the Republican primaries. We felt there was still a fair amount of promise downstream, so it was not entirely a fatuous notion.

—THE CHICAGO DEBATE—

BRODER: I wanted to ask Dick Wirthlin two quick questions: one, is Anderson right that the Chicago debate had relatively little impact? Two, was there ever a point that you all thought that John Anderson might be a potential problem in terms of the Republican nomination?

WIRTHLIN: The debate was critical for very different reasons than the New Hampshire debate. On March 9th, our daily trackings, as a matter of fact, showed John Anderson leading Ronald Reagan marginally in Illinois. We were very concerned because we didn't have many resources to build the kind of image we felt was needed to roll back the Anderson challenge without the debate. I remember clearly Bill Casey and I discussing long and hard whether or not we should allocate $18,000 dollars for radio in Illinois. Now, that's the point our campaign had come to in terms of having the leverage we felt we needed to keep the momentum going in Ronald Reagan's favor. The debate event itself had impact not only in terms of the number of people that watched it but also in the kind of clips that were then played by the media that had secondary and tertiary impact.

ANDERSON: The reason I made the statement about the debate was because I have been told by many people, and of course this is not on the basis of any objective findings based on a poll or anything of that kind, but enough people convinced me that the perceptions of that evening were quite different with respect to people who watched it from within the hall there at the Continental Plaza Hotel, and the people who saw it on television. It was an entirely different event. People who were watching it *did* think Reagan really sparkled, those who were watching it there in the hotel. But the portions of it that were carried on the media were not that impressive in enhancing his image.

WIRTHLIN: You've got to be very careful, again, about the kind of image collage that was important for us to build from the base that we started from. Competence and strength were never issues. But thre was always the question: "Is Ronald Reagan such an ingrained conservative that we can't live with some of these issue positions, and is he a man who has a human empathy for some of the kinds of problems that a president must deal with?" Not only did Democrats raise those issues but so did Republicans. And the key element in the Illinois debate had been the humor that the governor displayed—again, on the age issue; secondly, in terms of not taking himself quite so seriously, as well as the dynamic of that debate, which, in essence, put him as the unique person on the podium. Phil Crane and George Bush had their slings and arrows aimed primarily at you, John, and so we had this dynamic: a rather heated, direct confontation, with Reagan almost assuming the role of senior statesman, if you will.

ANDERSON: Above the storm.

WIRTHLIN: Above the storm, which was exactly what we needed to pull those moderate Republicans back into the Reagan camp. After the debate, we continued to widen almost on a daily basis, the gap between Reagan and yourself. As I said, just prior to it, on March 9th, you were ahead of us.

NOLAN: Looks like, John, that Dick is suggesting the instant replay showed that you did take your foot off the bag. (*Laughter*)

BODE: We still haven't gotten to Pennsylvania, where George Bush finally got his one-on-one shot against Ronald Reagan.

—THE CONNECTICUT PRIMARY—

MAHE: Ken, let me ask a question. You jumped Connecticut. I was under the impression, albeit from the outside, that Reagan's situation was fairly good in Connecticut, that you had a lot of strength up there. That could have been a knock-out blow, and yet you backed down on that one state, at spending money. You really backed away from it. Did polls show that you could not win Connecticut? I was shocked as to why you never talked about Connecticut.

CASEY: No, we didn't. We'd decided that we could afford to lose Connecticut.

MAHE: But would that not have been the knock-out blow, if you would have beat George in his home state?

CASEY: That's a close question.

MAHE: Let me ask Dave: If you had lost Connecticut, what would have been George's—

KEENE: He would have been in very, very deep trouble. We suspected that they might try and do that. We didn't know if they would. We knew their financial situation was precarious. But we knew we *had* to win Connecticut. If we had lost, regardless of what they had done, we would have been in terrible shape, and we probably would have had to drop relatively soon thereafter.

MAHE: Grand. And then your money problem's solved, in the Reagan campaign.

WIRTHLIN: I think it goes back to our basic decision—and I think it was a sound one—to always have backup options. We were not willing to put all our political chips on Connecticut. We felt we could do well in Connecticut and live to fight another day and still be in a good position.

CASEY: We knew we were going to come out way ahead in New York, the same day, with delegates. We felt if George Bush won his own state, that wouldn't impress anybody. We'd live with it. We decided not to spend the money there.

WIRTHLIN: Also, to impact Connecticut media-wise is a very expensive proposition, and up to that point, there'd been thirteen direct primary contests. Narrowly, we lost two of them, Massachusetts and Connecticut. So, even with the loss, given the races we were facing afterward, we did not feel it wise to go for the jugular at that point.

KEENE: It was a must-win for us, but it wasn't for you.

CASEY: Connecticut's a small jugular. That question would certainly be better for Pennsylvania. If we had the resources, we could have knocked him out in Pennsylvania.

BODE: How much did Bush spend in Pennsylvania?

KEENE: $800,000?

BODE: $800,000? How about Reagan?

CASEY: About $30,000.

BODE: $30,000!

CASEY: Yes. Just radio spots.

TEETER: That was key to Connecticut. I mean, I think that the Bush campaign went to Connecticut knowing that Reagan couldn't spend a lot of money. It was a major part of the decision.

KEENE: We'd looked at these states, and at that point, frankly, from George Bush's standpoint, we felt it was important for him to demonstrate strength to protect his future potential—and there was always the chance that something could happen, that you could knock 'em a good one and they'd stumble. But in Connecticut we also discovered two things: Connecticut was George Bush's home state; he did have resources that we could apply there that we didn't have elsewhere. In addition to that, the style of the campaign changed, to an extent, and George Bush found himself as a candidate. He was a better candidate and a better campaigner by the time he got to Connecticut than he had been in New Hampshire and Illinois.

And when we got to Pennsylvania, we developed this half-hour format on television, which cost a lot of money, but which put him in a very, very attractive position to show his knowledge and some humor, and at that point we became convinced that, the spending aside, we had ourselves a pretty good candidate who could do pretty well and that we ought to demonstrate that.

—THE PENNSYLVANIA PRIMARY—

CASEY: I think getting the act together in Pennsylvania was more important than the amount of money you spent. . . .

KEENE: That's what I mean, exactly.

CASEY: And you were ahead on the issues.

KEENE: Right. For all we said about the Nashua debate, and about the difficulties we had after Iowa, and going into phase two, we finally got phase two in Pennsylvania. And when George Bush got into that, I would say that I think that he was as good a candidate in the field, on television and on the stump, as was out there this year.

BODE: So Bush wins Pennsylvania and is the only moderate left in the race because at this point John Anderson—

KEENE: But we never referred to him as a moderate, and John Anderson didn't either. (Laughter)

BODE: John Anderson has made his decision, now, to go the independent route. Howard Baker endorses Ronald Reagan.

BAILEY: Before Pennsylvania. It is, I think, the automatic assumption of candidates who drop out that the race is over. It was very clear that the train was leaving the station, and the time to get on was right then.

—BUSH IN MICHIGAN AND TEXAS—

BODE: We're going to skip to one last primary, and that's Michigan, where George Bush once again loaded up for bear and went after Ronald Reagan. Everybody else knew it was over by that time, David. Isn't it true that when you had the support of a governor like Milliken and the kind of money you could outspend Reagan with in a state as big as Michigan, you were really trying to nail down the vice-presidency by—

KEENE: We were really trying to nail down Michigan. We weren't playing for the vice-presidency, but we were certainly playing, to an extent, to make a point, and playing for George Bush's future. We were demonstrating clearly that he was a pretty good candidate, that he could put it together, and that he had appeal in certain parts of the country, regardless of whether he was later picked as vice-president. It's easy, you know, after the selection is made, to say, Well, weren't you guys really shooting for that? The answer is no, but certainly we had his future in mind; he was a young candidate and had a lot going for him. We wanted to demonstrate that. We wanted to make certain that he would have future influence, that he was somebody that the people were going to say, "There's a candidate who ran a good race, a fair race, and got a great deal of support and won some primaries."

BODE: How about you, Bill Casey, were you impressed that George Bush could appeal to certain kinds of constituencies from that?

CASEY: Yes. I think George Bush had to do what he did in Pennsylvania. If he had dropped out after Illinois, at a time when he was finished as far as getting the nomination was concerned, he'd have come out as a weak candidate, a real loser. As it turned out, what he did in Pennsylvania, Texas, and Michigan commanded everybody's respect for him as having real campaigning ability and as being somebody with strength.

HUNT: Dick, I was really startled, since I thought that Texas was one of Ronald Reagan's strongest states, that Bush ran such a close race down there. What was that? Was that just due to lack of resources, or was there some—

WIRTHLIN: Lack of resources was surely part of it. Secondly, however, Texas is Bush's home state. He ran for statewide office there. He also hailed from Houston, which was the fastest growing area in the state, and was able to pull in a lot of the suburbanite Republican vote there as well as in Dallas.

HUNT: Did that showing weigh in your mind when you came to the vice-presidency? He'd done well in Pennsylvania, Michigan; you knew he was strong there. Did Texas—

WIRTHLIN: That was one of the factors. However, independent of that, our national survey research showed that with George Bush, we had a moderate who could, in fact, attract a constituency in the suburbs North and South, and—as we'll perhaps discuss later—winning Texas and Florida were the two lynch-pin states in terms of our geographical strategy in winning the presidency. So we looked with a great deal of interest on his vote pull there.

TEETER: That answered the question about whether or not George Bush was really a Texan. You began to see during that campaign, as we began to run some media in those markets outstate, that he was viewed, even in other areas outside Houston and Dallas, as a Texan. I mean, he was seen not as a native but as a legitimate Texan there. And that had been a debated question not only in the campaign but in the media for a long time.

BODE: Well, we've got George Bush positioned for the vice-presidency now, and that means it's time to take a break.

4 THE REPUBLICAN CONVENTION

Plans for Detroit. The Platform Committee. Abortion and E.R.A. Ford on the Ticket. Cronkite and the Co-Presidency. Political Impact of Reagan-Ford Mishap. Sharing of Power? The Focus on Bush.

CATHERINE MACKIN (network correspondent, ABC News): We wanted to start with the preconvention week, with the platform, and with some of the decisions that went into it and how that affected the convention. Some of the decisions, of course, addressed women, the defense issues, and abortion. Bill Brock, would you care to start off on how you think decisions on the platform affected the course of the convention and, perhaps even later, the general election?

—PLANS FOR DETROIT—

BILL BROCK (chairman, Republican National Committee): I was not particularly happy. We had very, very carefully worked to break several Republican stereotypes—by holding the convention in Detroit for one thing, trying to keep the focus, as always, on November. Detroit offered minority opportunities, blue-collar, labor unions, and primarily the economic mix of issues that we had determined in

Bob Teeter's work back in November of '79 were going to be the definitive issues. So when we got to the platform, I was obviously distressed to see the primary debate focused on what was described as the social issues. I felt that we were risking the under-forty target group that we had identified as our priority goal. And the more we talked about those issues, the more damage we did. I discussed at considerable length with the Reagan people the possibility of a quieter approach to the platform. We simply lost control of the situation. The people that were named to the platform committee were the ideological leaders of their states, self-defined, and they were not subject to the normal constraints of the campaign or of the party process. I don't know whether I can add much, except that it was a matter of real concern to us at the time. We were able to get it behind us quickly, fortunately, and it didn't, I don't think, in the long term do the damage that I had expected except on the women's issue, which did cost us into early October very, very handily.

MACKIN: Mr. Wirthlin, did you want to say something?

RICHARD B. WIRTHLIN (deputy director of strategy and planning, Reagan–Bush Committee): Well, I think that the goals that Bill has described were also very much our own. We looked at the convention as the single best vehicle we had—bar none—to present and position the candidate, and reinforce, both visually and verbally, the attractiveness that we felt Ronald Reagan would inherently have among nonpartisan, younger voters. I think if there's a single lesson to be drawn from not only our convention but also the Democratic convention, it is that these are, to a large extent, not completely controllable events. Given the way the platform committee was selected, we found some of our most ardent supporters, in their enthusiasm, if you will, building positions and creating media events that were inimical to what we recognized as early as March to be in our best interest for the fall campaign. We were caught, to some extent, on the horns of a dilemma because we had, really, three major objectives as far as the convention was concerned. First, to reinforce the perception held by the American electorate that the Republicans were united that year. I think that working in close conjunction with Bill Brock and with the other candidates who lost, through our unity dinners and those kinds of events, we had given, I think, strong support to the idea—widely held—that the Republicans, now that the primary was over, would fall in and support Ronald Reagan regardless of ideological cant or flavor.

The other major event was to lay the base for the general campaign. We had set out in March the strategic objectives of the general campaign, which indicated that we had to broaden the Republican base. There was no possible way Ronald Reagan could have won without bruising, if not breaking, the Democratic coalition of vote support in the South, among union members, among lower income voters. Catholics and urban ethnics also formed another key target for us. And the way the platform discussion went did not help us achieve that particular objective. Some of the balance we needed was established through the acceptance speech. We had our biggest single audience that particular evening, and the speech that Ronald Reagan drafted and delivered we found to be extremely effective in reaching out and raising the interest and the support of that larger coalitional body that we needed to have to win in November. Lastly, because we anticipated a personal and strongly confrontational campaign mounted against us from the Carter side, we attempted to preempt some of those charges by using various speakers to begin assailing, quite directly, what we considered the vulnerabilities of the Carter record. So, briefly, those were the major things we hoped to accomplish. Some of them we did relatively well; others we failed in doing.

— THE PLATFORM COMMITTEE —

DAVID S. BRODER (associate editor and national political correspondent, *Washington Post*): Is there something inherent about a platform committee that made it impossible for you all to manage it, or was it that somebody else was managing it who had a different agenda from your own?

LYN NOFZIGER (press secretary, Reagan–Bush Committee): It was inherently unmanageable because of the people on it.

BROCK: It stems from this explosion of the primaries, where we elect people as delegates by putting them on the ballot rather than requiring that they go through the party process. When you do that, you almost by definition elect your ideological activists. Certainly, in each state, there's always one—and that one's going to get on the platform committee.

BETTY HEITMAN (co-chair, Republican National Committee): Plus there are a lot of people who were elected delegates to this convention who had never been active in party politics, who knew nothing of the background of what had gone on before or what should come after. And they were answerable to themselves, really—would not take direction from anyone.

ROBERT M. TEETER (president, Market Opinion Research): Were there important planks in the platform, positions that you thought were very important?

Obviously there were some things that didn't make a whole lot of difference, but did you go to the platform hearings with the idea that there were some policy positions that you wanted to make absolutely sure were in there, or some that you were absolutely sure should not be in there?

WIRTHLIN: There were three major issues of concern that we held. One, we did want to focus on the economic issues, to begin laying the base not only for an attack on the failures of the Carter administration but to begin to form the elements of a cohesive strategy for economic growth that would deal with both the issues of unemployment and inflation. Secondly, we felt it was important to spell out in the platform a defense-foreign relations plank the governor could deal with. And thirdly, we hoped to defuse the Equal Rights Amendment issue, which, of course, we were not able to do at all. But those were the primary objectives we had in terms of setting a frame of reference. You'll recall that in 1976, Governor Reagan had run very hard on the platform, and we felt to be consistent we had to have a platform that we could, more or less, live with. We felt we could not walk away from it. We also felt that the Democrats would take whatever weaknesses were there and tie them around us, as they did on such things as the abolition of the fifty-five-mile-an-hour speed limit and other items.

BROCK: One of the mistakes that we made was in being too prepared. I think we did the right thing, with the extensive platform hearings around the country. We came in with a pretty well-prepared document. We worked very closely with the Reagan people to develop its tone and content and style, and frankly, made the mistake of eliminating things for people to do that would keep them occupied. That's a very honest statement. We just didn't give them enough busywork, so they had time to create all kinds of problems with fifty-five-an-hour speed limits and the E.R.A.

—ABORTION AND E.R.A.—

NOFZIGER: But there's one other thing here, and that is we were dealing with two no-win issues. Neither abortion nor the E.R.A. are Republican issues. They are individual issues, and they cut across party lines, and within the parties they cut across lines. No matter what we did—even if we'd ignored them—we couldn't have won.

MACKIN: Did you feel that way from your polling—that there was no way you could get to women who would be in favor of the E.R.A. as a group? Do you think of those people as just being totally Democratic? Lost to you?

WIRTHLIN: Oh, not at all. That's one of the hallmarks of single issues. They cut across a lot of different coalitions. And one of the things we did assess and measure early was the fact that there's a huge difference between those who favor or oppose one of those issues versus those who will vote on that issue. And what we found on the E.R.A. issue was that you had about 12 to 13 percent who were E.R.A. activists, and they broke about two-to-one in favor of E.R.A. Almost the mirror image of that on the issue of right-to-life. But at this stage it was, I think, recognized that it was not in our interest to highlight or raise the visibility of either of those issues in the context of the Republican convention.

BROCK: For example, on abortion—which is, I guess, the most emotional of all the issues—something like 63 percent of our delegates supported the Supreme Court decision. So the problem that we had, the decision we had to make, was whether or not to let it go from the platform to the floor. Basically, the decision was not to let it go to the floor—even though it would have heightened the issue. A lot more people would have seen the fight on the floor than would ever read the platform. And that's just about what it came down to.

ALBERT R. HUNT (correspondent, *Wall Street Journal*): Were there efforts where you tried to deal with some of the ideological hard-core there on any of these issues, and tried to get them to back off and were unsuccessful?

WILLIAM J. CASEY (campaign manager, Reagan–Bush Committee): I don't remember. (*Laughter*)

NOFZIGER: Well, there was some success. If you will look at the language in both of those issues, it was compromise language. It wasn't compromised enough for a lot of people, but nevertheless it was. . . .

ADAM CLYMER (correspondent, *New York Times*): I think you also got the language on the anti-abortion judges mushed up some. We still knew what you meant, and—

NOFZIGER: No, you just think you knew what we meant, but we didn't say what we thought you thought you knew—

CASEY: Well, I was one of the ones that wanted to clear it up on the floor, but it would have just heightened the issue.

BROCK: That's exactly what we're saying.

MACKIN: You said that you lost control. Was that exaggeration? Do you mean that?

BROCK: We could make some limited modifications as long as we stayed with their basic value goals. We could get them to agree to a little nuance, here and there, that would soften it. But otherwise it was out of control in terms of the campaign's ability. Bill had people in that committee all the time, and they were working assiduously on a couple of issues where there was no way to stop the movement.

HUNT: Were those just the social issues, Bill, or were there also some defense and foreign policy issues?

BROCK: No, we weren't that worried about defense and foreign policy.

CASEY: No problems there.

BROCK: No. It was the social area that we were concerned about.

BRODER: From what you were seeing, Pat, did you think that they made a mistake in not trying to take, say, the abortion issue to the floor and clean it up, or —

PATRICK H. CADDELL (president, Cambridge Survey Research): I think that once they had already had the committee situation they had given us as much of the issue as we were probably going to get. My feeling was that, in fact, they did the right thing by not heightening it anymore, that the one thing they did not need was to really open the issue for us in a way. They left us with sort of an issue, but one which we had to take and really intensify or give attention to or whatever. But if they'd gone to the floor and if they'd had an eruption, which is one of the things we were hoping for all along, that would have helped us a great deal, and would have given it a credibility as an issue that we could have played off of right away.

HEITMAN: May I disagree a little bit on what has been said?

MACKIN: Sure.

HEITMAN: Number one, I think we were aware, going into the convention, that we were going to be in trouble with the women's vote in the general election. And one of the things Bill and I were concerned about was the number of women delegates that we had at the convention, and we were tracking the number of women who were elected as delegates when it became apparent that we would not have as many women as we wanted. Bill and I then both made a concerted effort to encourage the state leadership to try and really push the election of women. In fact, I had contacted some of the Reagan people who I felt were in control of some of the primaries that were yet to come, and asked them to actively seek women delegates and support women delegates, which in many instances they did. Even though we had fewer women delegates at this convention than we'd had in 1976, it was approximately the same number that we had had before.

The other thing is that we recognized that we were going to have a problem with the E.R.A. I personally did not feel that abortion was ever an issue with most people. When the convention was over and I went out on the speaking circuit, I never had a single reporter ask me one thing about the abortion issue—it was all E.R.A. Every question was on E.R.A. We knew, going in, that they were going to take out the endorsement of the Equal Rights Amendment, even though Governor Reagan himself had said that while he personally did not favor ratification of the Equal Rights Amendment, he had no problem if the delegates and the party wanted to leave the platform as it was in 1976. We felt pretty strongly, given the delegates who were elected, that was not going to happen. But what we did was go to work about six weeks before the convention to draft wording for a strong women's plank that would do everything short of endorsing ratification of the Equal Rights Amendment, but which indicated a very strong support for equal rights for women, which is traditional within the Republican party. We submitted this, what we called a Bill of Rights for Women, to the platform committee. We did get a strong women's plank in the platform. The final product was not as strong as what we had submitted, which, incidentally, Ronald Reagan had signed off on, but we did get for the first time a separate plank on equal rights for women.

The other thing that we did, before the convention was over, was to invite the women leaders there who were working very hard and very outfront for the Equal Rights Amendment to sit down at a meeting with Governor Reagan and talk to him about their concerns, and about his position regarding the Equal Rights Amendment. We had people like Margaret Heckler, who can be very strident on the issue, feels very strongly about it; we had Helen Milliken; we had a number of women who are very strong proponents of the Equal Rights Amendment. After we met with Governor Reagan, I think every one of those women, while not satisfied with the governor's position, were reassured in their minds that the governor was going to do exactly what he said, and work at the state level to try and address the problem of equal rights for women. So I think there were some pluses that came out of it, and I think most of it was through the personality and obvious sincerity of Governor Reagan.

ROBERT J. KEEFE (political consultant, Carter–Mondale Re-election Committee): Was your activity on behalf of securing additional women delegates enforcement of an Affirmative Action program or through institution of quotas? (*Laughter*)

HEITMAN: Republicans are very strongly opposed to quotas. They believe very strongly in the merit system.

KEEFE: Affirmative Action?

HEITMAN: Affirmative Action, but not with a quota. . . . (*Laughter*)

DOUGLAS BAILEY (president, Bailey, Deardourff & Associates): Seems to me I've heard this song before.

HEITMAN: One of the biggest problems that we have in the Republican party is that most of our at-large delegates go to elected officials, and unfortunately most elected officials are men.

KEEFE: We have that problem, too.

MACKIN: On to the subject of Ford, and how that happened, why it happened. Who would like to begin? Mr. Casey?

—FORD ON THE TICKET—

CASEY: All the polls indicated Ford was clearly the vice-presidential choice who would add the greatest strength in the polls at that time. There was a strong disposition to see if he could be persuaded to be on the ticket. He had asked not to be considered. Nevertheless, there was a strong movement in the party from a lot of quarters which felt that it should be put to him strongly that if he wanted to defeat President Carter so badly he would have to make the great sacrifice and go on the ticket. He added some fuel to that fire himself on a talk show on Sunday, when he proclaimed he would do anything—anything—to bring about the replacement of President Carter. And that started to bubble around the convention, the feeling that if properly put to him he might come along. When he was asked to join the ticket, he was asked to sleep on it. He did, and he sent emissaries back to talk about his feeling that he didn't want to do it and that it would be difficult, but that he was ready to explore a vice-presidential role—if a meaningful role could be developed—that would justify the sacrifice he was making. There were discussions about what that role might be.

At the very beginning, when I first talked to President Ford after he stepped out of the race, said he wasn't going to run himself, he'd indicated that he wanted to be helpful, and he felt that there were two areas in which he was particularly able to be useful in the campaign and in a Republican administration: the appropriations area, which had been his strong suit in the Congress, and in the defense area. So the conversations went on around how we could find a role that wouldn't be an ornament, that would give him something specific to do.

CLYMER: Could I jump in before we trace the whole thing out? At the point when you folks were looking at Wirthlin's polls and whatever else you heard, and thinking it would be a good thing if you could get him, was the argument ever raised internally that, despite the polls, this would be an essentially unworkable idea once the public thought about it? Was the concern ever expressed that as a former president he might outshine the candidate?, Were the political arguments raised before you went ahead with it that said this might not be a terrific idea?

CASEY: Yes, those considerations were voiced and explored. They were not given the weight at the time that I think they deserved and they ultimately came to have as a closer examination revealed the difficulties and the public perception that might be created. The one that, in retrospect, strikes me most forcibly is that now there's no question as to what kind of mandate Ronald Reagan has. If we had a Ford–Reagan ticket, there'd be all kinds of discussions about what the mandate meant.

MACKIN: Mr. Wirthlin, as I watched the Republican convention with three television sets, I wondered if Ronald Reagan would ever be able to recover from this. I mean, it was an incredible display to watch this thing in your living room, thinking it looked as though he had really lost control. I would say that the concluding speech helped, but again, from the point of view of management and the decisions that went into this, weren't you terribly concerned as this thing evolved, how he was looking to the people you were going to ask to vote for him?

WIRTHLIN: There were concerns, and I think that day in American politics is going to be examined historically very carefully. Most of the action that was taking place was taking place behind closed doors out of the vision of the unseeing eye of television, with a good deal of rumor running rampant as to what exactly was the course, what the status of those discussions might have been.

MACKIN: Let me interrupt you right there. You could have controlled that by cutting it off, by ending the speculation and the rumor at any moment, if you decided that it was adversely affecting the candidate. Why didn't you?

WIRTHLIN: Keep the time frame in mind. Ford was approached initially, as I recall, on Tuesday; he slept on it overnight Wednesday; Wednesday morning we'd expected either a yes or a no—and we got a maybe. Discussion proceeded through the day under rather tight security. And then the former president determined that he would like, for whatever reasons, to let some of the process show in his interview with Walter Cronkite, which caught us somewhat by surprise.

NOFZIGER: Somewhat, hell! (*Laughter*)

HUNT: Can you just describe to us a little bit about, on Wednesday, who was saying what to whom—the papers that were exchanged, the proposed arrangements. Who was for it, who was against it? What Governor Reagan was saying to you all throughout that day, and how he felt about it?

WIRTHLIN: Well, I was, to some extent, out of the loop for a critical point of time, and I think if he feels so inclined, Bill Casey might describe it. Very briefly, as we understood it, they met almost through the night, Tuesday night and Wednesday early morning—

the Ford group. Again, we expected to hear an answer relatively early Wednesday morning. I had had another commitment, left the suite at eleven o'clock or thereabouts, and when I came back around two o'clock, a contact had been made. The issue was, "What could a possible role be if Ford could say yes, if he would be willing to be the vice-presidential nominee?" A short paper had been orated dealing with this issue. Unlike some of the discussion that centered on that paper, there were no massive changes in roles and responsibilities, and in fact it was explicitedly stated that nothing should be done to change any of the Constitutional rights or prerogatives of the president. That initiated a series of discussions that occurred from that moment through, as I remember, about 11:10 that evening when it was evident that we did have to cut it off. That's when there was no question that we had to move, and move quickly, or the whole issue would have been spilled over to Thursday, impinging on what we had felt—and I think correctly so—to be the seminal event of the convention, namely, the acceptance speech. And when it was evident that we could not come to a conclusion, we broke off the discussion.

HUNT: Were you using terms like "chief executive officer" and "chief operating officer" of the government?

MACKIN: "co-presidency"?

WIRTHLIN: I don't think the word "co-presidency" was used.

—CRONKITE AND THE CO-PRESIDENCY—

CASEY: The word "co-presidency" was used between Gerald Ford and Walter Cronkite. There was no such term in any discussions any of us had. No sharing of power was ever discussed. It was perfectly clear that if Ford had a role, it would be somewhat akin to the role Walter Mondale has had in the Carter administration and no more. The words, "relationship between a chief executive officer and chief operating officer," were used by way of illustration. But that was to illustrate that the chief executive officer makes all the decisions.

MACKIN: Which words were used specifically? Chief operating officer?

CASEY: Chief executive officer and chief operating officer. In fact, Jim Baker will be something like chief operating officer in the Reagan White House. Reagan will be chief executive; he will make the decisions.

MACKIN: Just to repeat again so there will be no question about it: those two descriptive phrases were used in the negotiations with Ford?

CASEY: Not in the negotiations with Ford. Just by way of defining to each other the kind of relationship that we were talking about. These words were used by way of analogy. I believe Alan Greenspan introduced them to reflect a generally understood relationship of the business world, between the person who has ultimate authority in terms of power and the person who implements, and runs the store on a day-to-day basis.

CLYMER: Didn't you have some people on your staff who were afraid that, as one or two of them said, you were giving away the store?

CASEY: Oh, that could well be, but I don't think they knew what was happening. They weren't in on the conversations. There was never any question on anybody's part of giving away any stores. And I might say this: nobody asked that the store be given away. Ford wasn't asking; his people weren't asking for anything that was unusual or improper.

HUNT: Lyn, what was Governor Reagan's attitude, both on the prospect of Ford and the role that Ford might play if he should choose to accept it, throughout that day? You were around him most of the day. How did the governor feel about it? What role was he playing in this whole process?

NOFZIGER: The governor was looking very carefully at the idea of a Ford candidacy and thought that if something could be worked out that was mutually satisfactory it would be something to go ahead with. But he's a very careful man, and at no time was he saying, "This is something we've gotta do, this is the only way we can win," or anything like that. That never arose. As a matter of fact, to the best of my recollection, while the time frame was very short, it was the governor who finally decided first to cut off the negotiations before Ford did, even though, as I say, they arrived at these things separately and almost simultaneously. But while the governor was talking in his suite about cutting it off, why, our friends who were negotiating—if that's the right word—were on their way down to say that Ford wanted to see him for the same purpose. In any event, the governor was looking at it very carefully. I don't think that he was ever married to the idea that Ford was the only vice-presidential candidate who could help him win.

KENNETH A. BODE (network correspondent, NBC News): How serious were the Constitutional concerns about residency in the same state?

CASEY: That was on Ford's mind all the while, but everybody said they were surmountable.

BODE: How were you going to surmount them?

CASEY: Well, all you've got to do is move. We had an opinion on that; eminent lawyers had no question about that as a matter of legality. There was still a question of whether it would look like too slick a trick. That concerned everybody. And I think that's one of the things that probably concerned Ford.

This was an exploratory talk to see whether something workable, and something novel and effective in the structure of the executive office in the White House, could be developed in a way which would attract Ford's interest and make him feel he was doing something important and perhaps precedent-making. And ultimately it didn't. Ford said he wanted to go down and see Governor Reagan, which he did, and said, "I've thought about this, and I just don't think it'll work. I think I can help you better the way we talked about at the beginning."

BRODER: I'd like to ask a highly non-objective question of Bill Brock. Every reporter that I know, when they first heard about this discussion, reacted, "That is the looniest idea I have ever heard of." Why was it not strangled at birth?

CASEY: I think because reporters are smarter than most other people.

BRODER: I'd like to believe that, but I don't.

CASEY: Well, look, let's try to answer it a little bit. This idea had infatuated the whole convention. Rather than loony, a group of eminent governors, senators, and whatevers thought this was the greatest thing since Swiss cheese, and called on Ford in delegations urging that it was something he had to do for the good of the party.

BRODER: Bill, you were in those meetings. In fact, I think you organized those delegations, if I'm not wrong. What was it you thought might happen? What were you thinking about?

BROCK: This was a subject that we started discussing as early as April. Dick and Bill Casey and I talked about it in April or May. The possibility of a magic ticket was attractive throughout the year. The polls were absolutely overwhelming. Gerald Ford brought a tremendous support base to the ticket. He solved an awful lot of questions about foreign policy experience, things of that sort, that could have been asked in the fall. I thought, and I think most of us very deeply involved thought, that it was an eminently logical thing to try to do. As Bill Casey says, those of us who were involved in the sessions with Ford throughout Wednesday, I guess, knew what we were asking him to do, the degree of sacrifice. But we felt that he could uniquely insure the election by being the vice-president on the ticket. I felt that it would be that much of an advantage, and I think Dick has some data that would at least validate that in part. I felt, frankly, George Bush was the choice coming in. But the possibility of putting a former president on a ticket, with the degree of support that he had in the country, the love that people in this country have for Gerry Ford, was deeply felt.

CASEY: Let me say, too, that there were some, and I was among them, who never really thought that Ford would do it, in the final analysis, but nevertheless thought that the effort should be made. The fact that Ronald Reagan would step up and agree to take Gerald Ford on the ticket contrasted markedly with the event four years ago between Ford and Reagan the other way. It answered once and for all the widespread speculation going on about whether Reagan would try to broaden the party and reach across the party or whether he would stay in what was perceived to be his own ideological corner. Discussing it with Ford and making the offer to Ford did a great deal to cure that, to answer those questions, and that was very important.

BROCK: I really disagreed with the press that were reading it as a disaster. But I think we were approaching a point where it could have become one, and that's why I thought that time was so crucial, and I think we almost went beyond the pale, to be honest with you.

CASEY: Well, I think the disaster consequences came from the misperception about what was going on, from what the press was handing out to the public.

—POLITICAL IMPACT OF REAGAN–FORD MISHAP—

BAILEY: Can we ask Pat Caddell and Dick Wirthlin whether there was a single shred of evidence in all of the polling in the fall as to whether this affected any votes negatively for Reagan whatsoever?

WIRTHLIN: It didn't.

CADDELL: After the Republican convention, I saw in a couple of measurements having to do with Reagan's judgment, post-convention, that there had been some minor impact. In other words, the gains he was getting on other questions he did not get on that, only that. But I differ greatly in terms of what the political impact of this would have been. We were initially concerned in the abstract of a Reagan–Ford ticket, Ford adding "credibility," if you will, as a former president, and help to solve some of Reagan's problems, particularly the doubts that existed about Reagan's understanding of the job and being able to handle it. As it unfolded, however—or as it seemed to unfold that day—I can't tell you with what anticipation we began to look forward to the idea that this was really going to happen, for one major reason. If you remember, we were having some problems, ourselves, at that moment, with Billy Carter and other members of the family, and one of our problems was to get some attention on Reagan where there were some seeds of doubt about Reagan's understanding and grasp of the job.

What was clearly emerging here was something that I didn't think the press would let go if Ford got on there, which was the nature of the deal which had been struck, the Constitutional crosses involved in terms of breaking up the presidency. You could answer all of those questions whatever way you wanted to, but the point is that the public perception would have been: here is Ronald Reagan, who we are not really sure about, clearly having done something that seems screwy and different, and in fact may be breaking up the Constitutional prerogatives of the president. Or something, but appearing very grievous in the sense of competence and understanding. I thought that if that happened it would be a story that would go on for some time, that it would begin to focus enormous attention at a very critical moment for any nominee—that point at which people first really begin to intensify their judgments and attitudes about a potential nominee—in a very negative way.

NOFZIGER: Yeah, but I don't think we'd have ever sent Ford to China.* (Laughter)

CADDELL: You might have wanted to by that time.

EDDIE MAHE, JR. (campaign director, John Connally for President): Since Dave Broder made such a strong statement of the consensus of the entire political press corps that it was absolutely loony—in order to keep the record totally clear and straight for those who read this book in the future, he ought to elaborate on this just a bit as to why he thought it was so loony. Maybe Mr. Caddell has done it to his satisfaction, now, but it seems to me that it was rather a bald statement just laid out there, and it was not really explained for us.

BRODER: My lawyer, Mr. Nolan, will respond.

MARTIN F. NOLAN (Washington bureau chief, Boston Globe): Thank you. I throw myself at the mercy of the court. I remember watching it and remembering what Mr. Ford said to Tip O'Neill once he had been appointed vice-president. He climbed into a limousine out here in Worcester when they were on their way to a golf

---

*From August 16–25, vice-presidential nominee George Bush visited Japan and Mainland China on a fact-finding and goodwill trip on behalf of the campaign which was complicated by remarks made by Governor Reagan concerning U.S.–China relations while Bush was abroad.

tournament, and said, "Tip, you know what this means for my pension?" (*Laughter*)

So the question I asked when I see him romancing Walter Cronkite and talking about co-president was, "Hey, will there be any change in his pension?" I think this was President Ford's moment in the sun, and he was having a good time, and I don't think he really meant it. I do think the media in this sense swept him up rather than vice versa.

CASEY: I felt at that time that he was having a hard time letting it go.

TEETER: First of all, I agree with Bill. I did not think he was going to do it, and I don't think I ever thought that he really would do it. I saw him in Detroit; he came Saturday or Sunday before this all took place. It was clear to me then that he was adamant about not doing it, and that he was very concerned that there might be a draft or some pressure for him to do it which might get out of hand. He was concerned to the point where he contemplated leaving Detroit and going home on Tuesday after he had given the speech on Monday night. I was aware of that concern as late as Sunday. But then sometime in the middle of Tuesday night, I talked to Bill Brock on the phone, and he said, "Would you like to come to breakfast and discuss the Ford situation?" I said, "Sure," but I was really astounded that there was a Ford situation at that point, that it had re-developed in some conversation I believe he had with Alan Greenspan and Henry Kissinger the evening before.

I think that from President Ford's standpoint there were three things that were important all the way through it. His position at any time, including during the day on Wednesday, was, "The answer at this moment is no, I'm not going to do it, but if some of the rest of you think it is important enough, I'm willing to listen and discuss it further." I don't think he was wavering in terms of saying, "I'm going to do it." Secondly, he was very concerned throughout his political career about not doing anything that looked conspiratorial or slick or tricky. The idea of changing his residence—I don't think he ever would have gotten over that hurdle. I recall, sometime when he was building his house in Palm Springs, someone at a low level, a Democratic precinct committeeman or something, was about to start a lawsuit in Grand Rapids, saying that he was not an eligible voter in Michigan anymore and that he shouldn't be allowed to vote in some election. It concerned him a great deal, to make sure that he was not viewed as trying to circumvent the law or do something slick. And thirdly, I think he felt the idea of a sharing of power, whatever the terms we used for the jobs, wouldn't work. He had tried very hard to give Vice-President Rockefeller more power and more authority and responsibility, and it hadn't worked. It wasn't because the staff didn't want it to; it was because institutionally it wasn't going to work.

There was a feeling on the part of a number of people in that meeting, in Bill's suite and with the president, including myself, that if it was important enough to the election for him to do it, if it was important enough to ask him to take a crummy job for four years, fine—but don't try to get him to do it under the illusion that in some way it is not going to be the same job he had before. He had been vice-president and he had been president, so he was fully aware of what both those jobs were about.

CLYMER: President was better.

TEETER: That's right. I think he probably understood better than any of us could have that president was better.

BROCK: He said that on several occasions.

TEETER: That's right.

BROCK: But never did he say, "Maybe." He really didn't.

TEETER: No. In fact, he emphasized, every time that I talked to him—before, during, and at the end of those conversations during the day—in almost exactly these terms: "The answer is no, but if there are people who think it's important enough to discuss it further, I'm willing to do that." But at no time am I aware that he ever wavered.

—SHARING OF POWER?—

MACKIN: Just to make your life difficult with people you may want to do business with, what were the words that you heard used to define the "sharing of power," to use your phrase?

TEETER: Well, I think there were some—I never heard the "co-presidency" used.

CASEY: There was no talk of a sharing of power.

TEETER: There wasn't really a sharing. I think there was some talk about, and I think Mondale did come into it, whether or not he might use the vice-presidency as a type of chief of staff, and the analogy was used of a chief executive and chief operating officer. Those are the only ones I'm aware of.

WIRTHLIN: Explicitly, the conversation was that there'd be no change in authority, powers, rights, or privileges.

CASEY: President Ford repeated time and time again that this would work out all right between him and Ronald Reagan. Where we'd have trouble would be with the staffs. The staffs would be juggling with each other and jousting for position. We talked about how we could get some kind of a common staff so this would not happen. That's not a sharing of power; that's an operational arrangement in an office.

TEETER: I think President Ford is convinced—I don't speak for him, but I think he may be convinced to this day—that one of the reasons that his situation with Vice-President Rockefeller may not have worked out better is because of problems with the staffs. He talked about that all day that day, at every meeting we were in. He understood it better than anybody else, and brought it up a number of times, that there was no way that the president could relinquish any of his power or executive decision.

HUNT: But, Bob, I'm confused here. You people talk in one breath about an analogy to Mondale, and then in another breath you talk about a chief executive and chief operating officer. Well, Mondale was not the chief operating officer of this government.

CASEY: Nobody's talking about the chief operating officer of this government. They were talking about the administrator in the White House, administering the staff in the White House, the White House staff—not the chief operating officer of the government. Dealing with the people instead and handling the assignments in a small staff in the White House.

TEETER: And essentially you're talking about the chief of staff job, that is, the implementer of—

CLYMER: In that case, you people who were inside can enlighten us in the reporting business on something. Where did the rumors about Ford running Defense, running the Office of Management and Budget, running this, running that, come from? Where did the concerns about giving away the store originate from that some of us heard from members of the Reagan staff not present here? I mean, everyone here makes it sound on a minor league level, and yet there were an awful lot of people in Detroit who seem to think you were considering doing a great deal more than that.

CASEY: I thought the press magnified it.

BODE: But we got it from somebody.

HUNT: But you're having Henry Kissinger negotiate what Gerry Ford's staff role's going to be? Come on. I mean, really.

BROCK: I think you've got to try to draw back and remember the kind of pressure cooker we were operating in and the kind of rumors that fly in that situation. In the conversations that Bob and I and our group had with the president—I guess it was mid-afternoon on Wednesday—we went through some discussion on sharing of authority, and he shut it down so cold it made your head swim. He said, "I have been there, I have been in the vice-president's office, I have been in the president's office, I've tried it," and he went through the whole scenario, as Bob says, with Rockefeller. I don't think there was one of us in that room that didn't agree that there was no way we could define roles and responsibilities, write anything down on paper, that would have any value whatsoever. President Ford did want to be a part of the administration if he was going to serve in it, and that was obvious. But to define it, I think he said that was impossible.

CASEY: I'd like to try to answer the question Adam has raised. Sure, there were people who were afraid of it; a paranoia developed.

The perception of Henry Kissinger was such that he would try to finagle something for himself, and that the thing might go beyond anything that was being talked about. It just wasn't true. Henry was there because Ford had called him in to consult. And as soon as he was there, people began to wonder about whether he would wind up with more power than they'd like him to have.

CLYMER: There were some people who thought that a condition was going to be that you make Kissinger Secretary of State.

CASEY: That idea was instantly rejected.*

BRODER: But these were not rumors.

CASEY: You couldn't make a condition like that. We haven't even picked a secretary of state yet. Could we have picked one back in Detroit? (*Laughter*)

NOFZIGER: It would have saved a lot of work.

BRODER: Two things. We know that President Ford had lunch with the *Newsweek* people on the day that was going on. *Newsweek* has reported that Ford believed that he had unique abilities to contribute to the success of the administration in at least the areas of budget-making and national security. But, he said, to be effective in that role, he would have to have available to him staff people in whom he had confidence. Now, if that is not some sort of sharing of power, what in the world were you talking about?

BROCK: Isn't it true that any president can designate a job for the vice-president to do and often does that?

BRODER: In this case it seemed to be the vice-president-designate who was designating the responsibility.

---

*Mr. Casey later stated: "President Ford put the idea forward only by way of illustration of the kind of advice he'd like to have considered. This embarrassed Kissinger, and he came down to say that under no circumstances could he accept an appointment that might be perceived to result from a deal which he was promoting in what he considered to be the national interest."

BROCK: Well, I just did not hear that.

HUNT: The job, Bill, was that—you know, it's not access to the White House tennis courts. The job is the budget-making and national security.

WIRTHLIN: Since this is a conference focusing on political decision-making, I think there are two critical things that should be brought into focus. There was no difference in terms of the consequence whether it was a "maybe" or a "no . . . but." We were chewing up time against a calendar that had a very short fuse on it, and given some of the problems that have been discussed here, it was evident relatively early that it wasn't going to go. Secondly, in regard to the impact this event would have on the game plan and on our objectives, I think from the data I have seen, it would be absolutely none. We tested that issue explicitly—over a period of ten days after the convention, not as it happened but as it was perceived to have occurred by the media—of whether that whole view had damaged Ronald Reagan's position with the electorate. To answer that question: there was absolutely no damage. If you remember, the last national study taken before the Republican primary was taken on the 15th of July by the *Los Angeles Times*; it showed Ronald Reagan running behind Jimmy Carter by ten points. The first study taken after the convention, by NBC, showed Ronald Reagan running ahead of Jimmy Carter by fifty-five to twenty-four.

CLYMER: Do you think he was actually ten points behind before, Dick?

WIRTHLIN: In my judgment it was a dead-even race going into the convention, and that we probably had, in the immediate afterglow of the convention, something between an eighteen- and twenty-two-point lead, which was shortly to be clipped by the next topic of discussion, namely, the Democratic convention.

HUNT: Dick, was Bush always the fallback? I mean, during the whole Ford thing, was it always obvious that if that fell through, you'd go to Bush?

WIRTHLIN: Always? No. But at least in that critical decision period, I think that was the case.

HUNT: By Monday, was it clearly either going to be Bush or Ford?

NOFZIGER: No, not by Monday. Not at all.

BODE: Who was still in it at that point?

NOFZIGER: Oh, just about everybody, really.

—THE FOCUS ON BUSH—

WIRTHLIN: There was not a firm decision on Monday; but Tuesday, Wednesday, the focus was Bush.

BODE: At what point did you hear Reagan say that Bush was his second choice?

WIRTHLIN: I can't pinpoint the hour and the day, but it was evident from things that he was saying Tuesday that it would very, very probably be Bush. When we made the decision between 11:10 and 11:30 Wednesday night to cut the discussion off, it was an easy and a quick decision.

CASEY: It was fairly well settled on Tuesday, if Ford did not do it.

WIRTHLIN: There was no heavy discussion once the discussion with Ford was terminated, as to who he would select.

NOFZIGER: I don't think it was really settled on by Tuesday.

CASEY: I sure had that feeling Tuesday night. Maybe not.

HUNT: Who else on Tuesday did you think had a serious shot at being vice-president?

NOFZIGER: I really don't know, but I do know that Reagan had had some reservations in his own mind right down the line about George Bush, and it took a while to get those resolved.

HUNT: Did it grow out of the Nashua debate?

NOFZIGER: I think there was a problem there, yes. But, you know, he had very strong personal feelings about Paul Laxalt, which he had to resolve in his own mind, also, that that probably wouldn't work; and he had looked at others like Vander Jagt. So in my own mind, I'm not sure the governor was convinced by Tuesday that he was going to go with Bush if Ford wouldn't do it.

BODE: You get the impression when you look at this whole thing that the Ford incident hung so heavily over everybody that there was no movement whatsoever until Ford lifted. Then as soon as Ford lifted, it turned and Bush got grabbed that quickly.

WIRTHLIN: It had to be that. There was no way we could begin opening the discussion with any other individual.

BROCK: We had to get the decision announced to the convention that night.

BODE: You said at one point that you thought you had a forty-five-minute window from the time you decided to the time that the press would announce your choice.

WIRTHLIN: That's right. Probably smaller than that.

MACKIN: What was it?

WIRTHLIN: Well, we beat the window, clearly. The press had rumors when Reagan walked out on that platform, but it was very evident that the press did not know what was going to happen for certain until Ronald Reagan announced his choice.

BROCK: You remember grabbing me by the tie, Mr. Hunt?

HUNT: Yes, I remember that very, very well.

BROCK: "Tell me what the hell's goin' on!" (*Laughter*)

5 THE DEMOCRATIC CONVENTION

The Kennedy Plan. Carter on Kennedy and the Rules Fight. Getting the Democratic Act Together. The Minority Reports. Emotions on Both Sides. Intention to Compromise. A Split Party.

CATHERINE MACKIN (network correspondent, ABC News): Why don't we start up by asking whether or not the Kennedy people actually had a plan when they went into the rules committee, or did they do what they did because they had no alternative in order to just keep going on into the convention?

—THE KENNEDY PLAN—

PAUL G. KIRK, JR. (national political director, Kennedy for President): We started off, after June 3rd, knowing the position was somewhat precarious in terms of being able to carry the campaign through to the convention. When the senator met with the president, he indicated a willingness to try and work things out with the economy and asked again for a debate. Then we went to the platform committee, and I think every vote was two-to-one, in terms of the Carter versus Kennedy forces. In the meantime there was a situation where everyone, every commentator, was saying it was virtually locked up mathematically. The bewilderment on the Kennedy side was if that was the case, then why did we still have a situation where you had the Hamilton Jordan memos put out about how to do a number on Kennedy? There was something still of a get-the "fat-rich-kid" psychology at work in the Carter camp.

What we hoped for was that perhaps, during this period from June 3rd to the convention, people would reflect on what had and hadn't happened. It was a factor in our strategy going forward from June 3rd that we looked back and said, "Jesus, the only good thing that's happened to President Carter in the course of the primary campaign are the Tuesday nights." Every other policy concern had either stayed the same or gotten worse. So we were not going to go forward from June 3rd in any confrontational way with President Carter, but let the Republican convention take place, and at that point Ronald Reagan was well on his way. After the Republican convention, the prediction was—and proved accurate—that the polls would show that basically Carter was way behind, and perhaps the Democrats going forward at the convention would reflect and say, "He can't make it in November." If indeed they had the convention locked up, why this show of insecurity and continual sort of pummeling? We read it as if what we thought might happen, they thought might happen as well.

So we went forward to the convention knowing that the Carter campaign and the Democratic National Committee had a virtual lock on all the apparatus. I met, for a number of weeks, with Carter's representative Dick Moe of Vice-President Mondale's office, and we talked basically about things on the economy, but not much came of it. As we moved forward after the standing committee meetings, we started some more serious negotiations about the convention itself. In the meantime, there wasn't a single voice from the party—perhaps other than Bob Strauss—who was saying, Kennedy's got to get out of the race.* So we went forward with a feeling on the part of the senator that if the party were to come back on track, the only way they could do it was to express themselves at the convention on the issues that were fundamental to the party.

We had a number of tough negotiations about how the convention itself would be structured. What we wanted, basically, was that the convention be fair. The question revolved around F3C considera-

---

*Robert Strauss was national campaign chairman for the Carter campaign.

tions.* The Carter campaign's concern was clear and repeated that they wanted that convention closed and closed as early as possible. Our hope and theory was that if we could break F3C, that there would be a fundamental reversal of what everyone had printed and had said publicly about who had this nomination locked up. If we could break the rule, then carry forward on the platform, this would be two days of victories on the part of a candidate who had been virtually counted out of the race months ago, and then the convention would take on a momentum, and there was a real chance for the nomination.

MACKIN: Maybe I could just ask Tim Kraft before he has to leave, as I covered the platform and the rules myself in committee, I wondered why you all didn't give the other side some of the things—in effect, pull their teeth, you know, give them some of the stuff in the platform that you eventually gave them anyway. You weren't going to give anything on open convention, but you could have given a few other things in there that they were asking for. But instead you played hardball right on in to the convention, where, in front of the whole country, you had to negotiate with Kennedy.

—CARTER ON KENNEDY AND THE RULES FIGHT—

TIM KRAFT (campaign manager, Carter–Mondale Re-election Committee): Okay. Inherent throughout Paul's and Carl Wagner's comments about Kennedy's candidacy and what he wanted, or what he felt was the mainstream of the Democratic party platform requirements, or what he thought was the best economic policy for the country, is a sort of assumption that here is a figure or an oracle that almost has the writ on this, and that why can't these Carter people see what the Democratic party philosophy is, and put the party back on track? as Paul just said. Well, not everybody feels that way, I don't think, among voting Democrats throughout the country, or among the representatives on the different platform committees, or

---

*Section F3C of "The Procedural Rules of the 1980 Democratic National Convention" reads: "All delegates to the National Convention shall be bound to vote for the presidential candidate whom they were elected to support for at least the first convention ballot unless released in writing by the presidential candidate. Delegates who seek to violate this rule may be replaced with an alternate of the same presidential preference by the presidential candidate or that candidate's authorized representative."

among the delegates at the convention that finally assembled in New York. Aside from not believing that Senator Kennedy had defined entirely the soul of the party and its platform requirements, we were also concerned with other factors relating to preparation for the general election.

As I said this morning, at a certain point in late March, early April, it was mathematically impossible for Senator Kennedy to get enough delegates to secure the nomination. We began looking forward to an April-to-August time frame wherein we could divert our resources and our efforts and our energies to raising money for the Democratic party—the Democratic National Committee, state committees—to prepare for what we could obviously see was a well-prepared and well-financed and coordinated Republican party effort. We looked upon the continual criticism and the constant hitting on the president's economic policies and his qualifications as a Democrat and his concern for the working people of this country, as sort of late hits, debilitating hits, efforts which did not help the Democratic party across the board and which certainly hamstrung any efforts that we might make to raise money for the party, both state and national.

We also saw efforts to change a rule which had been agreed upon in previous years—whereby if the delegates were released, the primary would continue all summer long, right up until the August convention, and we would not prepare for the general—as a continuing internecine skirmish, which would leave the nomination virtually not worth having in terms of being ready to face the Republican party and Ronald Reagan. In some instances, those members of the platform committee were not entirely at our beck and call. I mean, people that were supporting President Carter voted as they damn well wanted to. And they rejected some of the propositions that the Kennedy forces wanted to see in the Democratic platform. So it was not entirely as fixed or controlled as one might believe. We were concerned, as I say, about preparations for the general, and we felt like the F3C or the 11H thing was merely one more tactic to prolong the warfare throughout the summer.*

RONALD H. BROWN (deputy campaign manager, Kennedy for President): I think we were surprised, as many others were, by that

---

*Section 11H of the "Delegate Selection Rules of the Democratic National Committee" reads the same as Section F3C of the "Procedural Rules of the 1980 Democratic National Convention." See footnote on p. 169.

strategy, and I feel a little more comfortable in speaking to it since I was not identified specifically by Tim as one who was projecting the senator as an oracle on these issues. I do think that our feeling was that we were helped by that strategy. It was clear that many large segments of Democratic delegates that would be coming to the convention did agree on the issues with the position that the Kennedy campaign had taken, specific groups—women, labor, blacks, hispanics—and there were large numbers of delegates from those particular groups. The hard-line position that you defined was one that would, in effect, play into the strategy that Paul tried to define, in that when we got to the convention, the convention could take a life of its own. That's why it was important to tie the platform issue to the rules issue. Our thrust became: if in fact you don't eliminate this rule that binds you, you will not be able to speak your mind or vote your conscience on the issues. If you do, that could be defined as disloyalty to the candidate for whom you were elected to be a delegate, and could allow you, then, to be yanked from the floor of the convention. This was the line, of course, that we were taking during the campaign leading up to the convention. So I think we were as surprised as many other people at the kind of hard-line approach that was taken during that process.

JOHN RENDON (convention manager, Carter–Mondale Re-election Committee): There are two schools of thought in the negotiations that came up, as I can recall from the meetings that we had early on. When you negotiate, there are several outcomes. One is that you reach a successful conclusion in your negotiations. Another one is that in the course of those negotiations, during which you are claiming you have strength, people see that on some of these issues you've given in, which could very easily be characterized as your losing in the platform committee. Does this, in fact, mean that you have any strength at all? In the drafting subcommittee in some of those late-night sessions, we tried to reach an accommodation on a number of issues. We found subsequently as they started coming up again that there would always be a hard-line position, or that's the way we perceived it. So at one point, somebody characterized the drafting subcommittee as being a discussion between White House domestic policy advisor Stuart Eizenstat and Peter Edelman, Kennedy's representative, with Stuart having veto power. After having gone through the platform process, we just decided it would be best to hold all these negotiations to bring them to bear all at one time. Because if you give up something in the course of negotiations without having all the cards on the table, you would wind in the situation of constantly moving—

BROWN: John, to say that Carter delegates who were members of the platform and rules committee, were not clearly instructed, is just not the case. The image that Tim left was that people were voting of their own free will during this process. It was very clear there was heavy pressure to take a straight line on all of these issues.

ROBERT J. KEEFE (political consultant, Carter–Mondale Re-election Committee): On both sides.

RENDON: That's right. Earlier this morning, somebody said that a lot of our delegates, in terms of their profiles—the questionnaires they sent back to the Democratic National Committee—indicated that they tended to be more closely aligned with the senator's positions. I think that's true. But any time we went into a situation where we thought that a vote was extremely important, and we said this is a question that would rest or fall with respect to the nomination, our delegates were extremely loyal.

KENNETH A. BODE (network correspondent, NBC News): But, on extension of time, was that the kind of vote that you regarded as—

RENDON: I'll refer to that. Carl came up with two suggestions. I think we were in the rules committee, right? One was to expand the thirty-minute rule on the economic section to ninety minutes.

CARL WAGNER (director of field operations, Kennedy for President): Right.

RENDON: And F3C to an hour.

WAGNER: Right.

RENDON: At that point I think I asked you whether or not that meant that we would knock down the five or six minority reports we had on the economic section to one, and you weren't sure whether or not that was part of it. I think I'm being accurate.

—GETTING THE DEMOCRATIC ACT TOGETHER—

DAVID A. KEENE (national political director, Bush for President): One of the things that you spend a lot of time worrying about, as you approach the point where your candidate can't win it anymore, is how do you get out in a way that makes your candidate look all right and saves his future and yet helps the party so they can't come back after they lose and say it was all your fault? We understand the two guys don't seem to like each other very much. But wasn't anybody saying, Look, we got to get our act together?

WAGNER: Let me just shed some light on the calculation about the nomination because it was not resolved in our mind on June 3rd. There were really three concerns we had after June 3rd. The first, one that occupied a good deal of Paul's time, was the question of a political firestorm in the party, asking Senator Kennedy to get out now that the primaries were over. Much to our surprise, quite frankly, even from individuals and institutions who had endorsed the president, there was virtually no one in the party of any prominence who called on Senator Kennedy to withdraw from the race, collapse his campaign, and fold our efforts into the Carter campaign. That was in large part, at least in my judgment, a result of what was rather considerable political erosion in the Carter delegation on some critical issues; a good deal of the reason for that stemmed in part from the economic issue and the prominence it had been receiving. Not unimportant was the emergence of Billy Carter as a political issue. Just prior to President Carter's press conference on Billy Carter there was, in fact, by our own calculation, rather considerable erosion to the point where I don't think the president had more than 1,750 votes for his position on the rules fight. It was rolling away. . . .

KEENE: So you still thought you could break it open?

WAGNER: Oh, yes, it was rolling very hard and very fast.

KEENE: But did you think you could break it open only on those things, or on the whole—

WAGNER: It was very unclear to us if, in fact, we could tie together a victory on Monday on the rules and what dynamic we would set

loose Tuesday on the platform. I think it would have been very difficult for us, but nevertheless the nomination prior to the Carter press
conference on his brother was by no means locked up. I do think,
however, that Carter's press conference on Billy stopped the erosion
cold and did much to put their base back together. In fact, our survey of the convention delegates right after the press conference was
only thirteen votes off from the actual vote at the convention. After
we passed that threshold, then indeed did both the rules fight and
the nomination look very difficult. But moving through those platform committees, the standing committees, and then the negotiations Paul described with Dick Moe and Jordan, we had very definite
goals. One was the structure of the convention. The first offer to me
by the Carter campaign was twelve floor passes for us and the print-
ing press for them! I thought it a rather difficult circumstance in
which to manage 1,200 delegates, but nevertheless we had very little
leverage.

KEENE: They couldn't give because it could all fall apart on them;
is that why they were locked?

—THE MINORITY REPORTS—

WAGNER: Well, we had to create a circumstance where we would
have leverage, and we used the committees to do it so that the Kennedy campaign could dominate the agenda of the convention. We did
it essentially with minority reports. Much to my surprise, our positions at both platform and rules were received with a very hard line
by the Carter campaign, and they just voted them down, down,
down, down, and made available to us the opportunity to file minority reports and thereby secure leverage for a very big piece of the
convention time.

ALBERT R. HUNT (correspondent, *Wall Street Journal*): I remember in '76 the one thing the Ford people did when it came to platform fights as opposed to important fights like procedural fights, was
just to cave on everything. Did the Carter people ever consider caving
on all those platform fights?

ADAM CLYMER (correspondent, *New York Times*): The Ford people caved on some in committee and some on the floor. You could do it at either level.

KEEFE: I don't think the Kennedy people would allow us to cave on the minority reports. The minority reports were essential to their strategy and the Carter people could not cave—

HUNT: Once they opted for that opposition, you could take a dive.

KEEFE: At the end. Sure.

HUNT: You could take a dive in committee.

PATRICK H. CADDELL (president, Cambridge Survey Research): Minority reports are filed after the committee meets.

KIRK: And you could have taken those away from us by accepting them, is what Al is saying.

KEEFE: I just don't think that was ever really a question. Do you, John?

RENDON: No.

MACKIN: Wait, wait a minute. Why was it not practical?

KEEFE: What you don't understand is that strategically they needed the minority reports to operate, and they could file minority reports on any one of a hundred subjects.

KEENE: Yes, but by caving to them, you could force them to a nutty position. That's what Ford did in '76. They move over, and then if you want to fight that, you gotta write this nutty stuff up that nobody's gonna look at anyway.

WAGNER: I agree. That was the real pressure, the dilemma we would have faced had they not taken a hard line on all of the platform and credentials issues, would have been to contrive the preposterous issues positions at the platform committee. I think we probably couldn't have done that politically.

KIRK: From our point of view, if that had happened and we still were trying to barter for a timetable, then any plank or minority report we tried to put up would have been more and more frivolous, and we would have walked ourselves clearly into the exploiter role.

RICHARD G. STEARNS (chief of delegate selection, Kennedy for President): I think the best illustration is go back to F3C itself. All F3C was, was a rewrite of a rule we already had, rule 11H of the delegate selection rules. When the White House introduced 11H to the delegate selection rules, someone neglected to amend the convention rules, to bring it into sync with the new selection rules themselves. Our argument when we stumbled on this issue was, look, we have a delegate selection rule that says a presidential candidate or his agent can remove a delegate, an unfaithful delegate, but we don't have a convention rule that says that. Without a convention rule, the rule is unenforceable at the convention itself. What always struck me is the position I think I would have taken if I'd been in the White House, which is, "Oh, yeah, we'll see. We'll get to the convention and we'll see whether we have a rule or not." The worst that would have happened if you'd tried to enforce the delegate selection rule at the convention is that you would eventually have had an appeal of the ruling of the chair. Whether the chair would sustain the enforcement of the rule or not, which is a nondebatable motion, it would have been an up or down vote and that would have been the end of any debate over so-called F3C. Instead, for some reason, you guys decided, "My God, they must be right; we must need a convention rule in addition to the delegate selection rule. Therefore, we have to force a new convention rule through the rules committee." And that's what gave us the opportunity to bring the minority report, you know, and lay the foundation for the debate at the convention. But I think it could have been avoided very easily by just ignoring it.

CLYMER: Pat, in your counsels, again, did anyone say: "Look, we're right on the principle of bound delegates. But the way these guys are capable of framing the issue we're gonna end up looking silly. The PR arguments are on their side; therefore, we shouldn't fight, we shouldn't choose this fight."

—EMOTIONS ON BOTH SIDES—

CADDELL: There was some discussion of that. But let me say that I am not the best person to speak on it. I was worried about general election speeches and a few other things. I think we seem to be re-living here the emotions on both sides. There was a feeling on the part of the Carter campaign, at that point prior to the convention, that the Kennedy people would do whatever they could to destroy Carter, whether he was nominated or not. Whether that was true or not. On the other side there was certainly a set of feelings about the Carter campaign. You cannot deal with this as a rational process without having some sense of the emotions. The other factor in this is the president himself. On the platform questions, there were issues that the president was not going to yield on. He was not. There was some concern at some levels in the White House about abandoning positions we had taken policywise which would leave us open to other kinds of charges from the Republicans down the road in a general election. The fact of the matter was that on some of those issues Jimmy Carter wasn't going to do it. It wasn't really debatable. It was raised, but it was killed pretty quickly.

On the rules selection question, I think the feeling was that we had all operated under the same rules, the understanding on the delegate selection process, and that there was a lot of conviction as well as political tactic that it was the right thing. It had been the rule, and it had been understood to be that way. We weren't going to change it at this point. There was also the concern, frankly, I think in some circles, that once you open the door too much, serious erosion can begin. Remember, we are in the middle of the Billy Carter thing. We have a president who is in very, very deep trouble, intensified by the margin that we are now trailing Reagan, in that post–Republican convention phenomenon that we seem to have picked up in both '76 and '80. All of that lent to trying to keep it on an even keel and not open the door to floodgate. We never questioned the fact that Senator Kennedy could not get the nomination, and to this day I cannot believe that people would sit here and argue, knowing what the delegate's opinions were, that Senator Kennedy could be the nominee. We were somewhat concerned that if it took on a life of its own, we might find ourselves in a different situation, perhaps with somebody else, or at least a long battle.

HUNT: Patrick, I'm still interested in this platform issue. You're telling us that a president who submitted three budgets in seven months was really going to go up the wall on a Democratic party platform plank?

CADDELL: If that is the point you want to raise, I cannot argue with it. The point of the matter was that anybody sitting there involved with the discussion knew that there were certain issues on which the president would compromise on some of those, and others he would not at all.

HUNT: My question is, Was that a matter of substance or was that a matter of tactic?

CADDELL: It was some of both on the president's side, but it was more substance than it was tactic. I think in part he felt he had paid the price on these issues for a long time, and he believed they were right and he was not going to overturn them now.

CLYMER: I'm confused. I thought you were saying earlier, and maybe it's just a difference of time periods, when we were looking at the situation at about April, that if you took a whole series of losses, there was a possibility that you might lose the nomination. Now is it your view that once the delegates were selected, there was no series of calamities which could have cost you the nomination?

CADDELL: There was a 90 percent probability that you could not lose a nomination under any circumstances. There was a real belief that there was a 10 percent chance of a set of circumstances or forces that could go in motion which could open this thing up again, not for a Kennedy nomination but for some other outcome. Some people tended to believe that more than others, internally—and I won't get into who felt what, but there were some people who felt that way.

KEENE: To the extent that you think you can't lose, compromise becomes more rational.

—INTENTION TO COMPROMISE—

CADDELL: There was always the intention to compromise. The question was, How early and how much and when? You wanted to unify the party, but the feeling of the campaign, at least in some of the hearings at that stage, was that some efforts of compromise had been absolutely rejected out of hand by the Kennedy people. There was that sense, whether true or not, that if you gave up so much then, all it would do is up the stakes even further down the road.

BILL BROCK (chairman, Republican National Committee): But harking back to our own experience from '76, in effect what the Ford people did was to let Reagan write the platform, and then we went on with the nomination.

KEENE: And, in those circumstances in order to have a fight the opposition had to get so far out that it would be self-destructive.

BROCK: Yes, there was no way you could fight that out with any practical effect anywhere on the floor or anywhere else. Did anybody go to the president and say, "Why don't we give him the damn thing, if he'll make the trade on the rule?"

CADDELL: Yes.

MACKIN: Who did that?

CADDELL: I don't feel that I'm in a position to get into that—

MACKIN: It was definitely done? You're saying it was definitely done?

CADDELL: It was definitely raised.

HUNT: Can you tell us where you were on that then?

CADDELL: Listen, I'm a pragmatist. I was willing to do anything that was not going to hurt us and could unify the party. President Carter is not a person who simply follows the dictates of what some people advise, even in consensus, and there were other people who made other political arguments about it.

KEEFE: But the simple fact was that Stuart Eizenstat was personally the president's representative on the platform, which spoke to the point rather eloquently as to how important the president felt about it. I thought that was really swatting flies with a pretty big gun, and I thought it just demonstrated that he felt damn strongly about it.

BROCK: Ford felt strongly about it in '76. He just said, Hell, I'll run on my own platform.

KEENE: I get the impression that we were able to get along better when we were ready to kill each other than you guys did after the war ended. One of the reasons for that this time was that Bill Brock took the initiative to make sure that we didn't forget what the goal was. Granted, that's easier when you're out, but wasn't there anybody who was thinking about these other fellows out there who seemed to be after Carter's job?

KIRK: Right after June 3rd, when the senator and the president met, Dick Moe and I were designated to keep the lines open. We did meet within the next day or two, and the first item of discussion was basically the platform, the economic issues. I was trying to make a case that the president hadn't been out there, that it is tough economically; and the senator has put forth a position, we're going to have to come to grips with it, and so on. When we left the conversation, I said to Dick, If I have to come with the sports page and you have to come with the crossword puzzle, and we don't say anything, we should still meet once a week. It was a good idea and we did. (*Laughter*)

HUNT: Pat had mentioned that you all did consider a debate after June 3rd in order to placate Kennedy. Tell us about that.

CADDELL: There was a discussion, actually at the president's initiative, with the vice-president and myself, Hamilton, Jerry Rafshoon, and Jody Powell. I think those were the participants. It was after the president's meeting with Senator Kennedy and after about a week of this sort of back and forth, right around the time when the platform committee was going to meet, the prospect was raised by the president about an interest he had in considering announcing to Senator Kennedy or calling Senator Kennedy and saying he'd meet in a debate at the platform committee. If we wanted to have a debate, if that seemed to be the one stumbling block to a discussion of the issues, then he would be willing to have it. For about twenty-four to thirty-six hours or so, it was a very live option. Most of the people who were participants were strongly in favor of doing it. I think that some of us felt we dramatically needed to change the downward spiral we were on in terms of the president appearing to have manipulated the process. Also, we were just behind the curve at this point in terms of events moving against us, and this was a chance to break that and get on top and really take some wind out of the sails, if you will, of the Kennedy campaign.

HUNT: Why was it rejected?

CADDELL: There were some people, some who were at that meeting and some who were not, who strongly opposed it for a variety of reasons, including that no president debated a challenger. There were a variety of arguments. Some people just felt very strongly about not doing it, and eventually it died.

—A SPLIT PARTY—

BODE: So you had both camps pretty much separated right down to the convention. Through the platform committee, through the rules committee, right into the convention, you had a party that was pretty bitterly split. There was no neutral arbiter to meet the way Bill Brock was meeting with the Republicans. In retrospect, do you think it hurt you in the general election, first of all, and secondly, do you think it was a mistake to let John White ever abandon a neutral position as D.N.C. chairman so he might have done something like that?

KEEFE: Answer to the first question, sure, the division in a party costs us a lot in the fall. Not so much that the leadership, Senator Kennedy, jumps in and helps us actively work. That's not the problem. They did so and did so very well, but we lost a lot of time while all that was going on. I mean, I'm sure that Senator Kennedy and President Carter making joint appearances through the summer raising money for whoever wins in the fall would have put us in much better financial posture. We could have been working on a lot of stuff. So there are several ways it hurt us in the fall. As to the question of John's partisanship as opposed to Bill Brock's, Bill Brock was elected by the Republican National Committee in an open fight, fair and square, and he was his own man. John White was a chairman designated by the president. I don't know how, after he was first designated as chairman, he could step out and become neutral. I don't know if institutionally you can do that; certainly John White was not able to. He thought he owed some allegiance to the president because the president put him in that job. It would have been very handy to have a strong neutral force acceptable to both camps. There was none, was there? The speaker was at the convention. He was busy doing other things; he really didn't have the opportunity. Wouldn't you say, Paul, that certainly when we got to the convention itself, we were blessed by having Tip O'Neill there because he could communicate with all the principals and had their respect? He did a hell of a job, mind you. But he was not able to begin that process in May, in June, and just did not have the opportunity.

KIRK: I think that's probably right. I think it may be a lesson for the future. I don't know how it works internally, but clearly the National Committee was full bore for the Carter convention nomination and on through, and I think the horse was out of the barn at that point and probably nothing could be done about it.

KEEFE: Problem is you can't take politics out of politics.

KIRK: True.

KEEFE: If John White would have resigned on March 1st because it was impossible for him not to support Jimmy Carter, and the D.N.C. came back and elected, they probably would have elected somebody just as unacceptable to one side or the other.

MACKIN: Now, on to the general election.

6 THE GENERAL ELECTION
August and September

Anderson's Independent Candidacy. The Pollsters' View. Carter's Changing Image. Reagan's Appeal. Reagan's Post-Convention Dip. Defining the General Election. Changes from '76. Questions About the First Debate. Anderson and Baltimore. Anderson's Shift. Carter Versus Reagan. Strategic Changes. Targetting Carter Resources.

MARTIN F. NOLAN (Washington bureau chief, *Boston Globe*): Today, some three thousand miles away, in Beverly Hills, California, there is a very important event taking place we ought to note because there is some relevance. His friends in Beverly Hills are feasting the eighty-fourth birthday of a man who said so much about politics when he suggested that Tuesday might be someone's good-news day. Today is Ira Gershwin's eighty-fourth birthday. Just think of the political themes that we have covered today that Ira Gershwin foresaw fifty years ago—not to mention Alexander B. Throttlebottom, whom he invented. Now, he wrote "Nice Work If You Can Get It," which is, of course, the theme song of politics; and for the losers he wrote "I Can't Get Started," "I Got Plenty of Nothing," and "They All Laughed." For the winners he had "They Can't Take That Away From Me," "Love Is Sweeping The Country," and "It's Wonderful."

In this session we are going to cover something that people in this country last fall and people around here this afternoon want to know—"How Long Has This Been Going On?" So, onto the "Fascinating Rhythm" of the September campaign.

I want to start with the acceptance speeches given at both conventions, but this was a different campaign, and the difference was the Anderson difference. For the first time since 1924 a Republican had broken ranks to form a separate, independent candidacy, not to say party. So we have the perspective of Keke Anderson, whom I'd like to ask quickly why John decided to bolt and run?

—ANDERSON'S INDEPENDENT CANDIDACY—

KENNETH A. BODE (network correspondent, NBC News): Would you like to rephrase that question? (*Laughter*)

MRS. KEKE ANDERSON (National Unity Campaign): Well, being in Boston, maybe I should quote John F. Kennedy, who at one time said, "Sometimes the party asks too much." With that in the back of people's minds here, I think with John it was a question of the issues, the times in which we live; he felt so strongly that the decade upon us was going to face crucial questions that had to be addressed, planned for quickly, and done so without political expediency at the root of the decisionmaking process. That is why he made the decision to run as an Independent, hopefully to keep the issues alive and, I think to some extent, that was accomplished.

DAVID S. BRODER (associate editor and national political correspondent, *Washington Post*): You had to have some discussion, though, about how you were going to get from the point at which that decision was made to the White House. So what were your assumptions, and what did you think would have to happen for it to work?

K. ANDERSON: Well, this may come as a surprise, but I'd counseled against his running as an Independent. I think even my husband didn't believe that I meant it. The reason I counseled against his running was because we had gone through the Republican primaries. First of all, I knew how personally taxing it is on an individual. Also, the perception of "no win" had been built up to the point where I thought going into another campaign was inadvisable. Stories had already been written before John announced his candidacy that no independent candidate could be elected president. Stories about Teddy Roosevelt and other Independents who failed. So I cautioned him not to make the run because if the stories persisted it would have a negative impact on the campaign. He chose to do otherwise, and naturally, of course, I wholeheartedly threw myself into the effort.

BRODER: What were the arguments on the other side? Why did people think that it could work?

K. ANDERSON: I think they thought it could work because they believed so much in the man, in the candidate himself, David, that I believe John carried the campaign. Had we been fortunate enough at one stage or another to have the talent required to reinforce the candidate, maybe some things would have been different. I think they encouraged him to run because they wanted to keep the issues of the times alive.

ROBERT J. KEEFE (political consultant, Carter–Mondale Re-election Committee): Who is "they" in that context?

K. ANDERSON: The people in the states that had worked for him during the Republican primaries, his supporters.

BODE: Keke, in Wisconsin, in the Pfister Hotel, before the Wisconsin primary, I encountered an old acquaintance, Stan Shinebaum, who was up there talking to you about that, even back that early. Now Stan was an Anderson supporter at the time of the Republican primaries, wasn't he, and the folks around Stan Shinebaum?

K. ANDERSON: Yes, I believe, he was, though I think at the time we did not know it. Probably he had been discussing it with people in California and I think, if my recollection is correct, that late in the Republican primaries, he began to show visible interest in John Anderson.

KEEFE: By that, you're talking about Stanley Shinebaum who's a liberal Democrat in Los Angeles?

BODE: You're correct; that's right. I mean Stanley was interested in an independent candidacy.

K. ANDERSON: He was interested in the Republican primaries also, before John went into the Independent.

CATHERINE MACKIN (network correspondent, ABC News): You mean other candidates, other than Anderson?

K. ANDERSON: No, in Anderson, starting in January.

ALBERT R. HUNT (correspondent, *Wall Street Journal*): In that same hotel, I remember having drinks with you and John one night in your suite—this was maybe four or five days before the Wisconsin primary—and your husband seemed quite ambivalent on the question of an independent candidacy and, as I recall, you didn't seem at all ambivalent. At that point, at least, you were very, very much in favor. Did you change your mind later?

K. ANDERSON: I never let the press know my true feelings, Al. I think that's the biggest mistake anyone can make.

BODE: Does that apply even here today, at this table?

K. ANDERSON: No, only when it suits my purpose.

HUNT: You didn't go back and forth? You weren't for it in the beginning stages and then as he—

K. ANDERSON: I hadn't really come down on any decision, up until the time the stories of all of the failed independent candidacies started to appear in the press, before John had made a decision. It was after that, that I said, You're going to expose yourself to another no-win philosophy. Because of that I counseled against it.

—THE POLLSTERS' VIEW—

NOLAN: What I'd like to get from the two pollsters here is their frame of reference in helping the candidate prepare for the acceptance speech which is, in a sense, the beginning of the campaign.

What was their perception of the opponents' weaknesses? Obviously, Governor Reagan quoted Franklin Roosevelt a lot, so Pat Caddell figured that Carter was weak among blue-collar. How did you help the president prepare for both the acceptance speech and then moving on to Labor Day, the kickoff, establishing the themes of the campaign?

KEEFE: He was in charge of the balloon drop. (*Laughter*)

PATRICK H. CADDELL (president, Cambridge Survey Research): Let me start by saying that I think by the summer the general strategies of both campaigns weren't hard to figure out. We entered the situation after the June 3rd primaries in which Governor Reagan had done well. There had not been what we had hoped for, which was a Republican bloodbath that would carve up the eventual nominee. We had got the person we had wanted in the field that we thought could get nominated, but we had not quite gotten him in the way we had wanted him. The Republicans had a unified party, with less damage done to the candidate than we had had in '76. My concern in June was that we not come out of the Republican convention any more than fifteen to twenty points down, and, in fact, we reached that number in early July before the Republicans even went into convention and came out of that somewhere around thirty behind. The president's posture at that time was pretty grievous.

I went back and re-read the Ford memo—we all did at that point—and found an enormous number of similarities to the situation, except that we did not even enjoy the personal popularity as an individual at that point that Ford enjoyed in 1976 when he was far behind.* We came out of the primaries with the posture that the American people simply did not want Jimmy Carter as their president if they could possibly avoid it. In fact, we had tested that proposition in the abstract, and it was better than two to one that people did not want him to be president, and that gave the dimension of the problem that we had. The Democratic primaries in the course of the spring had done damage to the president, not just to his general job ratings, which had never been very good, but to his own personal popularity. Particularly he had been hurt in the North, with groups

---

* "The Ford memo" referred to was a strategy memorandum drafted for President Ford's fall 1976 campaign by Robert Teeter, Stuart Spencer, and Richard Cheney which candidly examined the strengths and weaknesses of Mr. Ford's candidacy.

we had not shown exceptional strength with even in 1976—particularly with Catholics, Jews, labor members, specifically in the Northeast. When we looked at the attitudes after the June 3rd primaries, just among hardcore Democrats—even before we extended at that point to the general population, in every one of the primary states that we had surveyed from late May to June 3rd, over half of the Democrats wanted the party to nominate someone other than the president, even though he was winning most of those primaries.

His job approval was a negative among hardcore primary Democrats in four of the six contests, even though he had won four of the contests. On the question we had that the president couldn't handle the job, in every one of those states the majority of the hardcore Democrats agreed with the proposition. And in terms of his competence and vision, we had found for some time that the feelings about the president's competence had a very high negative—the worst we had seen in the four years, in the three and a half years he had been president. We had a divided party, and worse than that, we had an ongoing struggle; as I said, our constituency groups with Catholics and Jews and liberal Democrats and the potential liberal defections to Anderson were great. Our base, if we had one, was in the South, and it was very weak, and we had some peculiar problems in places like Florida because of the Cuban refugee problem in a state that had been ours. On top of that, from '76, we were certain that we could not repeat the level of performance we had had in the small town rural areas which, in fact, had delivered most of the big states that carried in '76 to the president.

In addition to that, the events that we were looking at were not particularly good. The economy had gotten quite bad in the spring, particularly the inflation rate, and we had paid an enormous price for that, although one of the few hopeful signs was that people did expect the economy was beginning to turn around. We were suffering grievously over the irresolution of the Iranian situation, after the raid, and the sense that that was not going to be resolved. Our general situation had reverted to a state worse than we had seen at even our low point in 1979. There was a far greater personal hostility.

NOLAN: You haven't given us 5 percent of the total vote yet.

HUNT: What's the bad news?

CADDELL: The immediate thing was looking at Governor Reagan. When we assessed Governor Reagan both before and after the Republican primaries, some of the things we found were an interesting parallel to what we had seen in '76. In a number of leadership elements Governor Reagan was viewed as very strong, very decisive. He was viewed as having been a very good governor of California—after all, he was the Republican nominee—and in that he was also considered a man of vision. All of those were characteristics that Carter had had in the beginning of the summer of 1976; they were all characteristics that he had lost in the three and a half years of being president.

However, beyond that, we found that Governor Reagan did have some weaknesses. He did in terms of how much people thought he could actually do about solving inflation and unemployment. Although he enjoyed great edges on us comparatively, in a vacuum people were less sure that he would be able to do that. Also, there was enormous concern both about Reagan's judgment, the idea that his solutions perhaps were much too simplistic for the times. There was already implanted a sense on the part of a number of voters that he might be too old; also there was questioning whether he knew what he was talking about sometimes. Beyond that, you got to the personality negatives in terms of shooting from the hip—he had large percentages of people who thought that he did that too often. Enormous numbers of people thought it was a risk to make him president. We had known that question from '76, one of our drags in that campaign against President Ford. On the proposition that as president, Ronald Reagan would keep us out of war, that proposition during the campaign would fail steadily by twenty to twenty-five points. I read somewhere there was even at one point a percentage in the 40th percentile of people using the word "dangerous" with Governor Reagan.

The thing that surprised us the most was with regard to the assumption on the part of most people in the Carter campaign that Governor Reagan was considered a warm, likeable figure. What we found was that, as Dick Wirthlin mentioned earlier this morning, there were concerns of whether he really cared about ordinary people. He was not considered as warm a figure as I had expected him to be, and one of the comparatives we wanted to look at when we looked at the candidates was the quality of "slick." I was convinced that President Carter had done real damage to himself on that sort of attitude, and much to my surprise, I found that it was by an almost two-to-one margin that people thought Governor Reagan was more slick than President Carter. On the ideological end we had a situation somewhat out of balance. Although most people put the president flat in the middle, ideologically, or a little bit to the left, and he tended to track fairly closely with people, a good third of the people on our ideology scale put the governor to the extremity on that scale, and even very far away from where they were. At the same time, they rejected by better than a two-to-one margin the argument that he was too conservative to be president. When we looked at the areas of concern for voters, particularly in terms of blue-collar Democrats, we thought we had some opportunity, and we thought on the questions of "Does he understand this job?" and "Is he too simplistic?" that there was some room, and also on the question of what would eventually emerge as the war and peace issue.

NOLAN: Before I ask Dick for his review, there is one small point of tonality or protocol that has always bugged me, and I'd like to have Bob Keefe or Les Francis tell me why the Carter people always refer to him as Governor Reagan, nor Mr. Reagan. I presume things don't happen by accident, that they were trying to focus on his record as governor of California, which Peter Dailey was letting us know about six times a night on the television screen. You say that he had a good record as governor of California, that that was the perception. Why hasn't he called Mr. Reagan? A man out of office—

CADDELL: There was a decision, Hamilton Jordan and the president made the decision early on, that it would look a little bit petty—"petty" is the word—that he had been governor and that we should refer to him as that.

NOLAN: I want to ask Dick, specifically, about Carter's "meanness" becoming an issue in the first two weeks of the campaign. That is to say, his speech before the Ebenezer Baptist Church, which made a lot of allegations that seemed to be unproven relating to Governor Reagan's speech in Tuscambia, Alabama, researched by Lyn Nofziger, seemed to create in people's minds a new image of Carter as sort of mean. How did the changing notion of Carter track for you in the first couple of weeks in September?

— CARTER'S CHANGING IMAGE —

RICHARD B. WIRTHLIN (deputy director of strategy and planning, Reagan–Bush Committee): Well, I was sure that Pat was following, pretty much, the same exercise that we were. We were developing some of the key elements of our general campaign strategy as early as December of 1979, drafted a major memo in March of 1980 which pretty well set the frame of reference. Part of those strategy documents dealt with the key issue—what kind of a race can we expect from our opponent? The one thing that surprised us was the viciousness of the personal attack that the president launched in the first weeks in October. We felt very strongly in looking at the primaries, and we were watching the Democratic primaries almost as closely as we were watching our own, that Carter was very vulnerable. The surge that Kennedy experienced in Connecticut and New York gave evidence of how far an opponent could go against an incumbent president if he focused on the economic issues and on the leadership theme. However, Jimmy Carter also carried some great perceptual assets. Primary among those was he was viewed as an honest, forthright, well-intentioned individual. That perception was highlighted with the candor that he displayed when he went before the press and answered questions concerning the "Billygate" affair. That particular situation, in my belief, would have unstrung, if not severely damaged, most incumbents, but he handled it with adroitness and given the backlog of goodwill that he had, he shunted that aside with no perceptible damage. However, when he changed his role, if you will, and came out of the box as hard and as strident as he did, it gave us some options and opportunities that we did not enjoy before that time. Specifically, people looked at him more as a politician after those attacks than they did before, and secondly, while he was held in a considerable degree of esteem in terms of his honesty and his morality, nevertheless, we did see some of that fade.

It was our initial assumption that we could not beat Jimmy Carter simply by mounting a negative campaign, that we had to give the voters positive reason to support Ronald Reagan. This gave us credibility that we used, I think, quite effectively in the last two weeks of the campaign, to take on Jimmy Carter very frontally on the issues of performance and leadership. The campaign strategy focused around four or five basic elements. Having gone through the experience in

New Hampshire, we believed that all voters would display a degree of volatility that we hadn't seen before. Therefore, we said, we're going to save a good measure of our major resources to put into the campaign the last twenty and the last ten days of the campaign. In addition, we should be cognizant of Carter's strengths, and go as directly as we could to his weaknesses. We asked the question in the late summer, "Consider the fact that Jimmy Carter is re-elected to president of the United States, can you give me one good thing that you think he will accomplish as a re-elected president?" And almost half of the voters could not indicate one good thing expected to happen if President Carter were re-elected. Of course, that formed a lynch pin in the attack strategy that Pete Dailey developed and delivered in the month of October.

—REAGAN'S APPEAL—

The ideological issue was a key one, and we found something very surprising. We went back and interviewed and took all the interviews that we had collected during the primaries, to see where Republicans perceived Ronald Reagan to be vis-à-vis themselves and the other candidates. Those Republicans who voted in the primary were closer ideologically to John Anderson than they were to Ronald Reagan. But we also found that ideology was not cutting as a voting motivator. While there was skepticism about our ability to handle the inflation issue, nevertheless, there was enough ground-swell support, particularly from key coalitional groups, for us to believe we could go after that issue with a good deal of positive vengeance. Right from the beginning, it was recognized we had to solidify the Republican base and broaden it. As our key swing targets we selected ethnic Catholics, labor, blue-collar workers, and we felt we could make a major run at the Carter coalition in the South. As Pat has said, we looked at the '76 election and determined that a good deal of the Carter support did come from small towns, and our data gave us the clear signal that there would not be a repeat of that kind of strength for him in 1980.

NOLAN: I have to ask you, to interrupt you just at this point, if the concerns of the Moral Majority seemed to be rather prominent in these small towns in the South. How did that show up in your data?

WIRTHLIN: I think there was an impact on the Reagan vote that emanated from the Moral Majority, but not either in the breadth or depth as it's frequently described. If you take white, born-again Christians and compare their vote post–election with white, non-born-again Christians, the vote commitment across the board is exactly the same.

ADAM CLYMER (correspondent, *New York Times*): But didn't a lot of the born-again Christians who had not been registered, register and come out and vote for Reagan?

WIRTHLIN: That's where they did have their impact, in terms of their activisation as a cohesive group, which had not been involved in politics before, wielding, I think pivotal change in some of the key states.

BODE: Could you give us some notion of the geography of that and the dimensions of it? That was really kind of a mushy business; everyone had a hard time getting a handle on it. Reverend Falwell and the rest of those fellows made some pretty exorbitant claims that you could neither document nor could you really be sure weren't true during the period of the early general election.

WIRTHLIN: We're still in the process of analyzing post–election data, so what I'm saying isn't based on hard data but on some of the vote patterns that we have seen.

LYN NOFZIGER (press secretary, Reagan–Bush Committee): Fortunately, he did it faster than that during the campaign. (*Laughter*)

WIRTHLIN: From what I have seen, I think that they were critical in some of what we call the border Southern states—specifically North Carolina, possibly Kentucky, possibly Tennessee, perhaps Alabama, to a lesser extent maybe in Mississippi. But when you go beyond those regions the number in those groups was relatively small, and their ability to activate others or persuade others, especially Democrats to switch party or allegiance, was quite minimal. We estimated quantitatively that we are looking at a group that numbered in the range of 14 percent of the total electorate maximum.

—REAGAN'S POST-CONVENTION DIP—

HUNT: Before we get into where you got your vote, I want to go through a little bit of what happened after the convention. As you say, you did come out in good shape, you had this grand strategy, and then it appeared that the month of August, to put it mildly, was troubling for you. You had the "noble cause of Vietnam," you had evolution, you had the two-China policy, and then you capped it off on Labor Day with the Lyn Nofziger memorial Tuscambia, Alabama, remark.* Right after Labor Day—

NOFZIGER: It took me a while to get it just right. (*Laughter*)

HUNT: But I remember—I was traveling then—that Tuesday you all spent hours in hotel rooms in Detroit talking to Mr. Casey, to Dick Wirthlin, and others back at headquarters. What was your frame of mind then? What did you think you had to do, what mistakes had you made, and how could you correct them?

WIRTHLIN: You were right; the end of August and the first of September were not good days for the Reagan campaign. The only thing that gave us some solace during this period was reviewing what had happened to the Carter campaign in 1976, and I think the two campaigns were subject to the same force. That is, it is impossible for a campaign group or a candidate to understand the quantum shift that comes when you are no longer a possible nominee for the presidency, but you're running in a three-man race for the presidency. The degree of intensity with which statements are examined, the amount of pressure that's put upon the campaign organization, the extent to which virtually every comment has political overtones—all work together during those first couple of weeks, as they did with the Carter campaign, to put us very much on the political griddle.

The date sticks in my mind very clearly—September 4th—when we were taking some pretty heavy shots, and we decided to break stride, and take the attack to Carter. The determination was made

---

*On September 1, 1980, at the Michigan state fair, Governor Reagan remarked that President Carter had opened his campaign in Tuscambia, Alabama, "The city that gave birth to and is the parent body of the Ku Klux Klan." In some published reports, Mr. Nofziger was identified as the source of the political advice that led to this controversial statement.

that the best issue was the Stealth Bomber issue.* In other words, we found that the same forces that were beating us around the ears could be unleashed on an incumbent president if we selected and then used, primarily through surrogates, an issue of key concern. On that date, Bill and I, in conjunction with the campaign plane, determined that would be the vehicle we would use to get the focus off of the mistakes that we had made, and back upon what we felt would ultimately determine the election: namely, an election, a referendum on the performance of the incumbent president, Jimmy Carter.

HUNT: This is also the day you put Stu Spencer on the airplane?**

WIRTHLIN: Stu Spencer did not go on the airplane for another ten days.

—DEFINING THE GENERAL ELECTION—

CARL WAGNER (director of field operations, Kennedy for President): Dick and Pat, do you both agree—you tend to suggest this in your analysis of the fall campaign—that the general election in 1980 wasn't a right-left structure of the vote but, in fact, as you suggested, a referendum on Carter?

WIRTHLIN: My data show that very sharply. Ideology did not cut in the vote decision, even though I think there was a more conservative climate; the issues that were on the agenda of people's concerns were to some extent conservative ones. I think Pat and I agree on this point, but I would go one step further. I suggest that it wasn't only the issue agenda that was more conservative but also the solutions that were being offered by the two opponents tended to camp toward the conservative side. I guess this reinforces how mushy the whole concept of ideology is when it comes to assessing vote deci-

---

*Governor Reagan accused the Defense Department of compromising national security by deliberately leaking secret details of a radar-evading bomber in order to benefit President Carter politically.

**Stuart Spencer, a veteran political strategist who ran Mr. Reagan's first gubernatorial campaign and had served as political director for President Ford's campaign, was brought into the Reagan campaign as a consultant in September of 1980.

sions. The electorate still viewed Reagan, in spite of that, as considerably more conservative than themselves, and they did so right on through the election.

CLYMER: But this is an election in which each major party has selected its most conservative, serious candidate. With both of them moving to the right, which just hasn't happened before, that may set the agenda to a point where you can't get a left–right measure on the results.

ROBERT M. TEETER (president, Market Opinion Research): But that doesn't necessarily argue that it's an election that moved right. I mean, it may argue you can't get that difference between Reagan and Carter, but it doesn't necessarily argue that the country is off on some lunge in one direction or the other.

BILL BROCK (chairman, Republican National Committee): What we were trying to do from the very front end of the campaign, going back before we had a nominee, before we even had some candidates, was to try to keep the election non-ideological, to keep it focused on the economy because that was our issue. There was nothing the Democrats could do to defend against it.

NOLAN: There is one decisive thing that I think may have happened, and I would like to get Bill Brock on the record on it. Putting all that money into the idea of making voting for Republicans seem respectable. How long did you consider that? That struck me and a lot of other people as giving a lot of blue-collar people a reason — some exterior judgment values — to vote Republican.

BROCK: We started working on it first in 1978, did some testing that year with a different approach, and got very much more precise in the summer and into the fall of 1979. I made the final decision in November of 1979 and embarked on the program in January.

NOLAN: And spent $8 million, was it?

BROCK: Nine and a half million. We did it for two reasons. . . . "Vote Republican for a Change" had basically two purposes. One was to legitimize Republicanism. We had just about eliminated the net negative to being Republican. We had to proceed beyond that a little and make it a party campaign. But secondly, we had to establish the parameters of the debate, and we couldn't do it with press releases or speeches; we could only do it with controlled media, and that requires advertising. That's the only way we could force the focus to the economy, always.

NOLAN: If ideology was removed, I think we've all agreed, as a major strategic factor, I guess we have to get to the tactics, and that brings us back to debates again.

TEETER: Can I ask a question? You're coming off the Democratic convention in the end of the summer and Labor Day period, did you think that your coalition, if you could put one together to win, was essentially the same one that you had in '76? Or how was it different?

CADDELL: No. There were variances in it. It was obviously essentially Democrats you start with, that base; you have to hold your party. Where we needed to make some trade-offs were these. In 1976 Gerald Ford had run us very hard, as you know, with Catholics, in certain Northern states; in fact, he would do better with that than Reagan would, in my opinion, for much of the campaigns, and we needed to make some ground up there. We were going to trade off some of that small-town, rural support that we had. The place where I best saw we had the opportunity to do that, if there was going to be one, was to pick it up in some of the suburbs, where you really had a mix, where we had been, had our clocks cleaned in '76, particularly in the Chicago suburbs and some other places like that where we could make some votes up. And interestingly enough, in the South we saw some strange variances through much of the campaign. We would see changes in some Southern states and some metropolitan areas from 1976. We were tending to run better in the latter areas whereas, in some of the rural, white Baptist areas, more populous traditional areas, where we had run enormously well, in the 75 percent, we were not running as well as that.

TEETER: What about state changes, I mean what states didn't you carry in '76 you thought you could carry? At one point even if you thought you'd lose . . . you could . . .

CADDELL: We felt, first of all, that we had a better shot in the North than we had actually run in '76. We felt we had a shot at Michigan without Ford there. Despite all the unemployment problems, it was also basically a Democratic state presidentially. Illinois was a state that we felt we had real opportunity. It was one in which we thought the Anderson vote was a more complicated vote, particularly its effect in the suburbs, and we had some real strengths in Illinois. I never was very sanguine about New Jersey, but there was a period when we were actually doing better there than I expected. Connecticut, Maine, Vermont—a little state that hung close for a long time and where in fact we got a slight edge—and Washington and Oregon were states we thought we had a chance of winning. States that we were most concerned about that we had lost were Texas, where Reagan had very real strength—in fact, he was stronger there in some ways than he was in California. In Florida we had enormous problems for a variety of factors, but these Cuban refugees caused us an enormous difficulty. . . .

—CHANGES FROM '76—

BETTY HEITMAN (co-chair, Republican National Committee): Could I mention one other factor I think is significant? In addition to the television program that Bill put on, we spent the last four years trying to rebuild Republican strength at the grassroots level, and we had trained probably 16-17,000 people in campaign techniques.* So, in addition to Governor Reagan's organization that he had intact from 1976, we had a tremendous group of people that had been trained and brought in to the political arena on the Republican side.

NOFZIGER: Finally got those Ford people trained!

HEITMAN: Also, we had been able to increase our base, and we had greater strength in the state legislators, we had more congressmen, we

---

*The television program referred to, entitled, "Time for a Change," was a special production developed and financed by the Republican National Committee intended to define the Republican philosophy and establish a theme and base for Republican candidates for the 1980 elections.

had more governors, which provided a stronger base for Governor Reagan going in.

TEETER: Two questions which, I think, relate to that. One is, at this point in early September when you were making decisions of what your strategy was going to be for the last couple of months, it seemed to me that one of Carter's problems was that he just ignored his first four years almost, and he never really quite came to grips with what it was he had to say or wanted to say or about those four years. What was his thinking, or yours, or the other people in the campaign about how necessary that was, and if he had to talk about it, what should he say? I'll ask the second question, too, which is, did you anticipate at that time trying to turn the dialogue during the last two or three weeks of the campaign to foreign policy? Forget the last two days.

CADDELL: Let me go back to a point I want to make and fill in a little bit about the larger strategic assumptions we were operating under in the campaign. First of all, we knew that there were some variations from '76, particularly in terms of volatility or negative natures, and that their strategy was to make it a referendum on Carter's first term. We had known for a year that if it ever became a referendum on that, we were gone. It was very simple. We had to count on going back and looking at the historical structure of general elections. We would try to keep this to a choice for president.

As I said, we started with the understanding that by two to one, the American people did not want Jimmy Carter to be president, and so we had to find them a reason why they were going to be forced to keep him, frankly, and what we felt we had to do was to keep the choice to a president who could handle the job. We know the people bring in an enormous concern, as you knew from '76, on the question of the capabilities of the individual, how sure you were the person could handle the job, and particularly with the peculiar nature of it in terms of the awesome power that a president has, especially in foreign policy. So it was very clear to us that we had to attempt to control the definition of the campaign around two ideas. One was around the presidency itself—that it was an important job and the kinds of things that went into it—because we felt that by inference it worked somewhat against or at least went to the questions that existed around Governor Reagan. Secondly, we had to keep it to questions of the future, that this was not a time to have a debate after three and a half years on trying to change the country's attitudes, looking at fairly solid perceptions about the president's performance in a whole host of areas. We tested at one point fifteen or sixteen job areas, and in only two did he have a positive rating. Those attitudes, as we explored them, were not frivolously held. They were fairly strongly held beliefs, particularly on the economy, and understand that events were working to reinforce those.

BODE: Who had positive ratings, Pat? Carter? On two of sixteen Carter had positive ratings?

CADDELL: Yes. So we had to keep it to the future for some months, not so much for Reagan, necessarily, but because of some of the voters who were with John Anderson that we needed back. We had nothing to give them, and that was a constant source of debate inside the Carter administration, and you have to make some distinctions here about acceptability. The other thing we wanted was for Governor Reagan to have, as I think every challenger to the president has had—looking for a phrase—the problem of getting over the acceptability threshold. He had to make people comfortable enough to conclude that he could do the job. As the campaign wore on, that would intensify, and our objective was to move this campaign off domestic issues to foreign policy and the handling of international affairs and so on.

In fact, between the end of the Republican convention and early September, we maintained the leads we had on "trustworthy," which were fairly significant, and increased them; we increased our lead on "better qualified"; we were still losing "inflation" and "unemployment." But the areas that showed the most dramatic movement comparatively were in handling foreign policy, in handling international crises, which was a far more important issue in the regression structures in '80 than they were in '76, and we made some major movements there. So in the foreign policy realm, in keeping us out of war—those were then areas where we had in fact made the biggest progress going into September.

One last point—when Dick talks about the problems the Reagan campaign experienced in late August and September: part of our campaign assumptions, tactical assumptions, were that they would have those difficulties, that they would go through what we had been through, and that there was no way, unless you have done it, that you really can appreciate the change that takes place. In fact, I was hoping that we would come out of the convention less than ten points down, that Reagan would have a rough period, and we could get to some parity, and basically that is what happened.

BROCK: Didn't you have to resolve at least what I saw as a conflict between your desire to talk about the future and the other side of your campaign which said how complicated and difficult the job was? Weren't you creating a contradiction, or at least maybe a future that was sort of dismal as a prospect . . . ?

CADDELL: Oh, no. Politics is not often without some contradiction.

NOLAN: Bill is asking whether you were offering future malaise. (*Laughter*)

CADDELL: One of the things our campaign had tried to impose on the administration, and again it is somewhat difficult, was to get them to come up with some exciting things that we could, in fact, run on, including the economic revitalization program. You all can make your own determinations of how exciting it was. Conceptually, we wanted to pick some areas where we could come up with some more positive ideas for that future, and I think the problem was that we never really did that as well as we needed to.

NOLAN: That has brought us to the strategic vision, quite clearly, at Dunkirk, at Labor Day for the Carter campaign, so we have to go to the tactics of how we go onto the boats. There were serious tactical decisions facing the Carter people in regard to debates. Should you or should you not debate John Anderson? And a fresh element, a new thing in the ether about Carter's "alleged meanness." Les Francis, what about the decision whether or not to go to Baltimore and participate in a three-way debate? How did you vote?

—QUESTIONS ABOUT THE FIRST DEBATE—

LES FRANCIS (executive director, Democratic National Committee): It was not a decision made easily. I think it occupied a good deal of discussion at several meetings. Pat can speak with much more knowledge about the numbers, but essentially it came down to the fact that a large number of people were moving in the direction of Anderson at that time, at least more potential Carter voters than potential Reagan voters. So we felt that being involved in that debate would enhance Mr. Anderson's credibility as a candidate and make it harder to get those people back. It was a calculated political decision at the time.

NOLAN: Any regrets from anybody in the Carter side?

BODE: Les, if that's the case, you had this accompanying decision that you made early on to do all you could to keep Anderson off the ballots, and thereby got yourself a lot of publicity as the people who were trying to squash him and so forth, and elevated Anderson to a certain extent that way.

FRANCIS: Well, I don't know if it's accurate, but it was in the press that the Anderson campaign had to spend $2 million to get on the ballots. That's $2 million that could have gone into television, so I think it had some effect whether it built up his credibility or not. Neither of those decisions do I regret; I don't know if anybody else in the campaign did.

WILLIAM J. CASEY (campaign manager, Reagan–Bush Committee): How much did it cost you?

FRANCIS: Not a tenth of that.

MICHAEL F. MACLEOD (campaign manager–treasurer, National Unity Campaign): A quick question. We were able to make a fair amount of hay out of the fact that you all had theoretically or reportedly dedicated something like $225,000 at the National Committee to preventing us from getting on ballots in various states like Massachusetts, North Carolina, and elsewhere. Did the decision not to participate in the debates on September 21st take into account the fact that we were bound to have as much a field day with that as we possibly could?

FRANCIS: Yes, it was taken into account. All those things were, but we still did not want to reinforce that level of credibility.

CLYMER: One thing that I'm very curious about in this decision, which I heard again and again in the spring and the summer in the convention, was that it would really help the Carter campaign to debate Reagan because Carter knows the details; Reagan's a good actor and all that, but Carter was really going to succeed. If it was this important, did anybody say, Look, if we duck this debate, if we don't participate for all the reasons we're arguing but no one is taking very seriously outside, we may not get that chance to show up Reagan in a debate? Was it argued that it would be worth the possible inflating of Anderson with the deflating of Reagan?

FRANCIS: All of those facts were considered and discussed, and I can say that in the years that I've been in campaigns, this was the toughest political call I've seen anybody have to make. It was a close call. All those things weighed in and were considered, but I think when the decision was made we all felt comfortable with it.

NOLAN: Next question. Any hesitancy on the part of the Reagan campaign on debating John Anderson solo when the thing in Baltimore had been set up?

CASEY: There was a division of opinion as to whether it was a good idea or not, but the informed consensus was that he wanted the exposure and that we would do well. The "don't debate Anderson" school was a very small minority.

CADDELL: I would like to ask a question of the Reagan people. I had the sense, and maybe this was wrong, that you were a little surprised that we did not cave once the formal invitation was done, that, in fact, you thought we were going to debate.

CASEY: I thought you might do it.

CADDELL: If you had known for sure, if we had slammed the door as hard as some people wanted it slammed on the weekend before the League of Women Voters moved, would you have then accepted the debate with Anderson?

BODE: Are we talking about the first debate?

CASEY: Yes. We wanted you in the debate.

CADDELL: But if you knew for sure that we were not going to cave—it was absolutely clear that we would not and you were absolutely convinced of that—would you all have debated?

CASEY: Yes, because we kept the heat on you.

NOLAN: Is there also heritage of the Nashua experience in this?

BROCK: That Reagan wanted to debate with John Anderson there because of the Nashua experience?

NOLAN: And he did not want to exclude John Anderson?

CASEY: Absolutely. A consistent position. That same position he had taken in Nashua.

MACLEOD: I have an allied question to do with the polls which kind of intrigued me here. There was a time over the summer when it was clear from polls that were available to newspaper readers, which are the only polls available to us, that we were drawing roughly, I guess, two votes from Carter for every one we would shag from Governor Reagan. There came a point in the fall where it seemed to draw even, where the draw was almost equal, and I'm not sure exactly when that was. Was your decision to debate on the 21st of September at all predicated upon the way those polls were flowing and the way we were drawing votes from either you or from Carter?

WIRTHLIN: No. The Anderson coalition was a very complex one in the sense that to look at the aggregates, to look at the Reagan–Carter swing, really masked what the impact of that vote was in a state-by-state race. We debated primarily because: (1) we knew we would have a large audience; (2) we had walked through and beyond the hot coals of Iowa; and (3) we strongly felt that Ronald Reagan was the single best campaign asset we had—that the risk was relatively small in engaging in debate, and that the payoff was very high. But it was not accepted on the basis that we were concerned about too much of the Reagan vote bleeding off to Anderson.

—ANDERSON AND BALTIMORE—

BRODER: Baltimore was a big moment for the Anderson campaign. How did your game plan go with that debate; how much of the game plan was executed? And I'd like to hear some comments from the Reagan people afterwards about how they saw that debate.

MACLEOD: I suppose there were two principal areas of predebate activity for Mr. Anderson. In contrast with some of the other candidates in earlier debates who would repair to Kennebunkport or wherever for a couple of days of really intensive activity, our feeling was that in our case, that kind of briefing was not necessary. Instead we prepared a series of materials on various issues for the candidate and just kind of packed him off, let him have a few days before the debate—I guess it was about four and a half or five days—and let him review the materials at his leisure. In the meantime, the staff was reviewing some of the videotapes of the debates that had preceded the one in which he had participated, pulling out various segments of those debates where we felt that our candidate had not come off as well as he should have. A very prominent example is one that has already been discussed here, and that was in the Chicago debate, prior to the Illinois primary, when Crane and Bush and the others were going at him and our response was not effective, as Ken Bode suggested at an earlier session. We then sat him down and reviewed those with him, to give him an idea of how to respond if the debate should head off in that direction. That really was pretty much the sum total of the preparation. It ended on Friday, as I recall, and that was it until Sunday evening.

BROCK: Was it your objective to establish John intellectually or to attack Reagan or what?

K. ANDERSON: Well, the objective at one point became unclear because the press had established before the debate that this was a make-or-break for Anderson which put an added personal pressure on the candidate.

BROCK: I just wondered if you had discussed the possibility of whether you attack Reagan or attack Carter in absentia.

K. ANDERSON: No, it was never to attack.

MACLEOD: The purpose from an ideological point of view was to draw the distinction between Anderson and Reagan.

BROCK: And just forget Carter.

MACLEOD: For the most part, yes.

K. ANDERSON: To draw the perception between him and Reagan, yes. I don't know how left he went.

WIRTHLIN: I don't think there's any evidence that Reagan was hurt by it. I think it was a good decision for us. As a matter of fact, there is evidence that it did help reinforce again some of our key objectives, namely, to increase the credibility of the governor, to give him an opportunity to speak unencumbered to a large audience, and to be reassuring and dehorn the perceptions that he was dangerous and irresponsible.

MACLEOD: I confess to a certain amount of confusion because although we went into that debate knowing full well that we could not replicate the success that we enjoyed after the January 5th debate in Des Moines, we still felt that it was a real opportunity to ratchet our support up, maybe five points, maybe ten, who knows? It did not happen, and I still don't know the reason.

K. ANDERSON: The opportunity was diminished without the presence of the President. . . .

MACLEOD: Yes, but you still have 40 or 60 million people watching.

BROCK: I think you established the fact that you were not a candidate.

—ANDERSON'S SHIFT—

TEETER: I think there is an important question that takes place early in September in the Anderson campaign. If you take John's record as a congressman and as a moderate-liberal Republican, it left him somewhere, I suppose, in the middle of the country. But it seemed to me that as soon as he decided or got into the serious general election campaign, all of a sudden instead of sticking with many of the things I would have thought would have been attractive to the country, coming from his congressional record or positions he previously had, he did take a distinct turn to the left and essentially became a liberal Democrat and that kind of a candidate. I wonder if that was a conscious strategic decision, and if so, why? The second point is, if you are trying to get from a position from being a fringe candidate to a serious candidate in a year when things were focused almost exclusively on inflation and foreign policy, it seems to me that one of the things you do is never talk about anything other than those two issues. I don't know whether that's what you were doing and the press was covering you differently or not. There was a point at the end of August, I believe, when the candidate took a swing out on the West Coast or southwest Texas for a while, and either twelve or thirteen of those days out of two weeks, the main coverage had nothing to do with inflation or foreign policy. It had to do with Alaska lands one day and Agent Orange one day, and those kinds of issues. I wondered why you did that.

MACLEOD: Well, on the first count, and, Keke, correct me if you think I'm wrong, there was never any consious effort to veer left. In fact, my feeling was that we were almost entirely consistent with the record that he had built up over twenty years in Congress, or more specifically over the last ten years; you know, where he had shifted his philosophy on social issues, not fiscal. Apropos of the second question, I didn't travel all that much so I don't want to be too dogmatic about this, but I do know that we had a tremendous frustration in the campaign because although he would address the cosmic issues like inflation and foreign policy and the like, the cameras only turned on, and perhaps this pertains as well to the scribblers, when he was attacking Carter or Reagan or when he was talking about something other than the subject that these people heard about all the time.

CASEY: Tell me, Pat, were you surprised that Reagan accepted the Cleveland debate—the Reagan–Carter debate? Reagan decided he would debate Carter head-to-head, then changed his position. Was that a surprise to you, to your forces?

CADDELL: It wasn't necessarily a surprise at that particular moment. We had heard the rumblings. My problem was I couldn't understand why you didn't accept debating us head-to-head all along. I had lived in personal fear over the question that we would get a debate late, that when things got tough I thought you would go to a debate. As Reagan got on the defensive on war and peace and so forth, I thought the debate was the natural place for you all to be able to alleviate some of those concerns, and I think our mistake was in not shutting that debate off even sooner.

—CARTER VERSUS REAGAN—

BRODER: Can we back up on one point? For the reasons that Pat has made clear, Carter's strategy dictated that a number of negative messages about Reagan be delivered in the month of September. I'd like to ask the Carter people whether there was any serious discussion tactically as to who should deliver those messages and how they should be delivered. Was it considered that it might have been done by someone other than the president? Was nobody available to do it other than the president or did you just—

CADDELL: Initial intention had been not to have the president carry the attack but to have the vice-president in his traditional role, and surrogates, carry the attack. To the extent that we could have the president carry the attack in a general and indirect way—that frankly faded when the coverage of vice-presidential candidates faded when they became the "stealth candidates," and that was one tactical assumption that surprised us. The other thing was—and this goes to the point that David was raising—it never developed into surrogates. The other factor involved was that the president felt at times the instinct to get into it himself and did, and sometimes not necessarily to his total advantage.

NOLAN: If I were one of the Reagan people at this time, I think I'd start to worry about the war and peace issue, and I'd like to ask Peter Dailey whether there was any thought given to having Governor Reagan deliver a speech—say, on why he's against the draft—or to addressing the peace issue in some way, which I don't believe your media addressed directly anywhere along the line.

PETER DAILEY (deputy director (media), Reagan–Bush Committee): One of the most important things we tried to do throughout the campaign was to keep the focus. I think as Bill pointed out earlier, the Republican National Committee had done a superb job of setting the agenda as far as focusing on the economy which was *the* single issue before the campaign, during the campaign, and today. That was the issue we felt we were strongest in dealing with, and we wanted to stay with it as long and as hard as we could, not be diverted into a separate battle even when the media turned their guns. I think after the Carter mistakes, Pat or somebody was quoted as saying, "Why don't you press guys be fair? you got too much attention on the Carter campaign." I think you turned around and fired at the governor and started the whole dialogue about foreign policy or the war issue and even then, we kept our media focused directly on the issue of the economy and competence. Those two elements were the foundations of what we wanted. The last thing we wanted to do was to move away from that strategy because even when the press was talking about that issue, it was not one that concerned the public.

NOLAN: So you deliberately never went on the defensive and said Reagan's not a mad bomber.

BROCK: Wait a minute. Reagan did do a half hour show—

CASEY: I think it's important to say that we decided fairly early not to answer the kind of attacks we expected Carter would have to make on us. We just weren't going to respond; let him fall.

HUNT: What Mr. Casey is talking about, the three meanness occasions, I think, were: "racism and hatred" down in Atlanta; the "warmonger," the difference between war and peace out in Los Angeles; and "divide North and South, Christian and Jew," and so forth in Chicago. Pat, is it your understanding that all three of those were delivered as planned, those three sets of buzz words were what he had intended to say and exactly what you had set ahead of time and figured was the message you wanted . . . ?

CADDELL: No. The Atlanta one was, in fact, in the text and just was not caught as something that would cause the kind of reaction it did. The Los Angeles one I saw on television—the first time I saw the president doing his litany over good and bad futures, and war and peace, which had not been in the litany that way, was sort of thrown out at the end; it was the last one. It had not been the president's intention really to say it in that way, and he had not really caught it when he did it. But Jody Powell made an instant decision not to back off of it, other than to say that it was a misstatement that we stood by. The one in Chicago, frankly, apparently came from the fact that at a dinner several nights before he had used basically that text, had said that and had gotten no reaction whatsoever.

HUNT: Just as a historical point, didn't he use almost the same line, at least not Christian and Jew but North and South, about Kennedy during the primaries?

PAUL G. KIRK, JR. (national political director, Kennedy for President): Probably a year prior. I don't think it was attributed to the president himself, but it was either Jody or—

NOLAN: Jody used it a lot. On that Atlanta speech, I'd like to know from Pat, did the president have in mind certain worries that black turnout was not what it should be? It struck me that it might have been a motivation, and he needed something.

CADDELL: It's easier in retrospect to construct something and say that tactically it's exactly what we wanted to do. I think at that time it did serve that purpose to some extent. But the truth of the matter is that it wasn't said at that point necessarily to jack up the turnout among blacks.

NOFZIGER: As long as we're in that context, did that ad you guys ran in the black papers and, I guess by mistake, in the *Philadelphia Bulletin* do the job you wanted it to?

CADDELL: Seemed to at the time.

NOLAN: What did the ad say?

BROCK: In four years, Jimmy Carter's appointed thirty-seven black judges, etc. etc.—that's why the Republicans want him out of office. It was a nice touch. Soft.

CADDELL: It was clear that we were going to try to get the black vote. When you start with as few assets as we were beginning with, base-wise, that was necessary.

—STRATEGIC CHANGES—

TEETER: Can I ask Dick Wirthlin a question, or Peter Dailey? You had a really clear and pretty concise plan, starting out at Labor Day. If you take that period going up into early October, say the 5th or 10th or anywhere in there, was there a time that anything you saw caused you to think that you might have to make some strategic change from what you were doing? It seems to me you were faced with having to do the hardest thing in a campaign, and that's to hold your course. But was there a time when something came along that made you think about making a conscious change?

WIRTHLIN: Well, I think there were strong pressures to change the major strategic direction of the campaign later in the first two weeks in October. As I indicated earlier, we did go on a mild attack on Carter earlier than we had initially expected on the Stealth Bomber Issue. Aside from that, I think we kept pretty close to our basic media strategy as well as to the issue agenda we wanted the governor to address. There was a change that evolved in terms of where we felt we could get the easiest 270 electors, and that was one basic objective that we kept very much intact all through the campaign. Namely, by allocating our resources, we weren't gunning for a landslide, but we were gunning to maximize the probabilities of winning; and again the major changes from the plan didn't come in September, the period now under discussion, but they came in the 10th to the 17th of October.

DAILEY: There were tremendous pressures for change, and it was because of a fundamental difference in dimension of the '76 and the '80 campaigns, versus 1972. It was interesting to me to have been in both campaigns to see that change. In 1972, in going after the 10–15 percent of the undecided Independents and Democrats, the strategy and the tactics to reach them happened to be the same strategy and tactics to reinforce your own core vote. So everytime you ran an ad that was directed at them, your own people said, That's terrific. In 1980 the strategy to reach that undecided 10 or 12 percent—which we absolutely had to have or we would have had a marvelous Gold-water campaign and all gone home losers—did not necessarily re-inforce your core old-line Reagan votes. So, the campaign moved along; the core group, particularly the old-line people and the work-ers, became more and more incensed. For example, with the com-mercial that talked about his record as governor: after the basic people saw it twice, they objected. The rest of the electorate, that 10 or 15 percent you were trying to reach, weren't even aware that you were running the ad at that time. There were tremendous pressures to change some of the strategy and tactics in the media.

WIRTHLIN: There's a very basic decision again made early that was buffeted hard in September. We firmly believed that the electorate had to feel some positive proclivities toward Ronald Reagan before we could launch an effective negative attack. We started in Septem-ber with the knowledge that while name identification was high, Ronald Reagan had 90–95 percent; when we asked the question, Tell me how much you know about Ronald Reagan and where he stands, four out of ten probable voters said they knew very little about what Ronald Reagan really did stand for. The basic idea was to establish a base; we had to project and reinforce the images of strength early—namely, competence and leadership and vision—and then wait until that number who did not know very much about Ronald Reagan fell down into the 20 percent range before we opened up on the negative side on Carter.

BODE: Were you having some trouble then holding even the Repub-lican base in places like upstate New York and other places in the East, where you hadn't run media campaigns either in 1976 or dur-ing this period?

WIRTHLIN: Ken, that was one of the things that fell in place very nicely for us. We didn't ever see any signs that the Republican base was eroding, with perhaps the one exception of upstate New York which did not run as strongly for us as we expected.

BODE: I have one more question of Lyn and Dick Wirthlin. After the Nashua experience, the debate experience in Nashua, and you run a series of long, protracted debate negotiations, why did you have Jim Baker in charge of those negotiations?

WIRTHLIN: Because we felt he was more sensitive to mistakes on debates than anyone else. (*Laughter*)

—TARGETTING CARTER RESOURCES—

BROCK: I think one of our greatest assets in this campaign was the fact that we had a base that we almost literally could and did take for granted, and you know, we just had to work east of the Mississippi. We really frankly concentrated on about eight, maybe ten to twelve states. So we could focus our resources, our advertising, organization—everything we had—where it counted. How in the hell did you cope with the problem of prioritizing your response? I'm not being critical at all; I just think it must have been a terribly difficult problem.

CADDELL: It was. The short game list never got very short.

NOLAN: You were talking about California, a couple million bucks here and there.

CASEY: You never seriously were going to go to California, were you?

CADDELL: Not with that kind of money, no. There was a time, though, that I think both Dick and I saw California begin to close up some. The only states in the West we really felt we had an opportunity in were states where we felt relatively competitive all along, essentially Oregon and Washington. The California thing was amusing to watch, and at one point began to tilt some, but essentially our priorities were pretty well set. We had to make one gamble, and this was when we pursued the war and peace issue, which was essentially a move on independents and suburbanites and women. This campaign, of course, was the mirror of 1976. We're dominating women and just getting killed with men, and in '76 it was much the reverse.
Our problem was that we knew that the issues we were pursuing in the North were not helping us that much in the South, in the deep South, and we knew we had to come out of the deep South with most of those states, and we were running pretty hard in some of them. The one thing that we did know was we had to have the big states. If you had told me in the beginning of October that we were

going to lose by ten points, I would not have predicted to you that Mississippi and Alabama and Tennessee and South Carolina would have been virtually dead heats in those circumstances. Our biggest problem in terms of resource allocation was that there were states that should have been secure that were never secure. Arkansas was always a mess, and that was our strongest state in 1976. It was a mess because we chose to invite part of the Cuban population that did not invade south Florida to go to Fort Smith in Arkansas. As I kept saying, the problem with our refugee policy was that Cuba was not on the Pacific coast where we could move it into the far West. Massachusetts was a state where we resisted the pressure to put in the resources and kept having to put something in. We assumed it would come, and I think that had we had not suffered what we did at the end, it would have; but that state was dragging all along because of what Anderson was doing here, and because we just had innate problems with Democrats in the state who disliked the president. So there were always those kinds of problems in those states. We were always in the process of allocating resources, making decisions, trying to hold together.

On the other hand, there were states that constantly surprised us; Maine always looked good to us, Vermont. Most of the states that we needed were competitive: the Wisconsins, Missouris, and big states— Illinois was always for us. The one thing that we did know was how much of a national campaign this was. Most of these states were tight. When something happened in most of those key states it happened everywhere, and what you were playing for was enough movement to secure a whole bunch of them; a whole bunch were going to fall one way or the other.

KEEFE: I think right or wrong, there was a lot of discipline staying with the strategy; I mean, there was a lot of discipline exercised by the management of the Carter campaign in directing resources to the key states as they were defined. There were little more than eight but, for example, Massachusetts and some of the Southern states that were really begging for resources didn't get them, on the basis that we thought they would either come, or the whole thing would fall anyway.

WIRTHLIN: As we were looking at your problem, it was clear to us that you needed two things to beat Reagan, given the solidity of his base support not only in the West but also given our strength that you measured in Texas and Florida. You did need a boost across the board plus a big state strategy, and initially we thought that you were simply attempting to draw us into a trap back into California by the claim that you were going to spend funds there. When we ran some hypothetical breaks on the most probable states to take to win, it was clear to us that especially later in the campaign you were taking a run at California, that it wasn't out of the ballpark.

CADDELL: If it happened, if it was at a point where it would move and get close, we were going to put more resources in there. Other things happened to intervene with that, too. There was a limit on dollars, and we did make a run at it, but we never did as much as we talked about doing. We would have if we could have gotten some changes in other places.

7 **THE GENERAL ELECTION**
October and November

*Anderson's Decision To Persist. Reagan's First Weeks in October.
Carter Contends With Anderson and California. Preparing for the
'October Surprise.' The 'War and Peace' Issue. Kennedy As Team
Player. Independent Expenditures. The Moral Majority. Reagan
Decides to Debate. Carter Considers the Debate. Drawing a Con-
trast. Reagan's Final Plans. Carter's Return to The White House.
Reasons for Reagan's Victory. The Economic Issue. The Losers.
The Anderson View.*

DAVID S. BRODER (associate editor and national political correspondent, *Washington Post*): This is the session where the agony of
suspense is finally ended and we find out who wins the election.
What we're going to try to do is to deal with three fairly distinct
periods in the last thirty-five days of the campaign. First, the period
in October, prior to the eighteenth, when the decision is made that
there will be a Reagan–Carter debate. Second, the debate decision itself. And, finally, the frenetic last week. Then we want to give each
of you a chance to talk about the big picture, and what really happened and what decisions or factors in your view were critical in this
interesting presidential year. But first we want to put our minds back
to the first week in October, and I'd like to start with John Anderson. At this time you and your people are in hot pursuit of bank

loans, and with them, implicitly, is the decision that you are going to be in it all the way. Would you talk a little bit about what was going on in your campaign at that point, and whether or not the decision to seek those loans and make the commitment to stay all the way represented a change of thinking on the campaign's part, and on your part?

—ANDERSON'S DECISION TO PERSIST—

CONGRESSMAN JOHN B. ANDERSON (candidate, National Unity Campaign): David, there had never, I can assure you, been any question in my mind that I was in this race to stay. I was not going to withdraw because I continued to believe that that same volatility of the electorate that Dick Wirthlin has talked about at some length did exist, and that the same volatility that had led to a complete reversal in the positions electorally of Kennedy and Carter could yet occur in the final climactic phase of the campaign. We were confronted in this period with the fact that the strategy of our efforts had been on the operating principle that grand strategies don't have to be enormously convoluted and complicated to be successful. The predicate for all of this, the notion, the given, was that Carter could not win. We didn't have access to all of Mr. Caddell's sophisticated surveys, and despite what we were told in the public print by the leading pollsters about the relative closeness of the race, even at that point, we had operated from the very beginning with the assumption that it was a given that Jimmy Carter would not be re-elected. But we also realized that in order to appear to the American voters as the alternate to Jimmy Carter, and to give Governor Reagan a real contest, we had to show some progress in our campaign.

Since I was up here, I have been reading the *Harvard Political Review* and the article by Eugene McCarthy and John Armor where the statement is made that my goal to win the election was not important at all. My role was simply to be a footnote to history and to legitimize efforts on the part of third party or independent candidates, which I was, to win a presidential election. The trouble with that thesis is that isn't what we were in the race to do. We were seriously in the race to win and realized that American voters want their candidates to win. The no-win syndrome was the heaviest cross of all that we had to carry. To avoid that we knew we had to make some progress, and our hope had been that by this period in October, we would be in the high twenties, and that in turn would accelerate the collapse of the Carter campaign. If that occurred we would emerge you know as a rational and reasonable alternative to Ronald Reagan. Now—

LYN NOFZIGER (press secretary, Reagan–Bush Committee): You never viewed yourself as an alternative to Jimmy Carter?

ANDERSON: I was *convinced* that Jimmy Carter was not going to win. You know, the argument that a vote for me was a vote for somebody else never made any sense to me. The one decision that we did make in this period that I should mention is whether we would decide really to go for broke and spend what for us was a tremendous sum of money—about $1.2 million—for television in the final week or so of the campaign. We were risking the obvious—that if we did not achieve the threshold level of 5 percent of the vote, that I would end up being saddled with an enormous debt. We did make that decision.

BRODER: John, you say in your mind there was never any question whether or not you were going to stay in all the way. In this period, did you have to deal with any significant external or internal pressures to re-examine that position?

ANDERSON: No. You may have reference to the fact that, if not in that exact period, there were statements attributed to members of the Anderson campaign that I realized I couldn't win, and that this had become kind of a hopeless, hapless cause. I was terribly irritated by those reports because I had made it clear to the people around me that that was not my mood; I was sincere in my belief that it was still possible to win.

ROBERT J. KEEFE (political consultant, Carter–Mondale Re-election Commiteee): When did you first think you might not win?

ANDERSON: When was the earliest projection on the networks? I'm not trying to mislead anyone into thinking that I didn't recognize that there were some very, very bleak signs. When we were shut out of the debate process—and, of course, that occurred before the first week in October—it was clear to me, well, before the middle of September, I guess, that under no circumstances would the president appear on the debate platform with me. I realized that that would frame the election in the minds of the voters as strictly a two-man race, which indeed it did. So I was quite conscious of the great disabilities that we were under in that regard.

—REAGAN'S FIRST WEEKS IN OCTOBER—

BRODER: This was also the period when at least in the press, the Reagan campaign was seen as somewhat faltering, stalling, and not moving ahead. Let me ask the Reagan people, if I can start with you, Bill Casey, did you feel in these first two weeks of October any internal pressures to re-examine what you were doing? Was this in any way a kind of a critical decisionmaking period for your campaign?

WILLIAM J. CASEY (campaign manager, Reagan–Bush Committee): In the first two weeks of October? No, we thought we were going pretty well in the first two weeks of October. We had concerns in the first two weeks of September, with the alleged gaffes and the bad stories. However, we've been through that before. We had a baptism of fire; we'd had a lot of stories about inaccuracies and so on during the primaries. They seemed to wash away without hurting us, and I don't really think they hurt us badly, although the press made us think they did. We didn't like to read those stories every morning, but they didn't show up severely in the polls. Dick, am I correct in that?

RICHARD B. WIRTHLIN (deputy director of strategy and planning, Reagan–Bush Committee): Yes.

BRODER: But the race was tightening or appeared to be tightening in the first couple of weeks of October.

WIRTHLIN: Well, there were really two different periods during that juncture of the last week of September through the middle of October. We showed the race very close through most of September, marginally swinging back and forth till the very latter part of September and the beginning of October, when we started to break loose a somewhat more comfortable lead. We showed a six-point lead in that first week. However, beginning about the 15th of the month there was a critical event that lost us a good deal of momentum in the Great Lakes.

MARTIN F. NOLAN (Washington bureau chief, *Boston Globe*): The Northwest of the Great Lakes?

WIRTHLIN: The Great Lakes, not so much the Northwest or the Northeast, but we did go into a somewhat flat period in Michigan, and in Ohio, and in Illinois. We were judging our progress by three different measures, and the least important of those measures was the national ballot. The most important measure was how well we were doing in acquiring the sufficient electoral votes to win the election. This was an important period for us because from about the 11th through the 14th, that six-point lead nationally began to evaporate. We did see a shift of support from the Great Lakes to the South. Geographically, our strategy had always been to pick up Texas and Florida, which in my belief were never really seriously in doubt for us. While we were losing strength in the Great Lakes, we suddenly saw opportunities in the South that weren't there before. Tennessee, Kentucky, Alabama, all then began to look very possible. And beginning with what we felt was a fairly solid 205 electors—the West plus Florida and Texas and Virginia and Iowa—we only needed sixty-five more electoral votes to win. We suddenly saw opportunities to pick that up in the South, even if we lost, say, three of the four key Midwestern states. So it was a period of re-examination, but it was not a period of overconcern.

—CARTER CONTENDS WITH ANDERSON AND CALIFORNIA—

BRODER: Les or any of the Carter people, this was a period when a lot of the stories were written about the Democrats coming home. What did you think was happening to your campaign, vis-à-vis the Reagan campaign? Was there any effort at this point to try to do anything to manipulate or reduce the Anderson vote?

LES FRANCIS (executive director, Democratic National Committee): Let me take the last question first, and maybe Patrick can talk about what our figures showed at that time. The Anderson factor was continuing to trouble us in several Northwestern states: Washington and Oregon, California, Wisconsin. Within the Carter organization, it was about then that our field operatives started using the line in the field that a vote for Anderson was a vote for Reagan. It was at that time that we abandoned the posture of ignoring the Anderson candidacy in the field. In terms of individual key states, Pat's results showed that Florida never looked good; about that time in our figures Texas looked close, and we did accelerate some activity there. It was also around then that we saw Virginia looking possible, and we decided to put some effort there in the early part of October. But it was throughout that time that Pat's results just kept coming back: up two, down one, even in the key states. Going back to our earlier discussion, that's what made resource allocation decisions so difficult.

CASEY: Did you really intend to go into California or merely try to decoy us?

FRANCIS: At the time there was an indication that things were closing up and we thought we had a possibility. If it had the effect of drawing you in there more, so much the better, but that wasn't the main reason for doing it.

NOLAN: Do you have a money figure on California? I'd love to have a money figure.

ALBERT R. HUNT (correspondent, Wall Street Journal): You actually did spend some money there.

FRANCIS: Yeah, we did spend some money.

HUNT: And not an insignificant amount.

FRANCIS: That's right. We did spend money.

NOFZIGER: Did we ever close closer than 7 percent?

WIRTHLIN: Yes we did, as a matter of fact.

NOFZIGER: See what's wrong with the polls.

WIRTHLIN: We're talking about California, still. There was a time when it closed to about five points, and I think the Carter strategy at taking a run at California—while I was initially surprised that you would attempt it—did make a lot of sense because it was evident that you needed a big state strategy to win in the month of October. From our perspective, you needed an across-the-board move of four or five points plus focus of your resources on California, New York, probably Michigan, to close that gap. As time went on, that strategy made more and more sense, at least from the way we were looking at the election.

NOFZIGER: Pat, what did your polls show in California?

PATRICK H. CADDELL (president, Cambridge Survey Research): Well, it showed about that time the situation in California getting about five or six points down. We had always seen that the problem in California was that Governor Reagan, in terms of image and attitudes, was stronger in California than he was in other places, better known there. I mean, it was basically a set image. Our problem in California always had been that we'd never—I think we see it as one of the worst states for the president. But the fact is that we also were playing with it. The reason we were holding a decision on California so late was because California never tends to deviate that far from the national average. Secondly, if we began to get movements as we were in the big states on the issues that we thought were critical or having any chance at all to pull this out—those were the same kinds of issues, particularly war and peace, that were going to have an impact on California.

KEEFE: And then you have Anderson holding a lot of votes there.

CADDELL: We had Anderson holding a lot of votes, and then we looked at the states with him out of it, with Congressman Anderson out of it; it looked even better.

KENNETH A. BODE (network correspondent, NBC News): Dick Wirthlin, this point is the closest you are into a trough at the end.

What were you most worried that Jimmy Carter as president would do to pick up his momentum?

—PREPARING FOR THE 'OCTOBER SURPRISE'—

WIRTHLIN: As we started the month our greatest concern was two-fold. One, it was evident that the thrust of the Carter strategy was to mount a campaign of fear, raise the risk concern about Governor Reagan, using the vehicle of the war and peace issue, which we knew was a vulnerability that we had at that juncture. But our greatest concern was the vaunted "October surprise."* We started the campaign under the assumption that the president can't determine events but frequently can affect the timing of the event. Number two, because he occupies that position he can, even more than a challenger, acquire the media attention that's needed when there is some axial event that occurs, and we were very, very sensitive to that possibility. It was my judgment if there was an October surprise and if it was going to pound us, it would likely come between the 20th and the 24th of October; and we didn't have the margin at that juncture needed, from my point of view, to withstand the release of the hostages, say, in that time period.

PAUL G. KIRK, JR. (national political director, Kennedy for President): But Dick, I was going to ask that in addition to trying to condition the public about the possibility of the October surprise and put them on some notice, did you take other steps in preparation for a possible surprise of some specific nature, and if so, following such an occurrence, what steps would you take in order to try to rebut it even though you may not have known exactly what it would be?

NOFZIGER: We took the governor to church a lot, and we prayed often. (*Laughter*)

KEEFE: You did that personally?

---

*The announcement by the White House of a foreign policy development believed to carry a favorable political impact for the Carter candidacy, and probably involving the hostage crisis.

WIRTHLIN: When you get Nofziger praying, I know I've got to plan. During the first weeks we did start to track what we felt were the three or four very critical key perceptions about the release of the Iranian hostages that would guide a counter-strategy. Beginning about the 23rd or 24th of the month, there was a good deal of rumor that the hostages were going to be released. There was discussion about a parliamentary vote in Iran. That whole issue then came back into focus. At that juncture we created a campaign within a campaign. Every morning at six o'clock we met with Bill Casey and some other members —

CASEY: Six-thirty.

NOFZIGER: Those of us on the road didn't have to meet.

WIRTHLIN: And we met with Peter Dailey in that session. We created media response, we cut ads, we tracked the situation as best we possibly could to assess where it was going, and we developed four possible responses depending upon how that situation developed.

ADAM CLYMER (correspondent, *New York Times*): Dick, I'm just curious, not so much as to what you did but the fact that you were talking about an October surprise in September and early October. You were talking about how you were having strategy sessions. You were quite frequently on the record on it. It was something which you didn't necessarily have to talk about. Was this part of a basic strategy to be pushing people to think that if something happened, it was part of a political campaign and not part of foreign policy, and to take the edge off whatever Carter might get out of it?

WIRTHLIN: We felt we were most vulnerable to the experience that the Kennedy people had in Wisconsin on that Tuesday morning there. And yes, it was a conscious element of our strategy. We began talking about the October surprise as early as July. I think Bill Casey first opened that subject then, and it was designed to at least sensitize the electorate to some extent should some dramatic event occur in October that could have shifted the electoral balance.

CASEY: We saw a ten-point shift in the vote in Wisconsin, on the basis of a nonhappening, which was announced at seven o'clock in the morning when the voters were going to the polls.

NOFZIGER: The one thing it did, the constant repetition on it, made the press very aware. The travelling press was constantly talking about the October surprise, so it was thoroughly fixed in their minds. I think probably if there had been one, it would have been treated largely as a political event, at least by the travelling press.

BILL BROCK (chairman, Republican National Committee): But one of the reasons the strategy worked is because we were given that enormous asset from the press conference at seven-fifteen in the morning in Wisconsin. That had increased the level of scepticism to such a degree that we could then play on that for the rest of the year.

CADDELL: I'd like to pick up on the October surprise. That seven-fifteen press conference indeed had the same impact on us. It made the people in both the administration and the campaign absolutely gunshy of doing certain things governmentally that we thought might result in playing particularly to the press cynicism on that question, and it sort of backed us off.

BRODER: What kind of things were you inhibited from doing?

CADDELL: Well, announcing the release of the hostages, even when they weren't released. At one point over the weekend, someone suggested that we just bring actors in; no one would know. (*Laughter*)

KEEFE: They were using them.

NOFZIGER: It works.

CADDELL: I thought all the discussion about the October surprise was a valiant effort, probably the only thing you could do. But I never considered that if something as dramatic as the actual event itself took place, it would be anything but a straw being blown over by the event itself, that the thing would be so big and so real that it would wipe out any advance efforts to counter it.

NOLAN: You're sure of that, Patrick?

CASEY: Well, wouldn't that depend on when it happened and how it happened, and what the price was, and so forth?

CADDELL: Certainly, except that when you try to weigh it out, my assumption was that anything short of the hostages coming out wasn't going to help. The worst situation would be to have interest focused on it, to have hopes raised. . . . This plays back to the cynicism.

ROBERT M. TEETER (president, Market Opinion Research): I want to ask Pat: on the assumption that you were not going to get a break in Iran, and the hostages were not going to get out and you were not going to get something that would help you, during this first two or three weeks of October, did you plan some other kind of way to shift and focus the campaign on foreign policy or on something else other than Iran, that would be second best but would serve the same purpose?

— THE "WAR AND PEACE" ISSUE —

CADDELL: Well, the problem was that we never really expected that something would happen on Iran during this period. We weren't having a lot of success in the government with other dramatic actions, particularly in the economy. So our movement was obviously to move the nature of the debate to war and peace, Reagan's weakest area.

Our first survey sometime after the convention had us down about eight points, but by early September we were back basically to an even posture. I thought that in many ways it was our best point of the campaign. The debate with Congressman Anderson and Governor Reagan was very important because it had affected many of the image attitudes that existed about the governor; it reassured people and — I thought at that point — cost us a couple of weeks. But what it really did was de-rail our movement that was building at the time of the debate and moved Governor Reagan from an even situation to a couple of points ahead. By the 10th or 15th of October, though, what was striking was that there had been so little change. I mean, not only in the vote questions but, going back to early September, the opinions the people had about the candidates, the comparatives where they judged the candidates, were all relatively the same. We began to focus hard on the war and peace issue — we knew that our best ground was in foreign policy without Iran.

HUNT: Pat, in that connection, it seems to me sometime around September 20th the Iran–Iraq war started. Two questions. One, did you ever think of a way that you could use that as a vehicle to focus the campaign more on foreign policy? Secondly, did it surprise you that it apparently did not give you the normal benefit that a war, conflict, front-page news gives the incumbent? One would think it even more so given your advantages on the war and peace issue, but it didn't seem to.

CADDELL: It didn't seem to. . . . But we expected to get more out of the Iran–Iraq situation because of the focus on the war, and I don't think we got that. I think part of the problem in terms of projecting some leadership on it was the fact that, of course, we were not dealing with either country. If anything, it suggested that we had no control, but we thought that concern would arise over energy supplies and grow, and it did not.

CLYMER: That problem would have been better from your perspective if it had been Iraq against anybody else. Iran is not basically a word that you wanted in the public consciousness unless it was with news of the release of the hostages.

CADDELL: That's true, but they didn't consult us. (*Laughter*)

—KENNEDY AS TEAM PLAYER—

BRODER: We were beginning to get some awareness in October of three other sets of players. Senator Kennedy comes onto the screen prominently about this point; the independent expenditure groups on behalf of the Reagan campaign are operating; we begin to hear a lot more about the Moral Majority. I'd like to sketch in briefly some of the decisionmaking. Why did Kennedy decide to be such a prominent team player after being such a conspicuous nonteam player, Paul, up to that point?

KIRK: Nonteam as in challenger?

BRODER: Yes, that's all part of the process.

KIRK: Once the nomination was secured, I think the senator felt Jimmy Carter could not possibly prevail unless he had something going in the big states. Clearly there was a difference on a lot of the policy issues that brought Kennedy into the campaign; but nevertheless, when it comes to the bottom line in November, you're talking about a guy, and his family, who spent a couple of generations in terms of the Democratic party and what it stood for. Despite the wounds that existed within the party, I think he felt he could try to do his part and put his shoulder to the wheel. I don't think he felt that he could sit by. There were, I guess, some commercials that were cut, and he did take to the hustings and try to help out, but it was basically a guy born and bred in the Democratic party.

NOLAN: Did you keep a score card, Paul? I mean, I know Senator Kennedy went to the Chicanos in Texas and Hispanics in California and Jews in New York. I mean, you usually keep a score card whether you're on the varsity or not, right? How did he do?

KIRK: Did he make a difference? I don't think so. I think he hoped he would make a difference, but my own observation was that it didn't make any difference to middle-income families trying to make ends meet or to the steel worker who is out of work. I mean, Kennedy came back into whatever town he was in before, and they may have voted for him, and he's back here on behalf of Carter, against whom he ran before. Democrat or not, the guy out there or the family out there is saying that the choice is between two futures, and no matter what Ted Kennedy says, I'm going to make an independent choice on the thing.

KEEFE: Oh, I think there was some effect on the senator's ability to help Carter by the Reagan television use of earlier tapes of Kennedy campaigning against Carter. In Texas, for example, I thought that was very effective. When we had Ted Kennedy down there person-to-person, they had him on the tube on their side of the question, and I think that really blunted it.

NOLAN: Starting in '68, a lot of people could blame Gene McCarthy for Humphrey's loss and Ford's people blame Reagan for Ford's loss, and this time is it conceivable that the Carter people, if they ever achieve a resurrection in the next few years, can blame Kennedy in any way?

KIRK: This is a Kennedy spokesman talking; I can't see anyone wearing any hat, giving any credibility and credence to that.

BRODER: Bob, the Carter people seemed awfully eager to get Kennedy into this campaign, even at times fawning about this wonderful young man with this brilliant future. What did you all think you were buying when you bought his contribution to the campaign?

KEEFE: I think clearly, if you look at the results in the primaries, Senator Kennedy had some extremely strong support in areas of Carter's weaknesses, and we thought that he'd be very helpful in bringing back traditional Democrats in the big states—the ethnics, blacks, liberals.

CLYMER: Bill, did it seem to you that he was having that effect? Were you worried that he'd have that effect?

BROCK: Not really. Again, I thought that the media strategy of following Kennedy with some ads, talking about what Kennedy had said in the spring, was very capable of diffusing it. I thought Kennedy could make a difference in a couple of states that were really close, perhaps even Texas, but it did not turn out that way.

HUNT: Paul, right after the convention, wasn't there really more debate over how active a role Kennedy would play, and didn't a number of his associates, maybe you included, warn him that for his future, it was important that he get heavily involved, visibly involved?

KIRK: It was not a matter really of serious discussion or debate. It wasn't, Well, if you don't do this it may make a difference if you decide to do something in the future—that was none of the quotient. I don't think he himself, as a competitive fellow, wanted to be the guy sulking in his tent. I cannot tell you that he was totally comfortable going back out on behalf of Carter, but I think he would have been less comfortable doing nothing.

— INDEPENDENT EXPENDITURES —

BRODER: Doug Bailey and Dave Keene, the decision to run extensive independent operations on behalf of the Reagan campaign — was that decision essentially a clever way to get around the limits on what Reagan could spend himself or was it really a vote of no confidence on the ability of Casey-Wirthlin-Dailey-Nofziger to manage this candidate to victory?

DAVID A. KEENE (national political director, Bush for President): I don't think it was either of those. I think it was a reflection of the fact that we have a system now in which, particularly the presidential campaigns in the general election period, are financed by the federal government in total. They are of necessity rather closed operations relying heavily on media, and do not involve a lot of people who have historically wanted to be involved, either in activities or in contributing money, which is one of the ways people historically want to express their political views. The independent expenditure groups are really a creation of the Congress, not a creation of the management of any of the campaigns or a vote of no confidence. As long as people want to be involved in politics, and there is a legal way for them to do it, they will be, and I think that's really what we're talking about. With the people I talked to, there wasn't any sitting down and asking, Is there some way we could get around limits so Reagan can have more money spent on his behalf? The talk was, Here are a lot of people who want to do something to help Ronald Reagan be elected president; what can they do?

KEEFE: Was it more of a profit motive?

KEENE: There was some fellow this time in Texas or Florida or someplace who essentially raised money for himself, went into business using that as a way of defrauding contributors, but I don't think that was a motive on the part of any of the larger groups. Now there was, early on, a great deal of legitimate concern on the one hand and exaggerated reporting on the other about what these groups might do. Legitimate concern in the sense that the law created the ability and necessity of forming and organizing completely independent vehicles which are out of the control of the managers of the formal campaigns and therefore may be, on the one hand, counterproductive because of what they might do and, on the other hand, may be doing things inconsistent with the strategy that the formal campaign is carrying on. One of my concerns in being involved in this was that if any of these groups did something that was completely beyond the pale, it would make all of it look bad. Fortunately, I don't think that happened with any major groups. The second thing was exaggerated reporting at the beginning. There were stories that $25, or even $50, million was going to be raised by these people, and the fact of the matter was that such a thing was never possible.

NOLAN: How much was raised?

KEENE: I don't know. In total, I suspect that four to six major groups perhaps had a million dollars apiece.

DOUGLAS BAILEY (president, Bailey, Deardourff & Associates): Americans for an Effective Presidency, the only one that I can talk about, raised $2 million. They spent, I'm surprised to hear, the same million that the Anderson campaign spent in media. The only other large bill that we had were legal fees to combat Carter's rather massive effort to close these activities down or to keep them from getting any air time.

KEENE: The only one I can speak to is the effort that the National Conservative Political Action Committee (NCPAC) ran, and they spent approximately $6-$700,000, concentrated really in three states, on television, direct mail—

J. ANDERSON: I suppose that's exclusive of what they spent on senatorial races.

KEENE: It was an entirely separate thing. It wasn't separate in the sense that it was a different group, but it was money that was raised and given for that purpose exclusively.

BAILEY: I think there was a broad suspicion in the land among the press and among the Democrats.

BRODER: Bill Casey, did you know or care what these folks were doing?

CASEY: In fact, I was worried about it. I didn't think it would be significant in terms of the contribution it would make, and at an early stage we felt they might cut across our strategy and would make Reagan look harsher and more rightwing than we wanted to look and than he was. It was more of a hazard in terms of campaign strategy.

BRODER: What did you do about it—nothing?

CASEY: Oh, we didn't do much about it. Actually, we did send out all kinds of cautions to our people about having any conversation at all, and we did talk about the possibility of repudiating. Bill Brock made a very strong statement. We talked a lot about how we could dampen them down. The real danger in my mind was that it would take money that would more effectively go into the state organizations with which we could coordinate and use in grassroots organizing.

CLYMER: There's at least one ad that Reagan himself questioned?

CASEY: That's right.

BODE: The Dallas conference, the famous evolution press conference, Reagan renounced one of the ads without being specific about which one it was.*

CASEY: That's the one shown in California. He was nervous about the whole thing.

HUNT: I remember one time calling to do a story on the party money in late August. You gave a statement saying you hoped that people wouldn't give money to those independent groups. Did you do anything else like that?

*On August 22, after speaking to a group of evangelical Christians in Dallas, Reagan told a press conference that he felt there were "great flaws" in the theory of evolution, and that the Biblical account of creation ought to be taught in public schools along with the evolutionary account.

CASEY: We put out a policy statement to our whole organization that we'd prefer to see contributions go to the state parties, where under the law we could cooperate and coordinate our activities with them.

HUNT: Did you get a real sense of competition for that money, Bill, or was there enough so —

BROCK: The fear dwindled as we saw their inability to raise money. I think we were really able to shut off the spigot pretty well, and we very aggressively tried to do it, and I hate to say that with my friends here, but I was scared.

KEENE: We never targeted more than that because we didn't think it was realistic. We were perfectly satisfied.

CLYMER: I have the sense, and you would be in a better position to judge, that the Common Cause and Carter administration legal actions, scared a whole lot of potential, let's say, corporate executives who might have given $1,000 who saw themselves being subpoenaed and spending time explaining, No, I never did have anything to do with Reagan.*

BAILEY: Absolutely. I genuinely thought that except for the legal actions of Carter and Common Cause and so forth, that Americans for an Effective Presidency, because of its contacts with corporate America, could probably have raised $10 million. Let me say, however, that there are many examples throughout history, like the Iowa caucus suddenly in 1980 becoming giant in its size and impact. What's going to happen in 1984 is that everybody and his brother is going to figure out that independent expenditures is a good thing to do. That is a problem.

KEENE: Okay, if Ted Kennedy, for example, had been the nominee of the Democratic party, there would have been independent spending groups springing up because it's partly a response to the fervor of the base, and Carter didn't have that kind of base.

---

*The "Common Cause and Carter administration legal actions" were separate actions taken by those organizations which challenged the independence of expenditiures made in support of the Reagan candidacy by groups claiming no formal affiliation with the Reagan campaign.

EDDIE MAHE, JR. (campaign director, John Connally for President): There was one thing that was missed. Nobody ever really wrote a great deal about the vast volume of independent advertising that was done for John Connally in Iowa, a vast majority of which was very counterproductive. I mean they were running those four-page newspaper ads out there—just outrageous, and you could do nothing about it.

KEENE: We figured you could coordinate. (*Laughter*)

BODE: Given all the press that goes on giving priorities of various campaigns and media strategies, things like that, you really don't need to talk to a campaign manager to have that kind of communication and spend your money effectively. David, you knew precisely where to put that money, didn't you?

KEENE: Exactly. Al Hunt prepared the strategy memo for us in the *Wall Street Journal* as to what the Reagan people were doing and what we wanted to do in that respect.

HUNT: Glad I could be helpful!

KEENE: If a group wants to assist, and I think most of these groups got in for that purpose, you first of all wanted to discover through publicly accessible information what it is that the campaign you want to assist is doing, what their strategy is, to the extent that it's possible to find out. Then you wanted to devise something with what limited resources you have that will assist rather than hurt that campaign. A lot of it was common sense. We targeted three Southern states which, if things broke right, Governor Reagan would have a chance to win, or which we might be able to have enough impact on to divert some of Carter's resources to, where the Reagan campaign was probably not going to be able to target a lot of money, and where we could be of maximum help. That kind of judgment can be made from publicly accessible information, and it doesn't require any coordination in the legal sense.

—THE MORAL MAJORITY—

BRODER: I want to ask one question of Eddie Mahe. You dealt fairly closely, I believe, with several of the Moral Majority groups in state campaigns that you were involved in during the fall. Tell us a little bit about what their leadership is like in terms of political decisionmaking. What was going into their decisions?

MAHE: The point should be made that nobody has a tremendous amount of influence, at least no one around this table has a serious amount of influence with these people. I think the thing that has to be said about the Moral Majority is that it became a code word for some massive group out there which really does not exist in fact. Basically, all the Moral Majority consists of is some independent Baptists—they don't even include, by and large, the Southern Baptists; and, as a matter of fact, in Oklahoma there is a tremendous confrontation between the two. To the extent that we were making an effort it was probably to try to keep them from consuming each other and at least occasionally to keep their eye on the ultimate ball, which was that they should devote their time to trying to register and turn out those who are registered within the various denominations to vote. They got caught up in the system—particularly, I suppose one would have to say, Reverend Falwell. I don't think that Falwell anticipated the intensity of coverage that was going to come on him, and he became very concerned though I won't say lost some of his commitment; but he became very sensitive about what he was accomplishing.

I do feel that the evangelical movement did have an effect particularly in Alabama, and not because of their involvement directly as regards the presidential race, but because of their commitment to Republican Senate candidate Jeremiah Denton. Reagan would have carried Oklahoma in any event. Downstate Illinois, I think there was a definite impact. Less so in some other states. Governor Reagan, I think, was always going to win in Iowa. But when you think of the Moral Majority as a monolithic entity out there, let me assure you it *is not*.

BRODER: Now let's get on to League of Women Voters and the debate. John, let me begin with you on that. Some of us thought that you had the League of Women Voters in your hip pocket. How did they get out, and what did you try to do?

ANDERSON: I wish I knew how they slipped away! Of course, from as early as the middle of the summer we had been in contact with the league principally through the counsel for our campaign, Mitch Rogovin, in an effort to convince them that if they undertook their role as the sponsor of these debates, they should include us. Subsequently we were able to meet their initial criteria of being a serious candidate in the sense that we were on the ballot of all states, and that we had the required 15 percent.

KEEFE: Would you have debated Libertarian candidate Ed Clark?

ANDERSON: Would I have debated him under what circumstances?

KEEFE: Someone proposed a two-person debate between you and Ed Clark.

ANDERSON: I think at one time we did, as a matter of fact, talk about a debate, and I guess I would have had no fundamental objections to it. But to get back to your question, David, I think it was a legitimate suspicion that the Carter campaign was in communication with Mrs. Hinerfeld and other officials of the League of Women Voters, and putting them under severe pressure to schedule this two-man debate first between Governor Reagan and President Carter. Ultimately they did, of course, cave in, as we put it, on the 18th of October, or whenever it was, and agree to do that. As to how they got away from us, I don't know. We tried very hard. We continued to lobby them through our campaign counsel as extensively as we could, to hold fast to the idea that it was to be a three-man rather than a two-man debate.

—REAGAN DECIDES TO DEBATE—

BRODER: So they caved, and they offered a two-man debate. Why did Reagan decide to take the debate?

NOFZIGER: He decided to take the debate because we looked at the situation and it had flattened out. There was just no movement out there, and we thought that one way to get some movement was to challenge Carter to a debate. At that time we weren't even certain that Carter people would take it. A lot of us felt that they felt they had the best of both worlds, that they could beat us on the head for not debating, praying all the time that we wouldn't. I should point out that Governor Reagan has great confidence in his ability to do well in these kinds of things. There was never any doubt in his mind that he shouldn't debate from the standpoint of whether he could win or lose. The decision that was made and had been made all along was purely a political decision and not one based on any fear or trepidation or anything like that.

WIRTHLIN: I had a somewhat different view of the political implications of a debate decision. It was a close call. Of course, the governor himself personally made that call after hearing discussions of both sides of the issue. The one argument and the one position that he took that no one could argue was, "If I want to succeed Jimmy Carter, I should be willing to face him one-to-one." The governor was sincerely concerned about the fairness and the unfairness of excluding John Anderson, and he attempted to do everything he could to keep that door open as long and wide as he could; that was not, again, a politically motivated decision but how he really felt. It went back to in part some of the things that happened in New Hampshire concerning the equity or fairness of including all candidates.

NOFZIGER: Very nice when the candidate's morality coincides with the campaign's politics. (*Laughter*)

PETER DAILEY (deputy director (media), Reagan-Bush Committee): To get a human decision on it, too, there's a lot of Gipper in the governor, and how could the Gipper not debate?

HUNT: We read a lot during that time about how this was a close call and you were all rather deeply divided on it. You were one of the doves, Dick, I guess, on the debate question; let me just ask of you or Mr. Casey or Lyn, what fears did Nancy Reagan have on that debate issue at this time, and how much of a factor was she in this decisionmaking process?

WIRTHLIN: In essence, she changed her view. I felt that we should again engage the debate format as a very useful vehicle to achieve our campaign objectives of rounding out the view that the electorate had of the governor. I had suggested that we close our Baltimore debate with the challenge issued to Jimmy Carter to then meet us in debate at that juncture, but that suggestion was not followed. Initially, Nancy Reagan felt strongly that we should not debate—that was early October. But, at least from what I was able to see, Nancy Reagan had very little direct input into that debate decision.

NOFZIGER: On the day that those of us on the airplane thought we ought to talk to the people at headquarters with the idea of going ahead with the debate, Nancy agreed to that. She did not play any role within the discussion. She sat in on the final meeting which included the governor, and we went over all the pros and cons of this, but she did not take an active role. I suppose had she been adamantly opposed at the time that she would have spoken up, but it's a mistake to assume that her position would prevail if it was counter to what the governor wanted or what the campaign people managed to convince him of.

CLYMER: One thing you fellows haven't made clear, at least to me, is the argument against Reagan debating. Why did those of you who thought he shouldn't, or even the ones who were mixed on it, think it was a mistake, since you tell us that you and he had great confidence in his ability in such situations?

BODE: Bill Casey, what was your position on this, just for the record?

CASEY: My position had evolved over time. I saw the governor on the same platform with Jimmy Carter on two occasions: one at the Italian-American Foundation dinner and the night before the final decision on the debate, at the Al Smith dinner. I felt that he would just start out way ahead because he looked better and appeared to handle himself better.

HUNT: Had you made your decision by the Al Smith dinner?

CASEY: Well, I would say it was jelling, but it was kind of formally made the morning after the Al Smith dinner. Those who opposed the debate felt we were doing well without it.

BODE: I'd like to hear Dick's comment on that.

WIRTHLIN: This was perhaps the first time when those on the plane rather seriously disagreed with the way those of us who were not continually traveling viewed the course of the election. It was my view that we, in fact, had turned the corner about the 15th of October and all of our data, not only our national data but our statewide data, showed the election trending toward us by the evening of that decision, and that was a relatively recent event. I think in terms of decisionmaking, the environment of the airplane is an interesting one to consider. Lyn and Mike Deaver and Stu Spencer were encapsulized in that aluminum tube and subject to some extent to the voices they were hearing and the kind of discussion they were having. I think this is a classic case where their view was different because of the environment in which they were living.

I felt that the campaign had turned the corner for several reasons. As I indicated, we showed a very tight race up to about the 10th or 11th of October, but by the 17th we showed, based upon our Political Information System (PINS), that the most reasonable projection of electoral votes was 310 and that our national study showed us with about a six-point lead. I had no doubt in my mind that Ronald Reagan would do well, but why lay the whole election on an event that you cannot control? I felt that we could win the election without the debate, though nevertheless it was a rather close call. But the argument I couldn't counter was the governor's belief that if he were going to be president, if he were asking for the affirmative decision from the people, he should meet Jimmy Carter one-to-one.

ANDERSON: There was not so *sotto voce* dissent at this table just a few minutes ago by the press or parts thereof that the governor thought it was unthinkable that he would somehow retreat in the face of a challenge to debate. From a practical standpoint, I wonder to what extent were you afraid of adverse reaction from the press if you appeared to be backpedalling in the face of this challenge from President Carter to debate. Because frankly, not to answer my own question, I was disappointed at the extent to which this was a non-issue as far as the press was concerned. You started this discussion by asking me what I did to try to keep the heat on the League of Women Voters. I did try to make it an issue. I spoke repeatedly in speeches about how important I thought it was that these debates occur and that they be three-man debates; other than a few editorial cartoons, it just seemed to me that it was a non-issue as far as the great majority of the media were concerned.

NOFZIGER: John, let me come back to what I said earlier. Those of us on the plane in that peculiar environment with, I might say, access to telephones and getting on the ground once in awhile, did feel that the campaign had flattened out. We came to the conclusion all on the same day—literally the four of us did, and I'm talking about Stu and the governor and Deaver and myself. There was just that feeling and inertia that was beginning to disturb us at exactly at the time we were turning the corner. I guess we were a day behind.

BROCK: I think it's a question of who gets encapsulated. You can be mechanically encapsuled in a plane, but you can be isolated by the pressures of the campaign in a headquarters, too, and I was in a brutal fight with my best friend, Bill Timmons, who was very much against the debate, as you know.*

WIRTHLIN: For different reasons, and I think we should put those reasons on the record. It was Bill's strong feeling that we had structured the campaign to have maximal impact during the last five days. All of his efforts, the organizational efforts, and the media efforts would provide us with the additional boost we needed to offset (1) an October surprise or (2) "the return of the native" phenomenon the last few days. And Bill argued very strongly and persuasively to let the campaign run its course without the debate because he was very confident that his activity in the campaign would drive the campaign very successfully in the last week.

BROCK: I have exactly the reverse opinion because we had, I think, the same sense Lyn had, that we simply weren't getting the motivation and the movement in the field.

—CARTER CONSIDERS THE DEBATE—

BRODER: Excuse me. Pat, you indicated yesterday briefly that you had some personal reservations about Carter's decision to go into this debate. What was the discussion like on your side?

NOFZIGER: And what did Amy say? (*Laughter*)

NOLAN: Were you surprised that they accepted the debate?

*William Timmons was deputy chairman of the Reagan campaign.

CADDELL: As I said, I had found it amazing throughout the campaign that they had not accepted a debate with us, a head-to-head debate, from the very beginning, or at least set up a debate schedule. The reason for it was fairly simple. All one had to do was to look at the information we had from the '76 debate. It was clear to us that it was the vehicle of the challenger and not so much for its immediate impact but its longer term impact in answering doubts and reassuring people. In terms of the presidential campaign itself, we felt that by the middle of the month the situation was not as Dick said, that they were well ahead, six points ahead, but in fact it was relatively close at that point. We had forced the campaign to our issue. Governor Reagan himself talked about being hampered by the war and peace issues; the Reagan campaign spent the week dealing with the war and peace issue, which was fine for us because it was contributing to the salience of an issue on which we had an enormous advantage. The more people focused on it, the more we would get out of it.

We also knew—and I knew that the Reagan campaign was aware of this because he had talked about it earlier on—the need for having a secure lead going in the last weeks because of the fact that traditionally, if you go back and look at the old Gallup polls, at the '64 and '72 races, the incumbent party nominee in the last week of the campaign has traditionally gained five to six points that week. The reason for this is simple, because people intensify their decisions about who should be president, and, unlike many other races, it is generally resolved in favor of the incumbent; we could see that in '76. In the big states as well as nationally, the South was sitting there dead in terms of movement, but in the North and in the suburbs particularly, we were getting the movement on the war and peace issue. If you look at the structure of the race at that point, the undecided voters were essentially our natives, and traditionally the move was for natives to come home. I think everyone was picking up on that, and that incumbent advantage was clearly being positioned to take place. There was great division in the Carter campaign about debate. My personal preference, as I said, was always against debating if we could find a way rationally to avoid it. In part, we reaped what we had sown here because of the decision not to debate Senator Kennedy in the primary, and then the decision not to debate on the three-way model. We considered debating Senator Kennedy, and when we decided not to, the president did go out and say—or Jody went back on the plane and said—in June that we would accept a head-to-head debate, and we would also accept the debate of all the candidates when some formula was determined. We had put that marker down to protect ourselves.

The most nervous point was the question of whether we could survive what happened in Baltimore, in terms of the reaction of what was supposed to be the firestorm—some people felt there would be a firestorm over the decision not to debate. There was no firestorm. The key thing about the Baltimore debate is what convinced me even more that the Reagan people would want to debate, and that is the benefit Ronald Reagan got out of the debate. John Anderson won the debate on points and lost the war, and Reagan was the one who got something out of it because he reassured; he moved. You could see it in all the survey notes as well.

BRODER: Your advice is generally quite influential with the president. What was the counter-advice that led him to . . . ?

CADDELL: Here was what was going on. Some people argued that President Carter would show his superior knowledge in a number of things and take Governor Reagan on. There was a feeling of confidence on the part of some people that there had been all year about the debate. I didn't disagree with the president's debating ability; I just disagreed about the structure of what the debate could do, particularly for an incumbent. There was also another set of beliefs which became very critical in early October. Some people in the campaign, Hamilton particularly, said that—even though intellectually he accepted the argument that the debates were not our vehicle, that they were challenger vehicles—he was always struck with the sense that sooner or later we'd want one. Somehow, he had a sense that we'd want to debate Reagan, that we'd want something to move the campaign. So there was ambivalence because we had come to a critical period.

The weekend before, we had read that the Reagan campaign said they would not debate unless they needed to debate. We then saw in our surveys the movement was taking place, and I finally managed to convince most of the campaign that we should move to shut the debate off. In other words, what we should do is move quickly to issue a statement or challenge and structure it in such a way as to demand a rejection—that Reagan either decide in twenty-four hours to debate and stop being a coward or whatever we could put together on that, or we weren't going to have a debate because we were going to plan the last part of our campaign. The one thing we knew we did not want was a debate, particularly during the last week of the campaign which would mess up the normal incumbent advantage that I talked about earlier. We were, in fact, moving to do that when the League of Women Voters decided they wanted back into the game. I don't know whose hip pocket they were in, but they were never in ours because they always reared their heads at the worst moment. And I disagree with Anderson—we were not pushing Hinerfeld or anybody else to have a debate. We also heard rumblings on that Monday that the Reagan campaign was now seriously also considering moving toward accepting the debate.

So our strategy at that point was to close the debate down; in fact, we issued the statement. It didn't matter. The League had already moved and Reagan had moved, and so we were left with that question. Our problem was that there was probably more ambivalence and unwillingness to shut the question down totally in the period of the 6th to 10th of October than all of the U.S. wished in retrospect.

CLYMER: Had the expectation that one heard frequently from people in the campaign staff in the spring and summer—that Reagan was so likely to do something dumb—had that diminished from exposure to Reagan's performance in debates earlier in the year?

CADDELL: I was at Nashua. I had an invitation from the press to go and watch. We had looked earlier at the films of the debates and so forth, and frankly, it seemed to me that if we could avoid it, we should; we wanted no part of it, particularly for one major reason. We were intensifying the fear and doubts about Governor Reagan to an extreme, and the one thing that Governor Reagan does not look like on television in a debate is an extremist or a dangerous person. His demeanor is not such.

Look at the concerns that people had and the degree in which they had those concerns. You had Dick saying better than 40 percent of the people felt Governor Reagan was dangerous to some extent. We had, two to one, people disagreeing with the idea that he would keep us out of war if he were president; you had half the people believing he was too much of a risk to be president. A whole series of things existed, and it seemed to me that the concerns were so extreme that there was no better vehicle for Reagan than a debate.

From my experience in '76, —and I never thought that we would have better than a 25 percent chance of winning that debate, even if we won it on points—a debate tended to put us in a position of having both to help ourselves and to make sure that Reagan was hurt in the debate. Governor Reagan was in the position of simply helping himself and, by helping himself, would help the electoral situation.

—DRAWING A CONTRAST—

FRANCIS: Let me just add to what Pat said. I think it was Hamilton's view that we had to draw a contrast somehow on issues. It wasn't so much that we expected Governor Reagan to make a mistake in the debate or make some *faux pas*, but that we had to get that contrast to get those undecideds to move back our way. We had to reemphasize the fact that Carter was a Democrat and there were strong distinctions on programs and policies between the two. We hadn't been able to do that in the campaign at that point, and the debate was a good way to do it.

KEEFE: One of the things that Les Francis contributed to the campaign very early on was to take it upon himself to get the rest of the people in the campaign to recognize the tremendous campaigner that Ronald Reagan is. He brought Jess Unruh and Bob Moretti, former Reagan adversaries from California, back in June, I guess, and sat one afternoon, talking about Ronald Reagan as they knew him as one hell of an effective campaigner who doesn't rattle and who does well in appearances. I guess Jess couldn't speak to the debate structure specifically, but they were rather eloquent on Reagan's ability as a campaigner. Also, one of the dilemmas in working against Reagan is that you can either select his record or his rhetoric, and the minute you try to make him ambiguous because his rhetoric doesn't match his record, you drive him into the middle and make him a moderate; and, for God's sake, we certainly didn't want to do that.

HUNT: Bob, do you think that advice was really heeded? Do you think the top people in the Carter campaign really believed Unruh and Moretti?

KEEFE: I think it lowered their thinking of the disparity between our candidate as a campaigner and Reagan. I don't think it totally convinced them. I think it helped sensitize them. I'm not sure it took 100 percent, but it did help.

BRODER: The famous quote from Hamilton on the floor of the Democratic convention on the night of Carter's nomination—it will be easier than you think to defeat Reagan. Was that just rhetoric or was that, in fact, the view?

CADDELL: I think when he did it—the night of the nomination on the floor—I think that was simply a comment. I mean, all we had to do was look at the structure of our situation going into the general election.

BRODER: Okay, the debate takes place; we all saw it and have our reactions to it. Now we are into the last five days with an absolute swirl of events, the aftermath of the debate, the issues that were raised there, the impressions that were created; and meanwhile here comes the hostage question barreling down the track. At this point in a campaign, is there any effective control? Pete Dailey, you had probably more resources than anybody else around the table at that point. You were at the 6:30 a.m. meetings. To what extent were you still able to make decisions that could have an impact on the outcome?

DAILEY: I was tired.

BRODER: How many resources were available?

—REAGAN'S FINAL PLANS—

DAILEY: There are two things that are unthinkable in a campaign as far as the media goes. One is that you don't have enough to stand heavily at the end, and the second is that you don't spend everything that you have; and going into the last two weeks of the campaign, we had about $7 million, about 40 percent of our budget, and we had husbanded those resources because of the research and everything that Dick had provided us in experience in past campaigns. The electorate doesn't really get serious until the end, and we wanted to have all the flexibility we possibly could. So we were sitting on those resources. They were commited, all right, but they could have been adjusted. So we had the resources at the end to cover the bases very strongly, and we were faced with really essentially trying to hold onto the course that had been established earlier. There is a tremendous weight in a campaign as it moves along, as I know all of you are surely aware, as the pressures build and as you get closer to the end. And there's that obvious date when it's all over, and you've either won or lost. There's tremendous pressure to do something, and as it builds in the campaign, doing something is good and not doing something is bad. So you really have to keep your eye focused on what essentially you are really trying to do, and the key judgments are not necessarily what you do but what you choose not to do.

As we went into those latter stages, we were working very closely on some kind of a counter-strategy on the hostages, since it looked like that issue was developing. The unfortunate nature of the timing from the Democrats' side was that it happened to break officially for the first time on the two Fridays before, about twelve days before the election, which was the date of the consumer price index report. We had structured our media to come in very heavily on the specifics of the consumer price index following up on the baseline work we and the R.N.C. had been doing, focusing very strongly on the economy. We were going to use that as a take-off point. We were fairly sure that the numbers would be in our favor, and I think on that day the hostage thing re-erupted. We looked at it as the October surprise, and continued to try to monitor it, but essentially we didn't change our strategy at that point. We hung to what we were doing.

NOLAN: You fellows on the Reagan side had deliberately managed to convert the October surprise into a self-fulfilling prophecy, and you had calculated it so that if indeed the hostages came home, the viewers on television would have the image of Gerry Rafshoon applying pancake makeup to them. Was that it, or had you planned to provide your own sense of drama to counteract the real drama?

WIRTHLIN: That was clearly part of it, but secondly, we did have the mechanisms available to us, even as late as Sunday. Radio ads. We had television ads already cut to use if the hostages came home that covered a rather wide range of responses to that event should the hostage situation begin cutting into our base.

BODE: For example?

CASEY: We didn't have to do anything because by virtue of the debate we had the polls going our way. The reason we thought the debate was desirable was that we had a cushion but not enough of a cushion to withstand a last-minute shock. By the time the hostage situation re-erupted the weekend before the election, although we were concerned about it, we had a kind of a cushion that we felt could stand the shock. At the same time, the prospect of a shock had substantially diminished. Six weeks earlier, a poll asked if people felt Jimmy Carter would deliberately manipulate the hostage situation to political advantage, and only 15 percent of the electorate said yes. By the time of the last week, there were two questions. Did people think the Ayatollah was trying to manipulate our election, and did they think Jimmy Carter was trying to manipulate the election with the hostage thing? The answer had shifted so it was about two to one, or better than two to one affirmative. So the public was sensitized . . . .

BODE: Set that out. Was it two to one on both questions? Or two to one affirmative that Carter would manipulate?

CASEY: One-third said the Ayatollah was manipulating it; one-third said Carter manipulated it; one-third said it was unthinkable that anybody would try to manipulate it. On top of that some of us began to feel that we had a better side of the hostage situation because if something did happen, all kinds of new considerations were there—were we moving into a dangerous war situation, or what kind of price are we paying? The ransom issue had resurrected itself. I thought Carter had a much more difficult situation with the hostages, whatever the development, than we did. In fact, what we talked about we never really had to get ready because it was all going our way.

HUNT: What did those ads say?

WIRTHLIN: Well, the ads were prepared in part from things that were stated by others concerning the consequence and causes of the hostage release, and I don't know—

DAILEY: I don't think we could have done much at all if they did come home. It would have been difficult to deal with in terms of any media strategy. I think that one of the things that really hurt the Democrats was the fact that the issue was raised at all the Friday before, and it wasn't resolved, and just dragged on.

NOLAN: Now, which Friday is this?

CASEY: This was the Friday before election day. The only effective response we could have made would have been if the hostages had been released and had come home, let's say, ten days or a week earlier, so that you had a response in the first two to three days of gratification; but after that you could raise the question, How did we get in this mess? We had to have time at the end to deal with that question.

DAILEY: At that time we also had our toughest ad on the air, which was the one where we had Carter smiling and the words of the promise over it, and with the frown, the lack of followthrough on the promise. That obviously was an implied attack on his credibility which was our strong suit, and the fact that it was running in conjunction with the once-again raised issue of the hostages only tended to heighten all the groundwork we did earlier, publicizing the issue, of an October surprise.

—CARTER'S RETURN TO THE WHITE HOUSE—

NOLAN: Can I ask Pat why the president broke up the campaign on that Sunday, broke that schedule, created his own sense of drama by doing that, and flew back?

CADDELL: Because he had no choice. The point was that we were not really sure what the Iranians had said. He needed to be there. The translation of the conditions was absolutely critical, and he had to consult with his foreign policy advisors.

NOLAN: Couldn't he do that on the road?

CADDELL: You try to do that from an airplane on an open line, you know, it's just not possible. He couldn't do it from there and also campaign, and at that moment it required attention. It was not even a matter of a debate about coming home at that point.

NOFZIGER: In some respects, wasn't that the best political move anyway?

CADDELL: I think you could argue about that in retrospect, but at that point once the thing is moving—

CASEY: Let me ask you this. What would the whole situation be if he had decided on that Sunday, I'm not going to deal with this thing on account of the election; whatever we do, we'll deal with it starting Wednesday morning?

CADDELL: Well, how can I put this? He was not unaware of a political option, leaving aside all of the substantive considerations. A political option, not on merit but purely on the political need to take that bull by the horns and reject out of hand the conditions as unacceptable because on their face they were not acceptable. Frankly, there was also the need essentially to demagogue the issue on the basis that the United States is not going to be blackmailed and I'm not to be blackmailed and so on. There was no one who supported that option. The problem is, when you carry the responsibility—and I didn't but there are people in the White House who did—you can't do that because we did not know then what the Iranian reaction would be and you still had those people's lives at stake there. What would they do? Would they put them on trial, what? The decision was that that was irresponsible and we just couldn't do it. You pay a price for being in that position.

NOLAN: On Sunday weren't your numbers showing that the campaign was pretty much over, anyway, and he might as well bag it and come home?

CADDELL: On Sunday morning?

NOLAN: Yes.

CADDELL: No.

NOLAN: What did your numbers show?

CADDELL: We had seen a drop after the debate, by Thursday and Friday, and we had started to see it moving back Saturday afternoon and Saturday night. It was on Sunday that we saw it beginning to unravel again.

—REASONS FOR REAGAN'S VICTORY—

BRODER: At this point the role of the moderator becomes that of Leo Tolstoy, and I want you to become historians and not just campaign managers and political practitioners. The question that we want to spend a little time on is, How much of an impact did all this decisionmaking really have? How much of it is the men and women involved, and how much of it is the objective conditions? I'd like to start with you if I could, Dick, reminding you and reminding the readers of this book that at the National Press Club three days after the Carter victory in 1976, Richard Scammon stood up and said, and I think I quote accurately, "There is nothing wrong with the Republican party that 12 percent inflation will not cure." Was the outcome of this election really dictated by that elemental a fact?

WIRTHLIN: Well, I think that clearly imposed the structure of the election to some extent, but I think there was something even more basic than that. I believe that Ronald Reagan won because he, more than Anderson or Carter, did have an approach to governing and had a view of what the American role of leadership would be: namely, the ability to motivate and move masses of individual citizens. I think also he had a sense of vision of America that provided a frame of reference for the strategy that gave us a consistent and directed thrust to the campaign right from the beginning to the end. One of the critical numbers that hasn't been mentioned here that was running counter to the conclusion that a lot of writers and observers have made—that this was simply a negative election—was the fact that in December 1979, 74 percent of the American electorate felt that this country had seriously gotten off on the wrong track. In ovember, that had fallen to only 56 percent. In other words, in spite of the serious problems we encountered, there was a sense that the country was going more in the right direction than it was when the campaign started. Nevertheless, perhaps at base a lot of the electorate had a great feeling of uncertainty, and we viewed it a primary function of the Reagan campaign to reduce that uncertainty about the future, not so much in providing ready-made solutions about all of the problems that this country faced, but rather to provide an overall approach to public policy in governing.

Specifically, the presidential election, again painting with a very broad brush, in my view, is an axial event that gives us in essence a major political opportunity to redefine, if we can, the political agenda. It isn't a bestowal in and of itself of political power. It did not represent, in my view, a restructuring of party allegiances. Rather it gave to Reagan a stewardship opportunity to reconcile and reconstruct the political agenda. The extent to which that agenda receives public sanction will determine the extent to which it will endure. The central features of Reagan's approach, I think, need to be reviewed as we sum up this discussion on political decisionmaking because his approach, the action parameters, if you will, that have guided his political life since 1966 provide a perspective not only for what happened in the course of the election but for what may happen over the next four years. To me, these were the base of his victory. It wasn't the polling, it wasn't the media, it wasn't organization. It wasn't how the press dealt and interpreted the course of the campaign. There are seven key Reagan imperatives that drove the campaign and that will provide a certain direction to his administration.

First, that we place trust in the values of American society that are largely responsible for sustaining its growth. Second, that we treat American leaders, both public and private, as accountable stewards, responsible for living up to what we identified in the campaign as certain commonly shared values of family, work, peace, freedom, and so on. Third, that we recognize the inherent value of individual initiative, and operate on the basic premise that in a representative democracy, goverment—whether it be federal, state, or local—should not perform functions that are better handled by the individual citizens on their own behalf. Fourth, that government's size and costs have exceeded what's reasonable, and result in the government doing things that are unnecessary and too often missing the mark on what is needed. Not only did the force of a 12 percent rate of inflation, the Iranian crisis, and unemployment, which we consider to be the triad of overriding issues, support this key imperative, but so did the fact that the American people, at least at this juncture of history, are looking for more conservative solutions to those things that impact them economically and psychically.

Fifth, and this is a more specific imperative, that the two demons of economics that we're dealing with, the sluggish economy and inflation, are principally caused by excessive government spending, taxation, and regulation. Sixth, Reagan strongly believes that a once-proud and strong America should not acquiesce to a secondary role in the world. Seven, that leaders have an obligation to translate not only the voters' but the people's best hopes and aspirations into public policy that will provide a direction and hope to the collective enterprise that was absent previously. That paints it in very broad terms, David, what I think was of most help to those of us who were involved in creating a strategy that attempted to be very consistent with the candidate's own views. It's so easy to get involved in talking about the mechanics of election that we forget that the bottom line is the candidates; it's the challengers and the incumbents and their records and the issue positions they take which, in my view, are the greatest determinants of who wins and who loses.

BRODER: To continue, were there, in fact, any decisions that any of you think were really crucial and that could have changed the outcome of this process, or did it have a historical inevitability?

CASEY: I think it did, I think it's been that way since '72, which was a mandate for the principles that Ronald Reagan had been espousing. That mandate was nullified by Watergate. In 1976, Jimmy Carter was a phenomenon. By 1980, the public had decided they didn't want any more Jimmy Carter. It would have been hard to lose that election.

—THE ECONOMIC ISSUE—

BROCK: I think there was one strategic decision that was of enormous consequence and more important than any other single decision made, and that was the decision to stay within the parameters of the economic issue. Going back to the comment about what Dick Scammon said, we took the frustration of 12, 14, 18 percent inflation, interest rates, unemployment, and offered the positive alternative. I think if we had allowed ourselves to do anything else, not only would we have been hitting the wrong issue but we would have had a divided party. We were able to go with the one issue that held all Republicans in line.

WIRTHLIN: And as well, that issue provided us with a vehicle to reach out and break up the Democratic coalition. Post–election analysis shows that we got a net shift from the Ford–Carter vote in a range of 14–16 percent positive to Reagan among Catholics, among union members, among the blue-collar ethnics, and it reinforced as well as solidified our swing vote.

BROCK: That's what I'm talking about: the strategic concept to go for a unifying theme that had no divisive component.

BRODER: Bob Teeter.

TEETER: I think there's a characteristic of this election which is very important and interesting, and I'm not sure whether it is permanent or not. It is that this, to a greater extent than any one we've seen in a long time, was a national election. Things that happened in individual regions seemed to be very much conditioned on what was happening nationally at a given point in time. I think there were several reasons for this. The first and foremost is simply the Carter record. It just seems to me that you can take this inning-by-inning or any other way you want, but the fact is you can't get away from the Carter record. The record is what people were voting up or down. The Reagan campaign and Republican party this year did provide an acceptable alternative both in terms of a candidate and in terms of a set of ideas on the economy. To try and put a lot of minor factors into it detracts from that one singular fact.

I think that at least two or three other things also contributed to the same phenomenon. There is the notion that there was one party in control of the government. It seems to me that's something we've missed in the past. It was pretty obvious and should have been more obvious to us: it is easier for voters to bring about party sweeps when you have one party in control of both branches of the government—in this case, an unpopular Democratic Congress and an unpopular Democratic president. Also, we had a very narrowly focused issue structure in this campaign. We did not debate housing or environment or consumerism or health care—we debated the economy and national security, almost to the exclusion of anything else. Lastly, we may have reached the point in mobility and the change in communication where people all get exactly the same information, whether it's from the networks or from the wire services or the news magazines. So these regional differences have been masked in many ways that we have seen before.

It is probably self-serving for anyone who is in the business of advising candidates to say it, but it struck me all through this seminar and particularly with regard to the Reagan campaign, that most of the critical decisions made in all of the campaigns, either to do something or not do something which had a significant effect—whether it was Howard Baker, Bob Dole, George Bush, Ronald Reagan, or Jimmy Carter—were ultimately made by the candidates themselves. For all the talk about pollsters, advertising agencies, staff people, and other geniuses about, the really critical decisions that either helped them get elected or helped them lose were, in many cases and most cases, made by the candidates themselves, and we ought not to lose sight of that.

BRODER: In the perfect democracy of Harvard, even losers are allowed to express their views. Paul. (*Laughter*)

—THE LOSERS—

KIRK: My view of it is basically what has been said by the Carter people. If the test came down to whether people felt better, whether we had performed satisfactorily for the last four years, we knew we were gone from the beginning, or words to that effect. Basically when the people went to the polls on November 4th and wielded their awesome power, thinking about their own lives and the country and its direction, the verdict was a resounding no, they were not satisfied with the record of the four years. And I think that is a fundamental threshold on which they make decisions. I'll have to agree with those who said that despite tactical judgments, decisions, timetables and so forth, ultimately the process belongs to the people.

Despite what any of us may do in terms of advice and so forth, the choice is basically going to reside with them and they will make the judgment on it.

CADDELL: I think we're representative of big losers. Let me put a few flies in the ointment, although I generally agree with most of the things said as we all begin to wax philosophically about the major process that we're in. First of all, I think in most politics there are certain historical imperatives at work, yet not absolutely determining. To some extent it was the events themselves and the candidates' reactions to those events that in the end determined the election. There is no question that this year began with historical forces moving against the incumbent president and against the Democratic party. But it did not mean necessarily that that would be the outcome. To that extent the effort, as I said earlier, to try to structure, to give the election a definition that did not necessarily fit that particular impulse, was critical. After the election I said, about being in the campaign, that I felt a little bit like the German army being sent to take Moscow without winter uniforms. To some extent it is not the fact that you didn't get to Moscow; it's somewhat impressive that you got to the suburbs.

In the sense of what the election said or didn't say, our tendency, particularly in wide-margin elections and in elections that may surprise us in their outcome, is to read more into them than perhaps they deserve. There is no question that this election, to repeat Paul's point and one I've made all along, if it were to be a referendum on four years of a very unhappy American public, this administration, president, was going to lose. But there's another thing to consider, and that is whether there is a mandate or not on what is being spoken about here. You have a country that is justifiably unhappy with the inability of its government, whether it's Democratic or Republican, or its various presidents, to solve some of what it believes are the problems that have been not short-term but long-term. We have been living now with double-digit inflation since 1973, 1974—not every month, but basically it has been with us since then. It is something we did not have for any long period before then. No one has yet found an answer to that. Those and other basic problems have clearly impacted the political process itself.

I congratulate the Reagan campaign on what I think was an excellent campaign, on its splendid victory. But let's not lose sight of the fact that the American people in rendering their judgment on November 4th did not render an enthusiastic judgment. You have here one thing that distinguishes this election, I think, from every post-war election—both candidates are very unpopular. If you go back and look just at general personal favorabilities that candidates have enjoyed since the war, leaving aside the job considerations, except for '72 and '64 when you had a positive candidate and a negative candidate and the negative candidate losing in a landslide, you have had essentially two positive candidates running. I remember '76 specifically, when so many people talked about what a terrible choice this was, and the American people were offended by this choice of Carter and Ford; the truth of the matter is, and I think Bob will back me up, that both of the candidates had very high favorabilities— almost 60 percent or more—at the end of the election. Neither Carter nor Reagan this year was able to get much beyond 50 percent, another 50 percent in the negative. It is a very different situation than we have seen. I think this presents Governor Reagan and the Republicans with a unique opportunity. The expectations of what Governor Reagan will do are not all that great, and they are not all that great not because of Governor Reagan, but because people have been through this before. They went through it with Jimmy Carter in the election of '76, with a fair set of expectations which were raised even higher in the early days of his administration, and were then disappointed. They do not start with great expectations, and if I were in Ronald Reagan's shoes I would appreciate that because it does provide opportunity.

American politics is being buffeted now as the American people search for answers and solutions to problems. They would like these things solved, whether it's foreign policy, the economy, or whatever, and the opportunity exists. I don't think this is a watershed election. It may in the end serve as a turning point when we look back in many years, and it may not. It may simply be another aberration— we have now had two incumbent presidents defeated in a row. It may be that we will have another or another party turnover. Or as I said, the opportunity exists that if Ronald Reagan and the Republicans can make some progress, solve some of the problems or at least leave the American people with a sense that they have set a course and a direction that is going to work and is working, they may be able to change the political landscape for some years to come. I specifically disagree with you, Bill, about 1972. I think this is a better opportunity in a sense than existed in those previous years. One thing I'd like to lay on the table as a last point is that you can look at the issues and the problems and forces at work and you have to argue that they are working against incumbent presidents and against parties in power. If chickens came home to roost during the Carter administration, there's a flock on their way in the future. Anyone who looks down the road in the next four- or five-year range can see that. So in a sense now, president Reagan gets to run against history and against that tide in the reverse way than he did in the campaign.

—THE ANDERSON VIEW—

BRODER: The puzzle is what really happened in 1980. Perhaps John Anderson can give us his almost 7 percent solution.

ANDERSON: I'm not sure that one month, three days after the election, as the only candidate around this table or participating in this seminar, I am sufficiently detached from the event yet to render the kind of totally objective judgment that ought to be reflected in the pages of the book that will be published. Maybe I ought to be satisfied with that remark I quoted earlier from Armor and McCarthy's article that it was not my goal that was important; it was the role that I was destined to play to legitimate further efforts by independent candidates. There's been so much talk about the historical correlation of forces here in the last few minutes, I thought that I was at a seminar on Soviet–American affairs. Bob Teeter made the point that the election was a referendum on the Carter record, but he appended to that the observation or the judgment that it also represented a decision by the American people on an alternative set of policies that they preferred. He didn't quantify that. Was 70 percent of that judgment made up on the basis of the voters' attitudes on the Carter record and only 30 percent on the alternative policies? I don't know; maybe in his mind it was evenly balanced.

Traditionally, I think we have always believed it's axiomatic in American politics that voters vote their self-interest, they vote their pocketbook, that they most commonly vote against rather than for candidates. Pat Caddell has just referred to the unique and high degree of unpopularity, as reflected at least in some surveys, of both candidates, Carter and Reagan. It was also he, I think, who talked about the traditional trend during the last week of the campaign that nets the incumbent administration five or six percentage points. If the CBS–*New York Times* poll, which came out about several weeks ago, is correct, this election, as I recall the figures, showed a 20 percent shift. One out of five voters shifted in one way or another in the final week of the campaign. I talked to a very distinguished national pollster a few days ago, and heard him say that never in his entire experience had he seen voters agonize as much over their final choice, their final selection, as they did in this election.

That might tend to corroborate the notion that they really basically at heart were not satisfied with either of the two choices who they finally decided were realistic possibilities to win the presidency. As I say, I make no pretense at this early date of having the kind of objectivity that probably exists in the minds of the pollsters and the election experts and the analysts. I do believe that it was essentially a negative kind of vote that was cast by the American voters, that they were not really trading in one set of policies for a new set of policies. The centerpiece of the Reagan economic program is certainly the Kemp–Roth bill, and the last survey I saw indicated that as of the present time, a majority of the American people still think that would be inflationary. So I have some doubts about whether or not they really believed that this policy or that set of policies was what they were approving when they cast their vote on the 4th of November.

I, too, want to congratulate Governor Reagan for a splendid campaign. Having listened to these experts around the table the last couple of days, I think I understand better now why I was defeated, although that was a very generous act on the part of Pat Caddell to refer to himself or his candidate as the big loser. That relieved me. (*Laughter*)

HUNT: I gather there is nobody at the table who disagrees with the notion there's nothing wrong with the Democratic party that 12 percent inflation won't cure.

ANDERSON: I made the comment this morning that anyone who thinks the Democrats are completely knocked out, dead and ready to roll over, should think again. The first story that greeted my eye was the soon-to-be minority leader of the U.S. Senate threatening to resurrect Watergate and defeat Al Haig if he's nominated as Secretary of State, so I suppose there is life in the party yet.

BRODER: Thank you all.

APPENDICES

SOME IMPORTANT CAMPAIGN DATES

NINETEEN HUNDRED AND SEVENTY-EIGHT

March

March 16 — Senate passes the first of two Panama Canal treaties.

August

August 2 — Congressman Phil Crane (Republican, Ohio) announces his candidacy for the Republican nomination.

September

September 17 — The Camp David agreement is signed at the White House.

November

November 7 — Democrats retain control of both houses in congressional elections.

November 9 — Harold Stassen announces his candidacy for the Republican nomination.

November 29 — Benjamin Fernandez announces his candidacy for the Republican nomination.

December

December 8–10 — Democratic mid-term conference in Memphis, Tennessee.

December 9 — Edward Kennedy's speech to mid-term conference delegates on health care.

NINETEEN HUNDRED AND SEVENTY-NINE

January

January 24   Former Texas governor John Connally announces his candidacy for the Republican nomination.

March

March 12   Senator Lowell Weicker (Republican, Connecticut) announces his candidacy for the Republican nomination.

May

May 1   George Bush announces his candidacy for the Republican nomination.

May 14   Senator Robert Dole (Republican, Kansas) announces his candidacy for the Republican nomination.

May 16   Senator Lowell Weicker withdraws his candidacy for the Republican nomination.

June

June 3   Sean Morton Downey, National Right to Life Committee, announces his candidacy for Democratic nomination for president.

June 8   Congressman John Anderson (Republican, Illinois) announces his candidacy for the Republican nomination for president.

June 12   Jimmy Carter is reported as saying at a White House dinner for sixty congressmen, "If Kennedy runs, I'll whip his ass."

June 27   Senator Howard Baker announces at a news conference that he cannot support the SALT II treaty without amendments.

July

July 1   Democrats vote to hold 1980 national convention in New York City.

July 15   President Carter gives speech on "Energy and National Goals."

August

August 16   The Federal Election Commission rules that unauthorized Draft Kennedy Committee in Florida can raise and spend unlimited amounts of dollars to influence presidential straw vote to be held at state party convention in November.

NINETEEN HUNDRED AND SEVENTY-NINE *(continued)*

September

September 6	Senator Kennedy's family reportedly gives approval for the Senator to run for president.
September 7	President Carter invites Senator Kennedy for a "secret" meeting at the White House.
September 8	Libertarian Party nominates Ed Clark for president.
September 20	President Carter orders Secret Service protection for Senator Kennedy.
September 25	Senator Larry Pressler (Republican, South Dakota) announces his candidacy for the Republican nomination.
September 28	Edward Kennedy, at AFL–CIO convention in Boston, comments on AFL–CIO endorsement of him for presidential nomination: "You'll be hearing about my response to that resolution in not too many days . . . and I don't think you'll be disappointed."

October

October 11	John Connally's speech on Middle East.
October 13	Florida Democratic caucus straw vote: 522 for Carter; 269 for Kennedy.
October 15	President Carter attends a large fundraising dinner in Chicago at which Mayor Jane Byrne praises the president's record but does not give an endorsement.
October 19	Former president Gerald Ford announces that he will not be an active candidate for the Republican nomination for president.
October 20	At the dedication of John F. Kennedy Library in Boston, President Carter recalls President Kennedy's response to a question of whether he recommended his job to his brother: "I do not recommend it to others—at least for a while," and adds, "As you can well see, President Kennedy's wit, and also his wisdom, is certainly as relevant today as it was then."
October 22	Shah of Iran arrives in the United States from Mexico for medical treatment.
October 28	Jane Byrne, mayor of Chicago, endorses Senator Kennedy.

NINETEEN HUNDRED AND SEVENTY-NINE *(continued)*

October 29	Stephen Smith announces formation of a Kennedy for President Committee.
October 31	Former New Hampshire governor Meldrim Thompson announces his candidacy for president as an Independent.
October 31	Carter–Mondale Campaign files complaint with Federal Communications Commission, arguing that the networks unfairly refused to sell a half-hour of prime time to show a film after Carter's announcement of his candidacy scheduled for December 4.

November

November 1	Senator Howard Baker (Republican, Tennessee) announces his candidacy for the Republican nomination.
November 2–3	Maine Republican forum–dinner: Bush 35 percent of the vote; Baker 33 percent; Connally 18 percent; Reagan 7 percent; Crane 5 percent.
November 3	Iowa Democrat straw poll at Jefferson–Jackson dinner: Carter 71 percent; Kennedy 26 percent; Brown received fewer than 2 dozen of 2,224 votes.
November 4	Roger Mudd interview with Senator Kennedy aired on CBS.
November 4	American Embassy overrun in Teheran and American hostages taken captive.
November 6	John Y. Brown, Jr., and William Winter, both Democrats, win gubernatorial elections in Kentucky and Mississippi, respectively.
November 7	Senator Edward Kennedy (Democrat, Massachusetts) declares his candidacy for the Democratic nomination at Faneuil Hall in Boston.
November 8	California governor Edmund G. Brown declares his candidacy for the Democratic nomination.
November 8–9	Democratic National Committee meeting is held in San Antonio, Texas. A poll taken by ABC of the 162 members attending the meeting showed little change over one by CBS taken in early spring: Carter 64 percent; Kennedy 28 percent; Brown 1 percent; Undecided 7 percent.
November 10	President Carter orders the start of deportation proceedings against Iranian students living illegally in the United

NINETEEN HUNDRED AND SEVENTY-NINE *(continued)*

	States, cuts off direct American imports of Iranian oil, and freezes Iranian assets.
November 13	Former California governor Ronald Reagan declares his candidacy for the Republican nomination.
November 16	At a meeting of the Compliance Review Commission of the Democratic National Committee, Maine's early caucuses and Massachusetts' early primary are okayed.
November 17	Florida Republicans one-day state convention in Orlando straw vote of first choices: Reagan 36.4 percent; Connally 26.6 percent; Bush 21.1 percent; Crane 13.8 percent; other 2.1 percent.
November 17	Pennsylvania Republican state committee elected six at-large delegates, the first delegates to Republican national convention chosen.
November 18	Florida Democrats' three-day state convention straw poll: Carter 1,114; Kennedy 351.
November 20	Republican governors' conference in Austin, Texas, does not endorse any presidential candidate.
November 25	Communist Party nominates Gus Hall for president and Angela Davis for vice president.

December

December 3	Kennedy makes anti-Shah remarks.
December 4	Jimmy Carter declares his candidacy for the Democratic nomination.
December 8	Republican David Treen is elected governor of Louisiana.
December 10	Gallup poll reports President Carter's public approval rating at 61 percent, up from 32 percent in a survey taken November 5, the largest monthly increase in a president's popularity that the Gallup organization has ever recorded.
December 12	For the first time in almost two years, the Gallup poll reports President Carter leads Senator Kennedy 48 percent to 40 percent in a survey of Democrats across the nation.
December 12	John Connally announces his decision not to accept federal matching funds for campaigning in the primary and caucus states.

NINETEEN HUNDRED AND SEVENTY-NINE *(continued)*

December 15	The Shah of Iran flies from Texas to Panama.
December 27	Filing deadline for all presidential candidates in New Hampshire.
December 27	Soviet Union invasion of Afghanistan.
December 28	Carter withdraws from Iowa debate.
December 31	Filing deadline for presidential candidates in Illinois.

NINETEEN HUNDRED AND EIGHTY

January

January 1	All Democratic state delegate selection plans finalized with the Democratic National Committee.
January 3	President Carter asks the Senate to postpone indefinitely consideration of SALT II.
January 4	President Carter orders restrictions on trade of grain and technical equipment to the Soviet Union, in retaliation for its invasion of Afghanistan.
January 5	Republican debate is held in Des Moines, Iowa, sponsored by the *Des Moines Registrar.* Baker, Bush, Crane, Connally, Dole, and Anderson participate; Reagan does not.
January 12	Senator Larry Pressler withdraws from race.
January 20	President Carter announces he will request U.S. athletes to boycott the Olympic Games in Moscow in the summer.
January 21	Iowa precinct caucuses. Carter beat Kennedy almost two to one; Bush edged Reagan 32 percent to 29 percent, with Baker 16 percent, Connally 9 percent, Crane 7 percent, Anderson 4 percent, and Dole 2 percent.
January 22	Hawaii Republican precinct caucuses.
January 23	Republicans choose Detroit for their convention.
January 28	Senator Kennedy makes speech at Georgetown University.
January 28	Bani–Sadr elected president of Iran. Six U.S. Embassy people, who had been hiding in the Canadian Embassy in Teheran, escape Iran with Canadian help.

NINETEEN HUNDRED AND EIGHTY *(continued)*

February

February 1	Republican town and city caucuses begin in Maine.
February 2	Arkansas Republicans select congressional district delegates to the national convention.
February 4	Republican precinct caucuses in Wyoming begin.
February 6	Ronald Reagan celebrates his sixty-ninth birthday.
February 10	Maine Democratic municipal caucuses held: Carter 45 percent; Kennedy 39 percent; Brown 12 percent.
February 16	Arkansas Republicans select at-large delegates; John Connally wins a single delegate.
February 16	Georgia Republican precinct caucuses.
February 17	Puerto Rico Republican primary.
February 19	Nevada precinct meetings.
February 20	Republican debate in Manchester, New Hampshire.
February 23	Republican debate in Nashua, New Hampshire.
February 24	U.S. hockey team wins Olympic gold medal.
February 26	Bill Casey replaces John Sears as Reagan's campaign manager.
February 26	New Hampshire primary. Carter beats Kennedy, 47 percent to 37 percent; Reagan beats Bush almost better than two to one, with Baker and Anderson trailing.
February 26	Minnesota precinct caucuses.

March

March 1	Former president Gerald Ford says that Reagan cannot win the general election, and that he would entertain a request by the Republican party that he run again for president.
March 1	Administration supports U.N. Security Council resolution condemning Israeli settlements on the West Bank.
March 4	Massachusetts and Vermont primaries. Kennedy 65 percent, Carter 29 percent in Massachusetts; Carter wins Vermont. Bush narrowly wins Massachusetts over both Anderson and Reagan; Reagan edges Anderson in Vermont.

NINETEEN HUNDRED AND EIGHTY *(continued)*

March 5	Howard Baker withdraws from race.
March 8	South Carolina Republican primary. Reagan 55 percent, Connally 30 percent, Bush 15 percent.
March 9	John Connally withdraws from race.
March 10	Iowa county conventions.
March 11	Alabama, Florida, and Georgia primaries. Carter and Reagan handily win in all three states.
March 11	Hawaii Democratic precinct caucuses.
March 11	Oklahoma Democratic precinct caucuses.
March 11	Washington precinct caucuses.
March 14	Carter presents new anti-inflation package.
March 15	Robert Dole withdraws from the race.
March 15	Mississippi Democratic precinct caucuses.
March 15	North Carolina and Wyoming Democratic precinct caucuses.
March 15	Former president Gerald Ford announces he will not be a candidate.
March 16	Puerto Rico Democratic primary.
March 16–17	Hawaii Republican state convention to select congressional district delegates.
March 17–18	Delaware Democratic district meetings (first tier).
March 18	Illinois primary. Carter beats Kennedy 65 percent to 30 percent; Reagan 48 percent, Anderson 38 percent, Bush 11 percent.
March 22	Virginia Democratic city-county caucuses (first tier).
March 23	Shah goes to Cairo from Panama.
March 25	Connecticut and New York primaries. Kennedy beat Carter 47 percent to 42 percent in Connecticut and 59 percent to 41 percent in New York. Bush beat Reagan in Connecticut 39 percent to 34 percent; Anderson 22 percent; Reagan reportedly picks up 60.7 percent (seventy-one delegates) of delegates in New York to Bush's 5.9 percent (seven delegates).
March 29	Alabama Democratic at-large delegates are chosen .

NINETEEN HUNDRED AND EIGHTY *(continued)*

March 29	Florida Republicans select at-large delegates.
March 31	Puerto Rico Democratic state convention.

April

April 1	In the early morning, Carter announces a "positive step" toward release of hostages in Iran.
April 1	Kansas and Wisconsin primaries. Carter wins both easily. Reagan wins Kansas big and takes Wisconsin with 40 percent of the vote compared to 30 percent for Bush and 27 percent for Anderson.
April 1	Jerry Brown withdraws from race.
April 5	Mississippi Democratic congressional district caucuses.
April 5	Louisiana primary. Carter and Reagan win handily.
April 7	Oklahoma Republican precinct caucuses.
April 12–May 3	Virginia Democratic congressional district conventions.
April 12	South Carolina Democratic state convention.
April 13	Citizens' Party nominates Barry Commoner for president.
April 17	Phil Crane withdraws from race.
April 17	Idaho congressional district caucuses.
April 17–19	Missouri and North Dakota Republican state conventions.
April 18–May 20	Minnesota Republican congressional district conventions.
April 19	Georgia Republican and Democratic congressional district conventions.
April 19	Iowa and Mississippi Democratic congressional district conventions.
April 19	Louisiana and Oklahoma Democratic congressional district caucuses.
April 19	North Carolina Republicans select congressional district delegates.
April 19–20	Alaska Republican state convention.
April 19–May 4	Minnesota Republican congressional district conventions.
April 22	Pennsylvania primary. Kennedy wins a squeaker, and Bush overtakes Reagan 50 percent to 42 percent.

NINETEEN HUNDRED AND EIGHTY *(continued)*

April 22	Missouri and Vermont Democratic caucuses.
April 24	John Anderson announces his intention to run as an Independent candidate.
April 24	U.S. mission to rescue the hostages in Iran fails; eight marines die in Iranian desert.
April 26	Louisiana Democrats select at-large and add-on (elected officials) delegates.
April 26	Michigan Democratic caucuses. Kennedy gets seventy-one delegates; Carter seventy.
April 28	Supreme Court says Kennedy supporters cannot challenge Carter's use of federal money and personnel to help his re-election bid.

May

May 3	Texas Democratic precinct caucuses.
May 3	Texas primary. Carter beats Kennedy two to one and Reagan out-distances Bush 51 percent to 47 percent.
May 3	Guam selects both parties' delegates to the national conventions.
May 3	Georgia Democrats select at-large and add-on delegates.
May 3–4	Oklahoma Republican congressional district conventions.
May 5	Colorado precinct caucuses.
May 6	District of Columbia, Indiana, North Carolina, Tennessee primaries. Kennedy wins easily in D.C., Carter easily in three states; Bush wins in D.C., Reagan by almost three to one in other races.
May 8	Tennessee selects at-large delegates.
May 10	Illinois Republican state convention selects at-large delegates.
May 10	Michigan Democrats select add-on and at-large delegates.
May 10	Wyoming Democratic and Republican state conventions.
May 13	Maryland and Nebraska primaries. Carter and Reagan are victors.
May 16–17	North Carolina Republican state convention selects at-large delegates.

NINETEEN HUNDRED AND EIGHTY *(continued)*

May 16–17	Virginia Democratic state convention selects at-large and add-on delegates.
May 17	Delaware Republican state convention.
May 17	North Carolina Democrats select congressional district delegates.
May 17–18	Alaska Democratic state convention.
May 19	Utah district mass meetings (first tier caucuses).
May 20	Michigan Republican and Oregon primaries. Carter and Reagan take Oregon, while Bush beats Reagan in Michigan 57 percent to 32 percent.
May 23	Maine Democratic state convention.
May 23–24	Georgia Republican state convention to choose at-large delegates.
May 24	Arizona and Delaware state conventions.
May 26	George Bush withdraws from race.
May 27	Arkansas, Idaho, Kentucky, Nevada primaries. Carter and Reagan sweep all primaries.
May 27	Oregon state conventions.
May 29	President Carter, in Columbus, Ohio, on first campaign trip since the seizure of the U.S. hostages, says the economic tide is turning in America.
May 29–31	Minnesota Republican state convention.
May 30–31	Hawaii Democratic state convention.

June

June 3	"Super Tuesday": California, Montana, New Jersey, New Mexico, Ohio, Rhode Island, South Dakota, and West Virginia primaries; Mississippi Republican primary. Kennedy wins California, New Jersey, New Mexico, Rhode Island, and South Dakota; Carter wins Ohio, Montana, and West Virginia. With Bush out of the race, Reagan sweeps all races.
June 3	Missouri congressional district conventions.
June 6	Iowa Republican congressional district convention.

NINETEEN HUNDRED AND EIGHTY *(continued)*

June 6–7	Virginia Republican state convention.
June 7	Colorado and Iowa Republican state conventions.
June 7	New Mexico Republicans select delegates.
June 7	Washington Republican state convention selects congressional district and at-large delegates.
June 8	Kansas selects at-large delegates.
June 8	Minnestoa Democratic state convention.
June 9	Indiana Democratic state convention.
June 12	New Jersey Democrats select add-on delegates.
June 13	Indiana Republican state convention.
June 14	Colorado, Iowa, Missouri, Washington state conventions.
June 14	Nebraska Republican state convention.
June 18	New Jersey Democrats select at-large delegates.
June 20–21	Texas Democratic state convention.
June 21	California and North Carolina Democrats select at-large and add-on delegates.
June 23	Deadline for the selection of delegates to the Democratic national convention.
June 27–28	Utah Republican state convention.
June 28	Idaho Republican state convention.
June 28	Deadline for selection of delegates to the Republican national convention.
July	
July 8–9	Rules committee of Democratic party meets in Washington.
July 12–13	Democratic credentials committee meeting.
July 14–17	Republican national convention in Detroit.
July 25	Shah dies in Cairo.
July 31	Meeting between Kennedy and Anderson to discuss strategies; Kennedy indicates that if he were to win the Democratic nomination it could "eliminate the need" for Anderson candidacy, and Anderson says he might abandon Independent race if Democrats nominate someone other than Carter.

NINETEEN HUNDRED AND EIGHTY *(continued)*

August

August 4	President Carter holds press conference on Billy Carter's connections with Libya.
August 10–14	Democratic national convention in New York.
August 11	Ted Kennedy withdraws from race.
August 22	Reagan speech in Dallas states doubts about the theory of evolution.

September

September 9	Governor Reagan makes economic policy speech in Chicago.
September 12	Khomeini issues terms for release of hostages.
September 21	Reagan and Anderson debate in Baltimore.
September 22	Iran–Iraq war begins.
September 29	Administration decision to send four radar warning planes to Saudi Arabia.

October

October 17	Reagan agrees to single, head-to-head debate with Carter.
October 26	*New York Times* endorses Carter.
October 28	Reagan and Carter debate in Cleveland.
October 31	*Washington Post* endorses Carter.

November

November 2	Iranian Parliament adopts Khomeini's conditions for release of hostages: President Carter interrupts campaign and flies from Chicago to Washington to respond.
November 4	One-year anniversary of the seizure of U.S. hostages in Iran.
November 4	General election. Reagan wins with 51 percent of the popular vote. Carter receives 41 percent, and Anderson collects 7 percent. Reagan gets 489 electoral votes, Carter 49, and Anderson none.

In the preparation of this chronology, *Congressional Quarterly, National Journal*, and ABC special events division's election factbooks, among other sources, were drawn upon.

SOME CAMPAIGN
STATISTICS

DELEGATE SELECTION AND ACCUMULATION

Delegates by Selection System

In 1980, the Democratic party held presidential preference primaries in thirty-two states (including the District of Columbia and Puerto Rico), and used a caucus-convention system in twenty states (three of which – Idaho, Michigan, and Vermont – have non-binding preference primaries). The Republican party had preference primaries in thirty-five states (including the District of Columbia and Puerto Rico, and delegate-selection-only primaries in New York and Mississippi), and caucus-convention arrangements in seventeen states (including Montana which had a nonbinding preference primary).

	DEMOCRATS					REPUBLICANS					
	Total Selected	Carter	Kennedy	Others	Uncommitted	Total Selected	Reagan	Bush	Anderson	Others	Uncommitted
Caucus states	933	596.1	231.8	0	105.1	478	397	36	1	5	39
Primary states	2,378	1,375.0	990.0	2	11.0	1,516	1,183	217	50	4	62
Totals	3,311	1,971.1	1,221.8	2	116.1	1,994	1,580	253	51	9	101

Delegates by Region

	DEMOCRATS					REPUBLICANS					
	Total Selected	Carter	Kennedy	Others	Uncommitted	Total Selected	Reagan	Bush	Anderson	Others	Uncommitted
East	948	415	531	1	1	498	310	109	19	4	56
South	793	645	125	0	23	475	415	48	0	5	7
Midwest	932	592	277	1	62	553	436	68	31	0	18
West	581	288.6	266.8	0	25.6	446	415	14	1	0	16
Territories	57	30.5	22	0	4.5	22	4	14	0	0	4
Totals	3,311	1,971.1	1,221.8	2	116.1	1,994	1,580	253	51	9	101

Stages of Delegate Accumulation

After the February 26th Massachusetts and Vermont primaries:
Democrats: Kennedy 86, Carter 44; Republicans: Reagan 37, Bush 36, Anderson 13, Baker 8, Connally 1, Uncommitted 8.

After the March 25th Connecticut and New York primaries:
Democrats: Carter 552, Kennedy 341, Uncommitted 1; Republicans: Reagan 296, Bush 68, Uncommitted 64, Anderson 46, Baker 8, Crane 1, Connally 1.

After the April 22nd Pennsylvania primary:
Democrats: Carter 911, Kennedy 506, Uncommitted 13, Brown 1; Republicans: Reagan 443, Bush 102, Uncommitted 102, Anderson 52, Undeclared 13, Baker 8, Crane 1, Connally 1.

After the June 3rd "Super Tuesday" primaries:
Democrats: Carter 1,764.1, Kennedy 1,138.8, Uncommitted 58.1, Brown 1, Byrd 1; Republicans: Reagan 1,409, Bush 254, Uncommitted 101, Anderson 52, Baker 8, Connally 1.

Source: All statistics are from Congressional Quarterly Inc.

1980 PRESIDENTIAL PREFERENCE PRIMARIES

The presidential preference primary returns listed below include vote totals and percentage of votes of all major candidates for each state holding such primaries. The vote percentages do not always add up to 100 percent nor do the total votes add up to the total turnout because minor candidates' results are not included in this chart. The total vote figures have been calculated from the percentage of the total turnout. The percentages are based on official returns with the exception of the following states where only unofficial returns were available when statistics were completed: Oregon, California, Montana, New Mexico, Ohio, South Dakota, and West Virginia.

REPUBLICAN			*DEMOCRATIC*		
	Votes	*Percent*		*Votes*	*Percent*
February 17 Puerto Rico			*(March 16th)*		
George Bush	112,009	60.1	Jimmy Carter	449,912	51.7
Howard Baker	68,957	37.0	Edward Kennedy	417,713	48.0
John Connally	2,050	1.1	Edmund G. Brown Jr.	1,740	0.2
Benjamin Fernandez	2,050	1.1			
Harold Stassen	745	0.4			
Robert Dole	559	0.3			
(Turnout: 186,371)			(Turnout: 870,235)		
February 26 New Hampshire					
Ronald Reagan	72,990	49.6	Carter	52,719	47.1
Bush	33,405	22.7	Kennedy -	41,750	37.3
Baker	18,983	12.9	Brown	10,745	9.6
John Anderson	14,421	9.8	Lyndon LaRouche	2,351	2.1
Philip Crane	2,649	1.8	Richard Kay	560	0.5
Connally	2,207	1.5			
Dole	589	0.4			
(Turnout: 147,157)			(Turnout: 111,930)		
March 4 Massachusetts					
Bush	124,256	31.0	Kennedy	590,673	65.1
Anderson	123,054	30.7	Carter	260,404	28.7
Reagan	115,438	28.8	Brown	31,757	3.5
Baker	19,240	4.8	Uncommitted	19,961	2.2
Connally	4,810	1.2			
Crane	4,810	1.2			
No preference	2,405	0.6			
Dole	401	0.1			
Fernandez	401	0.1			
Stassen	401	0.1			
(Turnout: 400,826)			(Turnout: 907,332)		

REPUBLICAN	Votes	Percent	DEMOCRATIC	Votes	Percent
March 4 Vermont[a]					
Reagan	19,749	30.1	Carter	29,023	73.1
Anderson	19,027	29.0	Kennedy	10,124	25.5
Bush	14,238	21.7	Brown	357	0.9
Baker[b]	8,070	12.3			
Crane	1,247	1.9			
Connally	853	1.3			
Stassen	131	0.2			
(Turnout: 65,611)			(Turnout: 39,703)		
March 8 South Carolina					
Reagan	79,589	54.7			
Connally[c]	43,068	29.6			
Bush	21,534	14.8			
Baker	728	0.5			
Dole	146	0.1			
Fernandez	146	0.1			
Stassen	146	0.1			
(Turnout: 145,501)					
March 11 Alabama					
Reagan	147,313	69.7	Carter	193,771	81.6
Bush	54,740	25.9	Kennedy	31,345	13.2
Crane	5,072	2.4	Brown	9,499	4.0
Baker	1,902	0.9	Uncommitted	1,662	0.7
Connally	1,057	0.5			
Stassen	634	0.3			
Dole	423	0.2			
(Turnout: 211,353)			(Turnout: 237,464)		
March 11 Florida					
Reagan	345,627	56.2	Carter	666,488	60.7
Bush	185,728	30.2	Kennedy	254,737	23.2
Anderson	56,580	9.2	Uncommitted	104,310	9.5
Crane	12,300	2.0	Brown	53,802	4.9
Baker	6,150	1.0	Kay	18,666	1.7
Connally	4,920	0.8			
Dole	1,230	0.2			
Stassen	1,230	0.2			
Fernandez	615	0.1			
(Turnout: 614,995)			(Turnout: 1,098,003)		

REPUBLICAN			DEMOCRATIC		
	Votes	Percent		Votes	Percent
March 11 Georgia					
Reagan	146,525	73.2	Carter	338,606	88.0
Bush	25,222	12.6	Kennedy	32,322	8.4
Anderson	16,814	8.4	Brown	7,311	1.9
Crane	6,405	3.2	Uncommitted	3,848	1.0
Connally	2,402	1.2	Finch	1,539	0.4
Baker	1,601	0.8	Kay	770	0.2
Fernandez	801	0.4	La Rouche	385	0.1
Dole[d]	200	0.1			
Stassen	200	0.1			
(Turnout: 200,171)			(Turnout: 384,780)		
March 18 Illinois					
Reagan	546,959	48.4	Carter	780,694	65.0
Anderson	414,740	36.7	Kennedy	360,320	30.0
Bush	124,309	11.0	Brown	39,635	3.3
Crane	24,862	2.2	La Rouche	19,217	1.6
Baker	6,780	0.6			
Connally	4,520	0.4			
Dole	2,260	0.2			
(Turnout: 1,130,081)			(Turnout: 1,201,067)		
March 25 Connecticut					
Bush	70,362	38.6	Kennedy	98,619	46.9
Reagan	61,794	33.9	Carter	87,264	41.5
Anderson	40,285	22.1	Uncommitted	13,458	6.4
No preference	4,193	2.3	La Rouche	5,677	2.7
Baker	2,370	1.3	Brown	5,467	2.6
Crane	1,823	1.0			
Connally	547	0.3			
Dole	365	0.2			
Fernandez	365	0.2			
(Turnout: 182,284)			(Turnout: 210,275)		
March 25 New York					
			Kennedy	582,558	58.9
			Carter	406,504	41.1
			(Turnout: 989,062)		

REPUBLICAN			DEMOCRATIC		
	Votes	Percent		Votes	Percent

April 1   Kansas

REPUBLICAN			DEMOCRATIC		
Reagan	179,801	63.0	Carter	109,758	56.6
Anderson	51,942	18.2	Kennedy	61,278	31.6
Bush	35,960	12.6	Uncommitted	11,247	5.8
No preference	6,850	2.4	Brown	9,502	4.9
Baker	3,710	1.3	Finch	582	0.3
Connally	1,998	0.7			
Fernandez	1,712	0.6			
Crane	1,427	0.5			
Stassen	285	0.1			

(Turnout: 285,398)   (Turnout: 193,918)

April 1   Wisconsin

REPUBLICAN			DEMOCRATIC		
Reagan	364,957	40.2	Carter	353,846	56.2
Bush	275,987	30.4	Kennedy	189,515	30.1
Anderson	248,752	27.4	Brown[e]	74,295	11.8
Baker	3,631	0.4	La Rouche	6,926	1.1
Crane[f]	2,724	0.3	Uncommitted	2,518	0.4
Connally	2,724	0.3	Finch	1,889	0.3
No preference	2,724	0.3			
Fernandez	908	0.1			
Stassen	908	0.1			

(Turnout: 905,853)   (Turnout: 629,619)

April 5   Louisiana

REPUBLICAN			DEMOCRATIC		
Reagan	31,221	74.9	Carter	199,819	55.7
Bush	7,836	18.8	Kennedy	80,717	22.5
No preference	2,209	5.3	Uncommitted	41,614	11.6
Stassen	125	0.3	Brown	16,861	4.7
Fernandez	83	0.2	Finch	11,121	3.1
			Kay	3,229	0.9

(Turnout: 41,683)   (Turnout: 358,741)

April 22   Pennsylvania

REPUBLICAN			DEMOCRATIC		
Bush	626,706	50.5	Kennedy	737,243	45.7
Reagan	527,426	42.5	Carter	732,403	45.4
Baker	31,025	2.5	Uncommitted	93,567	5.8
Anderson[g]	26,061	2.1	Brown	37,104	2.3
Connally	11,169	0.9			
Stassen	6,205	0.5			
Fernandez	2,482	0.2			

(Turnout: 1,241,002)   (Turnout: 1,613,223)

REPUBLICAN			*DEMOCRATIC*		
	Votes	*Percent*		*Votes*	*Percent*

May 3   Texas

	Votes	*Percent*		*Votes*	*Percent*
Reagan	268,652	51.0	Carter	769,941	55.9
Bush	249,689	47.4	Kennedy	314,037	22.8
No preference	7,902	1.5	Uncommitted	257,565	18.7
(Turnout: 526,769)			(Turnout: 1,377,354)		

May 3   District of Columbia

	Votes	*Percent*		*Votes*	*Percent*
Bush	4,977	66.1	Kennedy	39,581	61.7
Anderson	2,025	26.9	Carter	23,671	36.9
Crane	271	3.6	La Rouche	898	1.4
Stassen	203	2.7			
Fernandez	60	0.8			
(Turnout: 7,529)			(Turnout: 64,150)		

May 6   Indiana

	Votes	*Percent*		*Votes*	*Percent*
Reagan	418,848	73.7	Carter	399,052	67.7
Bush	93,204	16.4	Kennedy	190,389	32.3
Anderson	56,263	9.9			
(Turnout: 568,315)			(Turnout: 589,441)		

May 6   N. Carolina

	Votes	*Percent*		*Votes*	*Percent*
Reagan	113,832	67.6	Carter	516,821	70.1
Bush	36,709	21.8	Kennedy	130,495	17.7
Anderson	8,588	5.1	Uncommitted	68,565	9.3
No preference	4,547	2.7	Brown	21,381	2.9
Baker	2,526	1.5			
Connally	1,179	0.7			
Dole	674	0.4			
Crane	505	0.3			
(Turnout: 168,391)			(Turnout: 737,262)		

May 6   Tennessee

	Votes	*Percent*		*Votes*	*Percent*
Reagan	144,651	74.1	Carter	221,599	75.2
Bush	35,333	18.1	Kennedy	53,337	18.1
Anderson	8,784	4.5	Uncommitted	11,493	3.9
No preference	4,880	2.5	Brown	5,599	1.9
Crane	1,562	0.8	Finch	1,768	0.6
			La Rouche	884	0.3
(Turnout: 195,210)			(Turnout: 294,680)		

REPUBLICAN	Votes	Percent	DEMOCRATIC	Votes	Percent

May 13   *Maryland*

REPUBLICAN	Votes	Percent	DEMOCRATIC	Votes	Percent
Reagan	80,640	48.2	Carter	226,618	47.5
Bush	68,427	40.9	Kennedy	181,294	38.0
Anderson	16,228	9.7	Uncommitted	45,801	9.6
Crane	2,175	1.3	Brown	14,313	3.0
			Finch	4,771	1.0
			La Rouche	4,294	0.9

(Turnout: 167,303)   (Turnout: 477,090)

May 13   *Nebraska*

REPUBLICAN	Votes	Percent	DEMOCRATIC	Votes	Percent
Reagan	155,954	76.0	Carter	72,170	46.9
Bush	31,396	15.3	Kennedy	57,859	37.6
Anderson	11,902	5.8	Uncommitted	16,004	10.4
Dole	1,436	0.7	Brown	5,540	3.6
Crane	1,026	0.5	La Rouche	1,231	0.8
Stassen	821	0.4			
Fernandez	410	0.2			

(Turnout: 205,203)   (Turnout: 153,881)

May 20   *Michigan*[a]

REPUBLICAN	Votes	Percent	DEMOCRATIC	Votes	Percent
Bush	342,226	57.5	Uncommitted	36,389	46.4
Reagan	189,266	31.8	Brown	23,057	29.4
Anderson	48,804	8.2	La Rouche	8,940	11.4
No preference	10,118	1.7			
Fernandez	2,381	0.4			
Stassen	1,786	0.3			

(Turnout: 595,176)   (Turnout: 78,424)

May 20   *Oregon*

REPUBLICAN	Votes	Percent	DEMOCRATIC	Votes	Percent
Reagan	166,033	54.5	Carter	199,655	58.2
Bush[h]	105,713	34.7	Kennedy	110,119	32.1
Anderson	30,769	10.1	Brown	33,276	9.7
Crane	2,133	0.7			

(Turnout: 304,647)   (Turnout: 343,050)

May 27   *Arkansas*

REPUBLICAN	Votes	Percent	DEMOCRATIC	Votes	Percent
			Carter	269,422	60.1
			Uncommitted	80,692	18.0
			Kennedy	78,451	17.5
			Finch	19,276	4.3

(Turnout: 448,290)

REPUBLICAN	Votes	Percent	DEMOCRATIC	Votes	Percent
May 27 Idaho[a]					
Reagan	111,815	82.9	Carter	31,400	62.2
Anderson	13,083	9.7	Kennedy	11,106	22.0
Bush	5,395	4.0	Uncommitted	5,957	11.8
No preference	3,507	2.6	Brown	2,070	4.1
Crane	1,079	0.8			
(Turnout: 134,879)			(Turnout: 50,482)		
May 27 Kentucky					
Reagan	78,111	82.4	Carter	160,781	66.9
Bush	6,825	7.2	Kennedy	55,276	23.0
Anderson	4,835	5.1	Uncommitted	19,226	8.0
No preference	3,128	3.3	Kay	2,644	1.1
Stassen	1,232	1.3			
Fernandez	758	0.8			
(Turnout: 94,795)			(Turnout: 240,331)		
May 27 Nevada					
Reagan	39,338	83.0	Carter	25,172	37.6
No preference	4,976	10.5	Uncommitted	22,495	33.6
Bush	3,081	6.5	Kennedy	19,281	28.8
(Turnout: 47,395)			(Turnout: 66,948)		
June 3 California					
Reagan	2,015,421	80.2	Kennedy	1,489,068	44.8
Anderson	341,767	13.6	Carter	1,253,077	37.7
Bush	123,137	4.9	Uncommitted	378,915	11.4
Crane	22,617	0.9	Brown	132,952	4.0
Fernandez	10,052	0.4	La Rouche	69,800	2.1
(Turnout: 2,512,994)			(Turnout: 3,323,812)		
June 3 Montana[a]					
Reagan	66,973	87.3	Carter	64,501	51.6
Bush	7,441	9.7	Kennedy	46,501	37.2
No preference	2,301	3.0	Uncommitted	14,000	11.2
(Turnout: 76,716)			(Turnout: 125,002)		

REPUBLICAN	Votes	Percent	DEMOCRATIC	Votes	Percent

June 3   New Jersey

REPUBLICAN	Votes	Percent	DEMOCRATIC	Votes	Percent
Reagan	225,995	81.3	Kennedy	315,230	56.2
Bush	47,534	17.1	Carter	212,584	37.9
Stassen	4,448	1.6	Uncommitted	19,632	3.5
			La Rouche	14,023	2.5

(Turnout: 277,977)   (Turnout: 560,908)

June 3   New Mexico

REPUBLICAN	Votes	Percent	DEMOCRATIC	Votes	Percent
Reagan	37,647	63.7	Kennedy	72,607	46.1
Anderson	7,151	12.1	Carter	65,992	41.9
Bush	5,851	9.9	Uncommitted	9,607	6.1
Crane	4,433	7.5	La Rouche	4,725	3.0
Fernandez	1,773	3.0	Finch	4,567	2.9
No preference	1,300	2.2			
Stassen	946	1.6			

(Turnout: 59,101)   (Turnout: 157,499)

June 3   Ohio

REPUBLICAN	Votes	Percent	DEMOCRATIC	Votes	Percent
Reagan	690,813	80.8	Carter	603,584	51.0
Bush	164,154	19.2	Kennedy	521,923	44.1
			La Rouche	35,505	3.0
			Kay	21,303	1.8

(Turnout: 854,967)   (Turnout: 1,183,499)

June 3   Rhode Island

REPUBLICAN	Votes	Percent	DEMOCRATIC	Votes	Percent
Reagan	3,841	72.0	Kennedy	26,177	68.3
Bush	992	18.6	Carter	9,888	25.8
No preference	347	5.8	La Rouche	1,150	3.0
Fernandez	48	0.9	Uncommitted	767	2.0

(Turnout: 5,335)   (Turnout: 38,327)

June 3   South Dakota

REPUBLICAN	Votes	Percent	DEMOCRATIC	Votes	Percent
Reagan	72,515	82.1	Kennedy	32,617	48.2
Anderson	5,564	6.3	Carter	31,061	45.9
No preference	5,123	5.8	Uncommitted	3,993	5.9
Bush	3,710	4.2			
Stassen	972	1.1			
Crane	442	0.5			

(Turnout: 88,325)   (Turnout: 67,671)

REPUBLICAN			DEMOCRATIC		
	Votes	Percent		Votes	Percent
June 3 West Virginia					
Reagan	114,594	85.6	Carter	194,976	61.9
Bush	19,277	14.4	Kennedy	120,009	38.1
(Turnout: 133,871)			(Turnout: 314,985)		
Totals					
Reagan	7,634,328		Carter	10,013,174	
Bush	3,067,363		Kennedy	7,354,271	
Anderson	1,567,439		Uncommitted	1,283,286	
Baker	175,673		Brown	536,263	
Crane	99,562		La Rouche	176,006	
Connally	83,504		Kay	47,172	
No preference	66,510		Finch	45,513	
Fernandez	25,045				
Stassen	21,418				
Dole	8,283				
Total of these major candidates	12,749,125		Total of these major candidates	19,455,687	
Total of minor candidates	36,059		Total of minor candidates	82,751	
Total turnout	12,785,184		Total turnout	19,538,438	

Source: Votes percentages and turnout figures from Congressional Quarterly Inc.

a. Nonbinding presidential preference primaries were held by Democrats in Idaho, Michigan, and Vermont, and by Republicans in Montana.

b. Baker withdrew March 5.

c. Connally withdrew March 9.

d. Dole withdrew March 15.

e. Brown withdrew April 1.

f. Crane withdrew April 17.

g. Anderson withdrew as candidate for Republican nomination April 24.

h. Bush withdrew May 26.

APPENDIX B continues on Page 290

PRESIDENTIAL ELECTION STATISTICS

PRESIDENTIAL ELECTION STATISTICS
Popular and Electoral Vote, 1976 and 1980

1976

States	Electoral Vote Carter	Ford	Popular Vote Carter	Ford
Alabama	9		659,170	504,070
Alaska		3	44,058	71,555
Arizona		6	295,602	418,642
Arkansas	6		498,604	267,903
California		45	3,742,284	3,882,244
Colorado		7	460,353	584,367
Connecticut		8	647,895	719,261
Delaware	3		122,596	109,831
District of Columbia	3		137,818	27,873
Florida	17		1,636,000	1,469,531
Georgia	12		979,409	483,743
Hawaii	4		147,375	140,003
Idaho		4	126,549	204,151
Illinois		26	2,271,295	2,364,269
Indiana		13	1,014,714	1,185,958
Iowa		8	619,931	632,863
Kansas		7	430,421	502,752
Kentucky	9		615,717	531,852
Louisiana	10		661,365	587,446
Maine		4	232,279	236,320
Maryland	10		759,612	672,661
Massachusetts	14		1,429,475	1,030,276
Michigan		21	1,696,714	1,893,742
Minnesota	10		1,070,440	819,395
Mississippi	7		381,309	366,846
Missouri	12		999,163	928,808
Montana		4	149,259	173,703
Nebraska		5	233,287	359,219
Nevada		3	92,479	101,273
New Hampshire		4	147,645	185,935

1980

Electoral Vote		Popular Vote		
Carter	*Reagan*	*Carter*	*Reagan*	*Anderson*
0	9	636,730	654,192	16,481
0	3	41,842	86,112	11,156
0	6	246,843	529,688	76,952
0	6	398,041	403,164	22,468
0	45	3,083,652	4,524,835	739,832
0	7	368,009	652,264	130,633
0	8	541,732	677,210	171,807
0	3	130,231	23,313	16,131
3	0	105,754	111,252	16,288
0	17	1,419,475	2,046,951	189,692
12	0	890,733	654,168	36,055
4	0	135,879	130,112	32,021
0	4	110,192	290,699	27,058
0	26	1,981,413	2,358,094	346,754
0	13	844,197	1,255,656	111,639
0	8	508,672	676,026	115,633
0	7	326,150	566,812	68,231
0	9	617,417	635,274	31,127
0	10	708,453	792,853	26,345
0	4	220,974	238,522	53,327
10	0	726,161	680,606	119,537
0	14	1,053,802	1,056,223	382,539
0	21	1,661,532	1,915,225	275,223
10	0	954,173	873,268	174,997
0	7	429,281	441,089	12,036
0	12	931,182	1,074,181	77,920
0	4	118,032	206,814	29,281
0	5	166,424	419,214	44,854
0	3	66,666	155,017	17,651
0	4	108,864	221,705	49,693

(continued overleaf)

| | 1976 | | | |
| | Electoral Vote | | Popular Vote | |
States	Carter	Ford	Carter	Ford
New Jersey		17	1,444,653	1,509,688
New Mexico		4	201,148	211,419
New York	41		3,389,558	3,100,791
North Carolina	13		927,365	741,960
North Dakota		3	136,078	153,470
Ohio	25		2,011,621	2,000,505
Oklahoma		8	532,442	545,708
Oregon		6	490,407	492,120
Pennsylvania	27		2,328,677	2,205,604
Rhode Island	4		227,636	181,249
South Carolina	8		450,807	346,149
South Dakota		4	147,068	151,505
Tennessee	10		825,879	633,969
Texas	26		2,082,319	1,953,300
Utah		4	182,110	337,908
Vermont		3	78,789	100,387
Virginia		12	813,896	836,554
Washington		8[a]	717,323	777,732
West Virginia	6		435,864	314,726
Wisconsin	11		1,040,232	1,004,987
Wyoming		3	62,239	92,717
Total	297	240	40,828,929	39,148,940

Source: *The World Almanac and Book of Facts*, 1982. New York: Newspaper Enterprise Association.

a. One elector in Washington for Reagan.

In 1976, McCarthy (Independent) received 739,256 votes; McBride (Libertarian) received 171,818 votes. In 1980, Clark received 970,869 votes, Commoner received 230,377, Hall 43,871, DeBerry 40,105 and Griswold 13,211. Anderson, Carter, Clark, and Reagan on ballot in all states and District of Columbia.

1980

Electoral Vote		Popular Vote		
Carter	Reagan	Carter	Reagan	Anderson
0	17	1,147,364	1,546,557	234,632
0	4	167,826	250,779	29,459
0	41	2,728,372	2,893,831	467,801
0	13	875,635	915,018	52,800
0	3	79,189	193,695	23,640
0	25	1,752,414	2,206,545	254,472
0	8	402,026	695,570	38,284
0	6	456,890	571,044	112,389
0	27	1,937,540	2,261,872	292,921
4	0	198,342	154,793	59,819
0	8	428,220	439,2-7	13,868
0	4	103,855	198,343	21,431
0	10	783,051	787,761	35,991
0	26	1,881,147	2,510,705	111,613
0	4	124,266	439,687	30,284
0	3	81,952	94,628	31,761
0	12	752,174	989,609	95,418
0	9	650,193	865,244	185,073
6	0	367,462	334,206	31,691
0	11	981,584	1,088,845	160,657
0	3	49,427	110,700	12,072
49	489	35,481,435	43,899,248	5,719,437

INDEX

ABOUT THE EDITOR

Jonathan Moore became the director of the Institute of Politics in 1974 after having resigned his post as associate attorney general in the U.S. Department of Justice. Immediately prior to that he served as special assistant to the Secretary of Defense, counselor to the Department of Health, Education and Welfare, and deputy assistant secretary of state for East Asian and Pacific affairs.

Mr. Moore has worked in various state and national election campaigns, and was a legislative assistant in the U.S. Senate. Earlier he served in the Departments of Defense and State and the U.S. Information Agency in the Kennedy, Johnson, and Eisenhower administrations, respectively.

Mr. Moore is a lecturer in Public Policy on the faculty of the Kennedy School of Government, and teaches a course in the political management of federal departments. He studies and writes about the presidential nominating process, the relationship between foreign policy and domestic politics, and the impact of the media on American political institutions. He presently serves on the Board of Directors of National Medical Care, Inc., the Dartmouth College Alumni Council, the editorial board of Channel 5, Boston, and is a member of the Council on Foreign Relations and Phi Beta Kappa.